ROCK
NAMES

THIRD EDITION

ROCK NAMES

From ABBA to ZZ Top

HOW ROCK BANDS GOT THEIR NAMES

Adam Dolgins

A Citadel Press Book
Published by Carol Publishing Group

A Citadel Press Book
Published by Carol Publishing Group
Citadel Press is a registered trademark of Carol
Communications, Inc.

Editorial, sales and distribution, rights, and
permissions inquiries should be addressed to Carol
Publishing Group, 120 Enterprise Avenue, Secaucus,
N.J. 07094

In Canada: Canadian Manda Group, One Atlantic
Avenue, Suite 105, Toronto, Ontario M6K 3E7

Carol Publishing books may be purchased in bulk at
special discounts for sales promotion, fund-raising,
or educational purposes. Special editions can be
created to specifications. For details, contact
Special Sales Department, 120 Enterprise Avenue,
Secaucus, N.J. 07094.

Manufactured in the United States of America

10 9 8 7 6 5 4 3 2 1

Library of Congress Cataloging-in-Publication Data

Dolgins, Adam.
     Rock names : from ABBA to ZZ Top : how rock
  bands got their names
     Adam Dolgins.—Third edition
         p.   cm.
     "A Citadel Press book."
     ISBN 0-8065-2046-9 (pbk.)
     1. Rock groups—Names—Dictionaries. I. Title.
  ML 102.R6D67   1998
  781.66′014—DC21   98-30717
                                         CIP
                                         MN

Introduction to the Third Edition

The third edition of Rock Names includes more than 125 new entries. They are: Ace of Base, Adam and the Ants, America, The Average White Band, Berlin, Better Than Ezra, Blue Cheer, The Bonzo Dog Band, The Box Tops, Bubble Puppy, Bush, Can, Cheap Trick, The Chipmunks, Chumbawamba, Cibo Matto, Collective Soul, Crash Test Dummies, Crowded House, Curved Air, Dash Rip Rock, Dexys Midnight Runners, Dog's Eye View, Drivin' and Cryin', Bill Haley and the Comets, Cornershop, The Crystal Method, The Darling Buds, Dawn, Dead Can Dance, Deee-Lite, Deep Blue Something, Electric Flag, The Elegants, The Emotions, EMF, Eugenius, Everclear, Fastball, 54-40, The Flaming Lips, The Fleetwoods, The Flying Burrito Brothers, Foo Fighters, Fugazi, Galaxie 500, Garbage, Giant Sand, Gobalee, The Go-Gos, GWAR, The Hollywood Argyles, The Hues Corporation, Jamiroquai, Jo Jo Gunne, Kajagoogoo, Killing Joke, The KLF, KMFDM, The Knickerbockers, The

Levellers, Lipps, Inc., Love Battery, M, The Manhattans, Marcy Playground, Marilyn Manson, The Marshall Tucker Band, Matchbox 20, MC 900 Ft. Jesus, MFSB, Milli Vanilli, Molly Hatchet, Mr. Big, Morphine, Mudhoney, Mungo Jerry, The Nice, Night Ranger, 999, No Doubt, Oasis, The Offspring, The 101ers, Paper Lace, Pavement, Phish, The Platters, Player, Buster Poindexter, Poison, Porno for Pyros, The Prodigy, Psi Com, Pulp, Pussy Galore, Radiohead, Bruce Hornsby and the Range, Right Said Fred, Rufus, Savage Garden, Shoes, Smash Mouth, The Sneaker Pimps, Soul Asylum, The Spaniels, Steam, Stiff Little Fingers, Stone Temple Pilots, Stone the Crows, The Strangeloves, The Stranglers, The Strawbs, Stryper, Tesla, Them, Third Eye Blind, 311, 'Til Tuesday, T'Pau, The Walker Brothers, The Wallflowers, The Waterboys, Wild Cherry, The Woodentops, X-Ray Specs, The Young Rascals, Maurice Williams and the Zodiacs.

The following entries have been revised or expanded: A Flock of Seagulls, The Champs, Chubby Checker, Counting Crows, Devo, Everything But the Girl, The Feelies, Goo Goo Dolls, Jane's Addiction, Los Lobos, Nine Inch Nails, The Rolling Stones, The Shirelles, Simple Minds, The Yardbirds.

In addition to everyone I thanked in the second edition, I'd like to add my editor at Citadel Press, Monica Harris, and to acknowledge two excellent books that I found very helpful, *The New Rolling Stone Encyclopedia of Rock & Roll* edited by Patricia Romanowski and Holly George-Warren, and *The Billboard Book of Number One Hits* by Fred Bronson. This book is dedicated with love to Jana Hollingshead.

I owe this book to the Jefferson Airplane—at least that's what I told interviewers while promoting the first edition of

Rock Names. When asked how the project got started, my standard spiel was, "I was listening to the radio one morning when a song by the Jefferson Airplane came on, and for some reason I said to myself that day, "What *is* a Jefferson Airplane anyway? And, for that matter, who's Pink Floyd? And why the Beatles?" And like any true obsessive, I was off.

In truth, I can't remember exactly what band it was that prompted the Andy Rooneyesque question, "Did you ever wonder how all those rock bands got their crazy names?" The Airplane was as good a band as any, maybe better, because their name was well-known, its origins obscure, and no less an authority than *Entertainment Weekly* had recently reported the story and blown it.

I began my research by combing through sources like *SPIN, Option* and a towering stack of *Rolling Stone*'s stashed in a closet. I quickly learned that it was a technique that left much to be desired. The stories behind band names were infrequently revealed, even when the sheer strangeness of some names seemed to demand it. And when the origins were explained, usually they were mentioned only in passing and were sometimes, I would later learn, flat-out wrong. This also held true for the rock encyclopedias found in bookstores and the library, and for the press releases and artist bios issued by record labels and public relations firms on file at the ARChive of Contemporary Music.

Ultimately, the best way to get to the bottom of things was to go directly to the band members themselves. Whenever possible, I set up brief phone interviews via their managers using a directory published by *Performance* magazine. While there were inevitable roadblocks due to recording and tour schedules, vacations, and occasionally, attitude, I was pleased to discover how cooperative and friendly most of the artists were. Unless a source is specifically cited, all of the interviews in *Rock Names* were conducted exclusively for this book, most of them by phone and a couple by fax.

I tried to be as inclusive as possible by covering bands from the 1950s through the present, from the mainstream and the underground. Sure, there are omissions, I was disappointed, for example, that I couldn't get the inside story behind Cheap Trick, although Lord knows I could certainly make a couple of good guesses. My great fear is that someone will open up the book, be it a kid in Indianapolis looking for a favorite death metal band or a critic in New York searching for a seminal No Wave ensemble, not find what he or she is looking for and toss it aside.

That said, I'm pleased with the result. The initial print run for the first edition sold out, and reaction from the media was terrific. *Rock Names* was featured on *Good Morning America,* MTV, VH1, NPR's "All Things Considered," the ABC, CBS, NBC, AP and BBC radio networks and over 50 local radio stations throughout the U.S. and Canada. In addition, *USA Today, Billboard, US* magazine, *The Chicago Tribune,* the *Los Angeles Times* and several other publications gave the book generous coverage.

The only person who didn't seem that interested in *Rock Names* was Andy Rooney, to whom I had written with the suggestion that he do a piece for *60 Minutes* that started out something like, "Did you ever wonder how all those rock bands got their crazy names?" Not long after I sent him a copy of the book, he sent me the following reply:

I looked through the book and was very impressed with all the work you did and monumentally disinterested in the product. I should think you might find a small market for the book. I hope so because good reporting should be rewarded. As someone who tries to appeal to a broad audience in both my television work and my newspaper column, I often worry about the great number of people who are attracted to something I don't know or care anything about. Part of it is age, of course, but there's something else going on there, too. I never understood the appeal of Frank Sinatra when I was sixteen or Elvis when I was fifty.

I would like to thank the following people, without whom *Rock Names* wouldn't have happened: Bob Mack, who helped set up and conducted many of the interviews, and who provided invaluable advice along the way; Steve Schragis, my publisher, who bought into the idea immediately and has stood by it ever since; Tad Kepley, who transcribed most of the interviews and also set up and conducted a few of them; Anne Kreamer, who gave me the initial kick in the pants; David Goldberg and Lisa Eskow, for their legal advice; Rob Rosenheck, for badgering me to finish "that unholy bastard of a book"; Deborah Feingertz, for helping to publicize the first edition; Emily Heckman, for her words of wisdom on the book business; all the band members and their managers and publicists, for their cooperation; and Daniel, Judith and Eric Dolgins, Gerry Blumenfeld, and, especially, Jana Hollingshead, for their love and support.

ROCK
NAMES

ABBA   The name of the Swedish pop group, which scored a dozen Top 40 hits in the 1970s, is an acronym of the four band members' first initials: Agnetha Fältskog, Benny Andersson, Björn Ulvaeus, and Anni-Frid Lyngstad.

ABC   The band began in Sheffield, England, as Vice Versa and changed their name when vocalist Martin Fry joined in 1980. Fry explains, "I wanted a name that would put us first in the phone directory, or second if you count ABBA; a name that didn't tie us to any one form of music; something big, bold, brash, and vague. It stands for nothing and everything—like the Band."

AC/DC   The hard-rocking band got their start in Sydney, Australia, in 1973, choosing their name because it fit their "high voltage" sound, "forgetting," as one bio put it, that the name was also slang for bisexual. This association dogged them for a time, leading publicists to play up the band members' heterosexual adventures whenever possible.

ACE OF BASE   Originally called Technoir, the Swedish dance-pop group renamed themselves Ace of Base reportedly because they considered themselves masters of the studio, their "base" of operations—not because they had mispelled "bass."

ADAM AND THE ANTS The Ants formed in London in 1977, their name a reference to the Beatles. In a VH1 interview, Adam Ant explained how he got his name: "My real name is Stuart Leslie Goddard. I . . . liked the idea of the 'first man' because I was shaped a bit more like a Renaisance painting . . . big shoulders and narrow waist, so I decided to enhance that. I think the Tubes wrote a song called 'Madam, That's Adam—There's no other woman that's had 'em. He's stronger than a tree and freshly molded from clay.' So I thought, 'Oh, that would be good,' and so I became Adam—and never looked back." For what it's worth, Atom Ant was the name of a TV cartoon character in the sixties.

AEROSMITH The band formed in Sunapee, New Hampshire, during the late sixties, before moving down to Boston and on to international fame as one of America's premier hard rock outfits. The band claims that their name has no special significance. They liked it because it sounded "cool." *Rolling Stone* reported in April 1990:

"No, Virginia, Aerosmith did not name itself after Sinclair Lewis's classic novel *Arrowsmith*. 'No way,' says [lead singer Steve] Tyler disapprovingly. 'That was just some book that they made you read in high school.'

"In fact, [drummer] Joey Kramer—who came up with the name—says he can't remember where Aerosmith came from. He just recalls sitting in high school, writing the word again and again on his math and biology textbooks, thinking that someday it would be one hell of a cool name for a rock and roll band. (Cooler even than the other, less original name the band considered: Spike Jones.)"

A FLOCK OF SEAGULLS   The band formed in Liverpool, England, in 1980. In a VH1 interview, vocalist and keyboard player Mike Score recalled: "The name of the band originally came because I read the book *Jonathan Livingston Seagull*. I thought it was a great book. I felt like I was, you know, flowing against the grain of society or whatever, and the book kind of said, 'You're not alone doing this; if you keep doing it you'll eventually arrive at the point you wish to be at.' So I thought that that would be a great name for a band. And also I was into the Stranglers, and they have a song called 'Toiler on the Sea' in which he yells out 'A flock of seagulls.' So the two things together just cemented the name. Once we'd used the name as a live band, people started making seagull noises—'Arh, arh, arh'—and things like that, and we became known as the Seagulls no matter what we tried to do. So the name stuck."

A-HA   The Norse trio of Morten Harket, Pal Waaktaar, and Mags Furuholem had a number one hit in the U.S. in 1985 with "Take on Me" and made a splash with their animated video for the song on MTV. "Originally, we were trying to find a Norwegian word that people would be able to say in English," Furuholem told *Rolling Stone* in November 1985. Instead, the name came from a song title that Harket spotted in one of Waaktaar's notebooks. "It was a terrible song, but a great name," he said. "I mean, you say it, 'aha,' all the time." Furuholem added, "Our manager says that this band has been on everybody's lips for years."

THE ALARM   The band formed in Rhyl, Wales, in the late seventies. Singer and guitarist Mike Peters explains: "We were called the Toilets originally—we were flushed with success. [Bassist Eddie MacDonald and I] met through being next-door neighbors, and then Nigel [Twist, the drummer] and Dave [Sharp, the lead guitarist] moved to the area. Then, as all the other local musicians started to drop out and get jobs and stuff, pressured to start a family, we were insane enough to keep going. Eventually it was just the four of us in the town who were really that committed and interested in making music. We were originally called Seventeen after the Sex Pistols song on *Never Mind the Bollocks*. That was '78 to '79, in Ryhl in north Wales. Started off as the Toilets, then to Seventeen. Then we kind of disbanded for a while because nothing was happening.

"We eventually started writing songs that later became the basis of the Alarm. We thought that we had something special this time. It was original for us, and we sat around a table looking for a name. We were all kind of throwing ideas into the hat based on our personal experience. We were just talking about musical experiences that we'd had, and we were hoping that someone would say a word or a phrase that would become the name of the band. I started telling about a song that I had written called 'Alarm Alarm.' It was the first attempt at writing a song and we all thought, 'Oh, that sounds good—let's call ourselves Alarm Alarm.' So we phoned up [influential BBC disc jockey] John Peel because we were doing a really early show of ours in London—probably one of the first gigs we ever had—and we said, 'Can you plug our gig over the radio?' And he said yeah. So it was, 'Alarm Alarm are playing tonight.' And then he said, 'It's funny, isn't it? There's Duran Duran, Talk Talk, now Alarm Alarm. Perhaps I should change my name to

John Peel John Peel.' And we thought, 'Let's just call ourselves the Alarm.' "

ALICE IN CHAINS   Grunge metal band Alice in Chains emerged from the same Seattle, Washington, scene in the late eighties that spawned Soundgarden and Nirvana. Recalls guitarist Jerry Cantrel, "We were partying one night and [singer] Layne [Staley] thought it up. He thought of starting a glampunk band on the side and calling it Alice in Chains. It started out as a joke, and after a while it seemed to be the best name that we could think of."

THE AMBOY DUKES   Motor City Madman Ted Nugent explains the origins of his garage band the Amboy Dukes, which he formed in 1966: "The name Amboy Dukes first came to my attention around 1960, when my Detroit band, the Lourds, were kicking ass during the dawn of man. Another rival band in the Motor City was named the Amboy Dukes and had a pretty good following. That band broke up around '62, so when I moved to Chicago and formed my new band, I thought the name was cool as hell, so I used it. Turns out that the original Amboy Dukes was a street gang in Amboy, New Jersey, with a controversial novel written about them in the late fifties."

AMERICA   Gerry Beckley, Dewey Bunnell, and Dan Peek—sons of American servicemen stationed in England—began playing together in 1969 while students at London's Central High School. Originally part of a five-man band called the Daze, the three took their name from an Americana brand jukebox found at a London pub.

THE ANIMALS   The Animals formed in Newcastle, England, in 1962. Singer Eric Burdon discusses the band's name in an interview: **How did the Animals get their name? I've heard a couple of different stories. You began as the Alan Price Combo.** "There were several bands playing in and around Newcastle. Basically the Animals came out of Newcastle University. [Drummer] John Steel was playing trumpet and I was playing trombone at the time in a traditional jazz band. Then rock and roll started affecting our ears. John went off into modern jazz and I started listening to more rock and roll and realized that for me that was where it was at. Then eventually he came around to that. But we used to fire off of each other—he used to turn me on to jazz, and I used to turn him on to blues and rock. That was the basis of the Animals, really. Then we needed a piano player, so we found Alan Price playing in a band called the Thomas Headley Trio, and he came and joined us, but he had his own band on the side as well called the Alan Price Combo. Just to make things less complicated, local newspaper people just said that the basis of the band was the Alan Price Combo, and that eventually became the Animals.

"The story that we were named the Animals because of our wild appearance onstage was just conjured up by some publicity man. The real reason the band was called the Animals was that we were sort of weekend warriors in a street gang. We—John Steel, myself, eventually Alan Price, [bassist] Chas Chandler—we were part of this street gang. We were the youngest members of the gang. They were mostly older guys—nineteen, twenty, twenty-one. We were like fourteen, fifteen, sixteen, seventeen at the time. We provided them with entertainment, and that's why we survived. We weren't just made hamburger and thrown out of the group because we entertained them. They liked us a lot and took us to heart. One of the main characters in this gang had been demobbed from the British army, who were involved in Cyprus at the time. The British were stuck in the middle—it was kind of like a mini English Vietnam, and there were a lot of vets who came back from that conflict with their minds pretty screwed up. This guy, who we liked a lot, his name was Animal Hogg, and he was the animal of the group. We liked him a lot and he liked us a lot, and we figured it would be good to name a band after him. It was fun to find out in later years that even on *Sesame Street* there was an Animal, a member of the gang called Animal. That's the real straight dope on the band. We named the band after our favorite character in the gang." **So the stories about you guys performing or looking like animals was—**"That was just an easy way to tell the story, because then we would've had to've gone into the politics of being a vet, talking about a guy who had been in the conflict. It wasn't good subject matter. In fact, just recently, when I tried to tell that story, in a book that I wrote, Pete Townshend [who was working as an editor at the British publishing house Faber & Faber] wouldn't let me. I went into how this guy, one night around the campfire, broke down and told me how he and his buddies had raped and pillaged in a village on Cyprus and how he had actually raped someone at gunpoint, and that's what destroyed him, he couldn't handle it anymore. Townshend's reaction was, 'You can't tell a story like that, you'll offend female readers. It'll be offensive to readers.' " **What happened to Animal Hogg?** "I have no idea. We left town shortly after that. We started traveling." **Do you remember**

any other names that you had considered? "I don't think we considered anything else. We just sat down in a pub one day, at one of our local gigs. It was when we'd heard that we were going to get a chance to go professional, and we'd heard that we were going to tour with Chuck Berry, and we knew we needed a name. Chas was in a band called the Contours, Hilton was in a band called the Wild Cats, John Steel and I were in a band called the Pagans, and we just sat down in the pub. I don't even remember who suggested it: 'Why don't we name the group after our favorite person, our favorite character?' " **Was he flattered?** "Oh, yeah. The reason we survived this gang was this guy was one of the toughest members—what he said went. He never went to movies, he never went to town, he just lived out in the country with his dog. He couldn't handle people." **Once you took the name and went on tour, were you pleased you chose it?** "Yeah, because it stuck in people's minds. I remember George Harrison and Georgie Fame on separate occasions, after watching our show at the Flamingo and the Ham Yard where the Who started out as the High Numbers—everybody played there—coming up and going, 'Hey, you guys are crazy calling yourselves the Animals.' It was pretty outrageous then. Pretty tame now, but back then it was pretty outrageous. We'd get people on the phone wanting to book us asking, 'What's the name of the band?' 'The Animals.' 'The Animals? Jesus, we can't put that on a poster.' I think only the French really under-stood what we were getting at with the name. We were really pissed off when we came to America because the American pop press would go, 'Okay guys, get down on your hands and knees and growl like animals.' And kids would ask, 'Which one's the tiger?' 'Who's the elephant?'

Y'know. But in the French press, we got reviews that said, 'This music lives up to the title. It's raw, it's animalistic, it has a wild soul.' They approached it in a different way. That's pretty much it."

ANTHRAX   Anthrax formed in New York City in 1981 and were one of the pioneers of thrash metal. Guitarist Scott Ian thought of the name, which the *American Heritage Dictionary* defines as "an infectious, usually fatal disease of warm-blooded animals, especially of cattle and sheep, caused by *Bacillus anthracis*. It is transmissible to man, capable of affecting various organs, and especially characterized by malignant ulcers." "I learned about the disease in science class in high school," recalls Ian, who grew up in the Bronx. "It sounded like a great name for a band."

THE ART OF NOISE   The intentionally faceless British techno-pop group Art of Noise met as part of Trevor Horn's production team in the early eighties. Their name was coined by ex-music critic Paul Morley, who ran ZTT Records with Horn, after a sociomusical diatribe published in 1913 by the Italian futurist Luigi Russolo.

ASIA   Asia was a so-called supergroup formed in 1981 by ex-U.K. lead singer and bassist John Wetton, Emerson, Lake and Palmer drummer Carl Palmer, and former Yes men Steve Howe [guitar] and Geoff Downes [keyboards]. In an interview, Wetton discusses how both Asia and U.K., itself a supergroup of sorts, got their names: "With U.K., we were trying to find something that conveyed the fact that we were British. We went through everything from British Legion to just using place names." **Like the names of different counties and towns?** "Yeah, counties, towns. It was a bit overdone, even in 1978—y'know, there had been a lot of bands that'd had place names, town names and stuff. So that sounded really corny. Actually, we were halfway between something that conveyed we were British, and something like an abstract thing, like K-1000, a number that was just completely off the wall. Somehow we just arrived at U.K. We just ran through every combination of British things and decided that that would work if people wouldn't mutilate the posters by putting a *P* at one end and an *E* at the other. Round about that time, it was sort of the postpunk era and there were lots of people called the 'U.K. somethings' by the next year. There was the U.K. Subs, and lots of other things. The band only lasted for two years, anyway, so it was no great thing. With Asia, we weren't thinking in those terms at all. It was a suggestion by our manager. All four of us were meeting in the office one day. The name game is one that everyone dreads, y'know: 'What are we going to call it?' All the good names have been had long ago. Basically you know that the name is only sort of unusual for the first three months. As soon as people get used to it, you can be called anything, people just get used to it. The Beatles is probably one of the worst names anyone ever came up with, but as soon as you get used to it, it represents the best band that's ever been." **You're right about that.** "What a grotesque pun. It's horrible, a horrible pun. But in fact, once you get past that, it's okay. It's just become a symbol of those four people. We were doing the name game in the office, and our manager came up with the name Asia. He said, 'No one's ever used that.' And everyone said, 'Oh, yeah, right, Brian, shut up.' Everyone told him to shut up and carried on. And about an hour later, I said, 'That's not a bad idea—four guys, four letters, graphically pretty strong, yeah, okay.' Gradually everyone came round to it. It seemed like a damn good idea. So we tried it out. In fact, we just put it on the back of *Melody Maker*. We just put a photograph of us and the word, to see what people's reaction was going to be, and everyone loved it, everybody really liked it. There was a real sort of buzz going on: 'Who are they?' 'What does it mean?' It was good, it served its purpose very well, I think. It wasn't intentionally a place name. It could have been any word that had four letters and was graphically strong." **But the four letters had something to do with it.** "Yeah, for me it was appealing because of the four letters and the fact that it was a four-piece band. Four units in one kind of thing, the fact that we were individuals." **I had heard that you did it so that you would be at the beginning of the record bin up by the A's.** "No, that's a little bit obvious. I mean, we could have done better than that, we could have done Aardvark. Then we could have guaranteed that we would have been at the top. It wasn't that at all. I remember, just before the formation of Asia, I'd got a thing about A's anyway. Words beginning with A and ending with A. For U.K.—it was a very long shot—Eddie Jobson [U.K.'s keyboard player and violinist] and I were toying with the word Alaska, but decided that was a ridiculous thing to do because none of us had anything to do with Alaska. It just happened to be a feeling for the shape of the word." **So that was your philosophy with Asia, 'cause you guys don't really have much to do with Asia.** "We had fuck all to do with Asia, but it's a good word."

THE ASSOCIATION   The Association sold over 15 million records in the sixties, among them "Cherish," "Windy," and "Never My Love." Keyboard player Terry Kirkman recalled the band's origins in an interview: **How did you guys decide on the name the Association?** "All but one of the original Association members had belonged to another group called the Men, a huge—originally thirteen, then eleven-member—folk group. We were the house band at the Troubadour in Los Angeles and were, honest to God, a pivotal band that was well-known in Los Angeles and known nowhere else. We came right along at the very, very end of the folk thing and were the first band that I know of in the United States to be called folk rock, which was a definition put on us by Doug Weston, who was, and is still, the owner of the Troubadour, arguably one of the most despicably powerful guys in the music business at the time. We'd added an electric bass and an electric guitar and drums, but we weren't making it because we were at the very, very end of the folk thing. It was really disheartening. We were really blowing everybody away and having an amazing time. We even had the likes of Bob Dylan ask if we would stick around after a Troubadour show to come down and discuss how we were applying electric music to folk music.

"We were together eight and a half months and we played all over town. But it was very big, it was very unwieldy, although very exciting. We just reached one of those impasses where, although we were all friends and I was the leader, we could not agree as a group on a direction that we wanted to go. And it was wearing me out. It was just exhausting me. We could not get beyond just doing the local club scene. Ironically, the week after we broke up—which is the time of this story—Warner Brothers offered us a contract. But I wasn't going to go back for that. Nor do I think it would have been successful. I mean, it was way after the fact for the folk scene. I got up and walked out of the rehearsal. I just apologized to the guys and I wished them well. No animosity, nothing. I just said, you know, 'I really have to split.'

"We were in a little village in the Hollywood area called Larchmont, and I walked out on the sidewalk from the rehearsal hall and was standing there thinking, 'What the fuck have I just done?' And Jules Alexander walked out, and then the rest of the guys walked out. And they were in agreement with me. There had been no conspiracy, there'd been no clique or anything. That was just the way it went down.

"We all went back to my apartment in the afternoon and sat down with a glass of wine and some joints. We sat there and thought, 'We just took eight and a half months of really hard work, just trying our hardest, our absolute fucking hardest, and threw it away. What are we going to do?' We're sitting there in that post-separation shock when one of the guys looked up and said, 'Don't look now, but there's six of us in this room and there's two tenors, two baritones, and two basses.' I just looked up and said, 'Well, fuck, I'm game if you are. We've already got this work ethic. We already know what we're doing. We're obviously all in agreement.' And we decided that we would try to become a group right there. I'm talking within an hour and a half. And then we jokingly started to muse over what it is we would call ourselves.

"There was this really despicable joke that I loved a lot at the time in which a family group comes in to audition for a show business agent and the show business agent says, 'Great. What is it you do?' And the joke went something like, 'Well, first I stick it in my wife's butt, and then my little kid jumps on me and the little sister does this.' The answer is this horrible, incestuous daisy chain of interlocked family sex. And the agent is totally aghast, and he says, 'That's so fantastic. What do you call yourselves?' And the guy says, 'We call ourselves the Aristocrats.' I don't know why that was funny then, but it was the funniest joke I knew. And we all started laughing and it was such an inside showbiz joke at the time that Brian Cole said, 'I'm for it. Why don't we call ourselves the Aristocrats.' We were fairly whacked by that time, and somebody said we better make sure of the true, true meaning. And we meant that as a joke—we were all kind of etymologically inclined. And Judy, my wife, looked it up, and while she was looking for *aristocrat,* she said, 'Here's a word that I think defines what you are.' The definition that she read was 'a group of people gathered together for a common cause.' And we went with that. We were named and formed within two hours. **Are you glad you went with that?** "No. I wish we had stuck with the Aristocrats."

THE AVERAGE WHITE BAND The band formed in Scotland in 1972 and topped the charts in 1975 with "Pick Up the Pieces." Like Vanilla Fudge, their name was a joking reference to the fact that they were a white group that played black music. The name was suggested by Bonnie Bramlett, one-half of the singing team of Delaney and Bonnie. They eventually shortened the name to AWB.

AZTEC CAMERA   Aztec Camera was formed by Roddy Frame in Glasgow, Scotland, in 1980. According to Frame's manager, Bob Johnson, Roddy "was only sixteen or seventeen at the time. Besides, he comes up with a different story each time he's asked." Johnson guesses that "he probably thought it was psychedelic sounding. He was listening to a lot of 13th Floor Elevators."

B

BACHMAN-TURNER OVERDRIVE   See **The Guess Who**

BABES IN TOYLAND   Kat Bjelland, Lori Barbero, and Michelle Leon formed the band in Minneapolis in the late-1980s. The name is a reference to the classic operetta by Victor Herbert that was adapted to film by Laurel and Hardy in 1934 and Disney in 1961. In *Babes in Toyland* by Neal Karlen, Bjelland says that they didn't "mean babes as in 'girls,' but as in babies. Boys and girls are all babes in the universe."

BAD COMPANY   The seventies supergroup, composed of ex-members of Free, Mott the Hoople, and King Crimson, formed in 1973. The band's name comes from the 1972 film of the same name starring Jeff Bridges.

BAD RELIGION   The band formed in Woodland Hills, California, in 1980. When queried about their name in a 1995 interview for this book, lead singer Greg Graffin said, "We've been asked this question at least a thousand times. It's worse for us because we've been around for so long. Well, in 1980, we were a bunch of teenagers. I was fifteen years old when the band started. And if you think back to what was going through your mind when you were fifteen, you'd think about pissing off adults more than anything." He laughs. "And we thought *Bad Religion* would accomplish that goal. Back then, I gotta say, the motivation for the name was pretty juvenile. However, it was a time when there was a lot of televangelism, if you remember. So it was sort of timely, that we would poke fun at some aspect of American culture. And it turns out that the name, although it started out on a juvenile foundation, became actually a pretty good name over the years, because we use religion as a metaphor for organized, dogmatic thought—really the opposite of what punk rock is all about, which stresses independence and individuality more than anything else. And so, actually, the name is still thought-provoking, because we have to combat dogma for our entire life." **So you're glad you chose it.** "It's not a name I have to be embarrassed about, which is nice." **Do you recall any other names you almost went with?** "We almost went with Bad Family Life. Then we almost went with Head Cheese." He laughs.

BADFINGER   The band formed in the midsixties in Swansea, Wales, and were signed to the Beatles' record company, Apple, in 1968 as the Iveys. Guitarist Joey Molland, who joined the band a month after they released their debut single, explains: "The story I heard was that Neil Aspinal, who was the head of Apple Records at the time, came up with the name. He got it from an old blues record called 'Badfinger Boogie.' It was a piano record." **When you joined the band, were they already called Badfinger?** "They were just changing their name from the Iveys." **Do you know where that name came from?** "No, I really don't. Tell you what, though—Mike Gibbins, the original drummer, is alive and well and living in Florida."

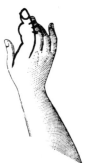

When asked how the Iveys got their name, Gibbins replies: "I've no idea. That's a name I think is really kind of—it's a shabby kind of name." **You think so?** "Yeah, it's kind of weak, you know what I mean? In Wales, in Swansea, where the Iveys originated from, bands were called, like, the Jets, y'know? I mean, they were really kind of masculine names. The Iveys to me was a little kind of prancing, mincing name, y'know? There was the Ivy League, which was a famous band from England, and people used to confuse the Ivy League with the Iveys, so that was kind of a bit of a damper, too, on the name." **So then how did you guys become Badfinger?** "In the early Apple days, when we got signed, the band itself didn't like the name. We were like, 'Wait, wait, this is not kind of strong enough for the new modern era,' y'know. So we used to write lists and lists and fuckin' lists all night and come up with different kinds of stupid names. Then we got really silly, and that was too useless, so Neil Aspinal came up with the name Badfinger." **Where did that come from?** "It was an old record of a black guy, a singer, y'know, 'Badfinger Boogie,' or something. It was the name of a blues tune. He figured 'Badfinger, what a great name.' And we went, 'Yeah! That's really fucking off the wall!' "

BANANARAMA   The British trio of Sarah Dallin, Karen Woodward, and Siobahn Fahey began performing as an unaccompanied vocal group in London pubs and nightclubs in 1981. After a string of hits in England, the group finally broke into the American Top 10 in 1984 with "Cruel Summer," followed by the dance-club smash "Venus" in 1986 and "I Heard a Rumour" in 1987. Their name is a cross between the sixties children's TV show "The Banana Splits" and the Roxy Music song "Pyjamarama."

THE BAND   The members of the Band met when they joined Ronnie Hawkins & the Hawks in the late fifties and early sixties. The group split from Hawkins over a financial dispute, becoming the Levon Helm Sextet and then Levon Helm & the Hawks before releasing their first single as The Canadian Squires in 1964. By the time Bob Dylan hooked up with them in 1965, at the suggestion of Atco Records secretary Mary Martin, they were calling themselves the Hawks. Between the time Dylan took them on his electrified world tour in 1966 as his backing band and the release of their debut album in 1968, the band had evolved into the Band. In *The Last Waltz,* Martin Scorsese's documentary of the Band's final concert on Thanksgiving Day in 1976 at the Winterland in San Francisco, pianist Richard

Manuel and guitarist Robbie Robertson discuss the name in intercut interviews: MANUEL: "Well, we were the Hawks." ROBERTSON: "And everything was fine, we were sailing along, and all of a sudden, one day the Hawks meant something else altogether [as in 'warmongers,' this being the height of the Vietnam War]." MANUEL: "And it was right in the middle of that whole psychedelia [craze]. Chocolate Subway, Marshmallow Overcoat—those kind of names, y'know?" ROBERTSON: "When we were working with Bob Dylan and we moved to Woodstock, everybody referred to us as 'the band.' He called us 'the band,' our friends called us 'the band,' our neighbors called us 'the band.' MANUEL: "We started out with the Crackers. We tried to call ourselves the Honkies. Everybody kind of backed off from that. It was too . . . straight. So we decided just to call ourselves . . . the Band."

THE BANGLES   The Bangles began as the Supersonic Bangs in Los Angeles in 1981, a name taken from the headline of an *Esquire* magazine article on sixties-style haircuts. The name was shortened to the Bangs, but then changed to the Bangles because a band from New Jersey had already laid claim to the name.

BAUHAUS   The band formed in Northampton, England, in 1978 after singer Peter Murphy joined guitarist Daniel Ash, bassist David Jay, and drummer Kevin Haskins, who were performing as the Craze. They began as Bauhaus 1919, named after the German institute founded that year for the study of art, design, and architecture and known for its

development of a style of functional architecture and its experimental use of building materials. *Bauhaus* is German for "architecture house."

THE BAY CITY ROLLERS   In an effort to give the Scottish pop rockers an American-sounding name, manager/producer Tam Paton randomly stuck a pin in the map of the U.S. and put a hole in Bay City, Michigan, a city of about 42,000 residents near the southern end of Saginaw Bay.

THE BEACH BOYS   Early names included Kenny and the Cadets and Carl and the Passions. They were calling themselves the Pendletones, after the plaid shirts popular with West Coast surfers, when they cut their first single, "Surfin'," in 1961. The single was released by the regional label Candix Records, which wanted to call the band the Surfers, despite the boys' wish to remain the Pendletones. When it was learned that there already was a band called the Surfers, Candix called them the Beach Boys, which was coined by Candix executive Russ Regan. In his autobiography *Wouldn't It Be Nice*, Brian Wilson recalls the day the band received the first copies of "Surfin'": "Gathering around, we lifted them out carefully, handling them more delicately than anything we'd ever touched. It was the five of us on that record. Our music. Our voices.

"There was only one problem. The label read 'Surfin',' by the 'Beach Boys.' We were the Pendletones!"

" 'That's not our name,' fifteen-year-old Carl said.

" 'What the fuck?' Mike added.

"Dad called the Morgans. There was an explanation. After the session, the Morgans struck a distribution deal with Candix Records, a small, independent label, to release 'Surfin',' and between then and the single's release on December 8, 1961, Russ Regan, a young promotion man, lumped us with Jan and Dean and young southern California surf bands and rechristened us the Beach Boys. The only problem was we didn't find out until we read the label.

" 'Well, change it back,' my dad bellowed into the telephone. 'Change it back to the Pendletones. That's what the kids call themselves.'

" 'No dice,' he was told.

"The records had already been pressed, the labels printed, and the whole kit and caboodle shipped. It was a small-time operation. Low budget. Reprinting the labels was too costly, my dad was informed.

"There was nothing we could do except shrug it off. That was easy. We had a record out. That was a considerable achievement by itself, far more important that a silly name."

THE BEASTIE BOYS Adam Yauch (MCA, as in "Master of Ceremonies Adam"), Adam Horovitz (King Ad-Rock), and Michael Diamond (Mike D) formed the Beastie Boys in 1981 as a hardcore band with Kate Shellenbach and John Barry. Prior to the Beastie Boys, Shellenbach and Diamond were in the Young Aborigines, while Horovitz was in the Young and the Useless. Shellenbach recalls that the name first appeared on a button made and worn by Yauch, and she seemed to think that the double *B* in the name was a takeoff on the Bad Brains, as was the band's mock-reggae song, "Beastie Revolution" from the *Cookiepuss* EP. Yauch, however, gives credit to Barry for coming up with the name and denies that it has any link to the Bad Brains. "It was more like a goof on the Angry Samoans," says Yauch in an interview. "It was like me and John sitting around my room in Brooklyn, just kickin' around names. It was like Beastie this, or Boys that. And we just said, 'Let's go with that one—it sounds pretty stupid, like some Angry Samoans hardcore shit.' Then we started making buttons and writing it on the back of our jackets with masking tape."

THE BEATLES   The Beatles began as the Quarry Men, a band John Lennon formed when he was a fifteen-year-old student at the Quarry Bank High School in 1956. Paul McCartney joined the band the following year, and after a brief stint as Johnny & the Moondogs, they became the Silver Beatles in 1959. In *The Beatles: The Authorized Biography*, published in 1968, author Hunter Davies reports: "In 1959, because it looked once again as if they were about to get an important audition, they got a new name. They started seriously trying to think of what to call themselves . . . [and] this is when the idea of the Beatles came up for the first time. No one is definitely sure how it happened. Paul and George just remember John arriving with it one day.

"They'd always been fans of Buddy Holly and the Crickets. They liked his music and also his name. They particularly liked the Crickets bit. It had a nice double meaning, one of them a purely English meaning which Americans couldn't have appreciated. They wished they'd thought of calling themselves the Crickets. Thinking of the name Crickets, John naturally thought of other insects with a name which could also be played around with. He'd filled his books as a child with similar word play.

" 'I was sitting at home one day,' says John. 'Just thinking about what a good name the Crickets would be for an English group. The idea of beetles came into my head. I decided to spell it BEAtles to make it look like beat music, just as a joke.'

"That was the real and simple origin of their name, though for years afterward they made up daft reasons each time anyone asked them. Usually they said a man with a magic carpet appeared at the window and told them.

"Though they now had a name they at last liked, they weren't called the Beatles for a long time. They met a friend who ran another beat group, Casy Jones of Cass and the Casanovas, who asked them what their new name was. He said it was rotten. You had to have a long name for a group, he said, like his. Why didn't they call themselves Long John and the Silver Beatles? Beatles on its own, he said, was far too short and simple. They didn't think much of his idea either. But when this important audition came up and they were asked what they were calling themselves, they said the Silver Beatles, which was a name they stuck to for the rest of that year, 1959."

It's worth noting that the Beetles was the name of the motorcycle gang led by Lee Marvin in the 1954 biker movie *The Wild One,* starring Marlon Brando, whose leather-clad look John Lennon, Paul McCartney, and George Harrison affected early on.

THE BEAUTIFUL SOUTH   The band was started by ex-Housemartins Paul Heaton and Dave Hemmingway in Hull, England in 1989. The band is not named after the American South, but is meant as an ironic comment on depressed South London. "I'd like to go down the Mississippi, though," Heaton quipped in a 1992 Elektra Records press release.

THE BEE GEES   First called the Rattlesnakes, and later Wee Johnnie Hayes & the Bluecats, the Gibb brothers—Barry, Maurice, and Robin—were renamed by Bill Good, a racetrack promoter they met while performing at Brisbane's Speedway Circus in Australia in 1960. Spotting their talent, Good introduced them to Bill Gates, a disc jockey on the local radio station 4KQ, who began to play their tapes on the air. When interest in their music began to build, Good magnanimously rechristened them the B.G.'s after his and Gates's initials, not for the Brothers Gibb, as most assume.

BELLY   Band founder Tanya Donnelly, quoted in *Playboy,* says that the name of the group is her "favorite word—soft, warm and female, like the music."

DION AND THE BELMONTS   Doo-wopper Dion DiMucci formed the group in 1958, naming them after Belmont Avenue, one of the main drags in the Bronx neighborhood where they grew up.

BERLIN   Bassist John Crawford formed the synth-pop band in Los Angeles in 1979, choosing the name to evoke the decadence of 1930s Berlin.

BETTER THAN EZRA   Formed in Louisiana in 1990, the band took their name from a reference to poet Ezra Pound in *A Moveable Feast*, Ernest Hemingway's memoir of Paris in the twenties: "I had heard complaining all my life. I found I could go on writing and that it was no worse than other noises, certainly better than Ezra learning to play the bassoon." The passage appears in the chapter "Birth of a New School," in which Hemingway describes being interrupted while attempting to write at a café.

BETTIE SERVEERT The name comes from a late sixties instruction manual by Dutch tennis star Bettie Stöve. It means "Bettie serves."

THE B-52s The band, which formed in Athens, Georgia, in 1977, took its name not from the U.S. Air Force bomber but for the Southern term for the towering bouffant hairdos worn at the time by band members Kate Pierson and Cindy Wilson.

BIG AUDIO DYNAMITE Singer and guitarist Mick Jones formed Big Audio Dynamite after leaving the Clash in 1984. When asked in a Manhattan nightclub, Jones said that it was Jane of Sigue Sigue Sputnik who suggested the letters B.A.D. He admits that it was only later that he tried to come up with the right words to make the acronym. Two of the names he considered were Before Alien Domination and Black and Decker.

BIG BLACK Big Black began in Chicago in 1983 and revolved around fanzine writer Steve Albini. In an interview, Albini explains why he picked the name Big Black, in addition to that of his later group, Rapeman: **Why don't you tell me how you came up with the name and whose Idea**

that was? "Big Black was a name that I came up with when I was in college. It was just sort of a reduction of the concept of a large, scary, ominous figure. All the historical images of fear and all the things that kids are afraid of are all big and black basically. That's all there was to it." **Was there any racial context at all?** "No. I kind of wish that there was, because then all the people that have been saying that would have some basis for their arguments." **So people would say that?** "Oh, people say that all the time. But, y'know, people are fucked, as we all know." **When you've been confronted with that, what has been your standard rap?** " 'Go fuck yourself' is my standard rap. There's no point in explaining something to somebody who's already made up his mind. You just tell them to eat shit and walk away. I found out after the fact that there was an African percussionist who called himself Big Black—not African actually, just a black guy from America, who made a bunch of sort of psychedelic-jazz percussion records. I actually have some of them. They're pretty horrible, but he was using the name ten years before I was. I think he started in '67 or '68, using the name Big Black." **Did someone bring this to your attention?** "No, actually. I just found one of his records in a record shop." **Did you recall any other names that you considered before going with Big Black?** "I was in a band before that called Small Irregular Pieces of Aluminum." **What was the**

origin of that? "We had trouble coming up with a name. Actually I considered just keeping that name because I like it. But at the time I was concerned with what it sounded like, and it sounded 'New Wavey to me, and that was a sin." **How about Rapeman?** "Rapeman is the title character in a Japanese comic book that I had come across through a friend of mine. The comic book is just a total mind-bender. There's a whole genre of comics in Japan, rape stories where women are raped in really graphic detail for whatever reason, and it's an amazing thing that this is just an accepted part of their sort of normal popular culture. Seeing one of these comic books really blows your mind if you're not familiar with the concept, and if you're looking at it as an American would look at a comic book, as something very lighthearted, and y'know, sort of children's entertainment. You open up this comic book and there's this superhero who rapes people, as his profession. It's pretty amazing. So Ray Washam and I—the drummer from Rapeman—he and I were both sort of obsessed with this comic book for a while, we just thought it was the most amazing thing and kept looking at it, and we just realized that we should call the band that." **It's memorable, that's for sure.** "I caught far more shit for calling a band Rapeman than I did for Big Black, not that it really mattered to us. There were far more picket lines to cross." **When you say picket lines, I'm sure you got some heat, but was there actually boycotting of shows, and—** "Oh, yeah, there was tremendous brouhaha. On our first American tour there were actual picket lines and news crews at three of the gigs. It was the typical motley alliance of housewives and lesbians at the picket line. Housewives offended by the concept of punk rock and lesbians offended by the concept of rape.

27

The really annoying thing was that the majority of the people on the picket line were precisely the kind of people that we would have liked at the gig, people that politically basically think like we do. But sometimes people are so dead set on being stupid that they won't allow themselves to experience something themselves. That's all part of the natural selection process that determines the audience of a band, and I can't really say if that's good or bad. When we were in England, there was an enormous brouhaha at a university that had rented out a hall to a promoter to do a show. The national press were called in, and there was an attempt to boycott the gig, and the university returned the money for the deposit and tried to cancel the gig, but the promoter wouldn't allow them to. Because of all the attention, it ended up being an enormous success." **That often turns out to be the case when there's a storm of publicity.** "Yeah, the gig ended up being a sold-out show, and since the university didn't take any of the money that they had contracted for, the band and promoter both made a whole shit-pot of money." **Are you pleased in retrospect that you took both these names? Any regrets?** "It's a matter of indifference to me. We picked the names for us, it made not a shit difference to us what anybody else thought of them."

BIG BROTHER AND THE HOLDING COMPANY Big Brother and the Holding Company is best known as Janis Joplin's band, but its history predated her arrival and extended beyond her departure. The band took shape in late 1965 at loose jam sessions organized by Bay Area impressario Chet Helms, who set up the group's first gig at the Trips Festival in January 1966. In the audience at the festival was David Getz, who soon joined the band, replacing the original drummer. In an interview, Getz explains the genesis of the band's name: "Chet Helms was the manager and the overseer. He was, in a certain sense, spiritually part of the band. The name Big Brother and the Holding Company came up, and I think that was chosen because he was sort of looked upon as the big brother. That was also, of course, a very conscious reference to Big Brother in *1984*—this was 1965, so it was still a long way off.

"*Holding* was a euphemism for possessing drugs—that was a word that was very common in the early sixties. Are you holding?' meaning, 'Do you have some stash?' That had the double entendre because a holding company was also a big corporation, and it went along with the Big Brother idea—some kind of megacorporation that was going to rule the future.

"But at the same time it had its other meaning, which was Chet Helms, who was running the Family Dog [nightclub] and was also managing the band, and the band itself, sort of being a loose-knit bunch of guys who got high. That's about it. It was selected. Everyone kind of stuck on that one.

"It worked for a while and then was always kind of a problem later on when Janis joined the band because people would say, 'Who's Big Brother?' That was a long time after we fired Chet. We fired Chet in mid-1966, so there really was nobody who was that figure, although people thought it might be James Gurley. There never really was a Big Brother after that, per se.

"Our fans, or our following, in that time, in '66 and '67, a lot of them just began calling us the Holding Company, and it didn't work that well. So nowadays, when we play, we just call ourselves Big Brother. The Holding Company part seems more dated. The Big Brother part still seems to have an image connected to it that has some kind of mythological power."

BIG STAR   Cult favorites Big Star pioneered power pop in the seventies. The band formed in Memphis in 1971, where ex-Box Tops singer/songwriter Alex Chilton joined Ice Water, a trio composed of guitarist Chris Bell, bassist Andy Hummel, and drummer Jody Stephens. One evening, as the band left the Ardent recording studio where they were working, they noted the name of the supermarket across the street, Big Star Foodmarket. And. thus, Big Star was born.

THE BLACK CROWES   The band began as Mr. Crowe's Garden in 1984 with brothers Chris and Rich Robinson in their native Atlanta. The name came from a favorite children's story. After they were signed to Def American Records in 1989, A&R man and producer George Drakoulias convinced them to change their name. Chris Robinson told *Rolling Stone* in May 1991: "Everyone just called us the Crowes when we hung out. And we came up with Black Crowes—blackbirds. That was it."

BLACK FLAG   Black Flag emerged from southern California in the late seventies to become one of Americas first and most influential hardcore bands. Guitarist Greg Ginn discusses their beginnings in an interview: **How did you come up with the name?** "Well, it was really a combination of reasons—the connotations of anarchy and also the aggressiveness the bug spray. [The black flag is the international symbol of anarchy.]" **Were you guys sitting around and saw the commercials, or . . . ?** "Not really. I think it came from the anarchist angle, but we liked the fact that there was a fun aspect, too, with the spray can. The third thing was just the sound of it—'Black Flag.' Y'know, Black Sabbath is one of my big influences. Just the sound of it—'Black Flag.' So really, those three things were about equal. It wasn't really triggered by one particular event. The name just came up, and after thinking about it, it stuck." **What were some of the other names you were bandying about?** "Originally the group was called Panic. That was before we had put out the first record—or played our first gigs for that matter. There were a few other groups called Panic out there, so we thought it'd be good to change the name." **When you guys first broke, the kids who were really into punk, the last people they wanted to hang out with were the kids who liked Black Sabbath.** "That was the thing with Black Flag. There was always some tension between us and our fans—us and everybody, really. My favorite band was the Grateful Dead, still is. One of my favorite bands is Black Sabbath, and at that point people didn't want to hear about groups like that, but I think that that's what made our group unique. We had an open mind. We didn't think, 'Oh, we're playing punk music.' To me, we were playing music that was influenced by Black Sabbath and the Stooges. I'd only read about punk rock. I had long hair, and that kind of stuff. Back then, our fans were very offended when we'd inform them that we loved Sabbath."

BLACK OAK ARKANSAS Black Oak Arkansas was a longhaired Southern hard rock band popular in the early seventies. The founding members all grew up in rural Arkansas near the town of Black Oak. Originally called Knowbody Else, they renamed themselves after their hometown when they moved to L.A. in 1969.

BLACK SABBATH Seventies heavy metal gods Black Sabbath were originally called Earth when they got together in 1968 in Birmingham, England, to play music much lighter than their trademark crunch. They were forced to change their name because another, then more successful band was already using it. They chose their new moniker from a song by drummer Terry "Geezer" Butler, inspired by an occult thriller by novelist Denis Wheatley.

BLIND FAITH Blind Faith, composed of Eric Clapton, Steve Winwood, Ginger Baker, and Rich Grench, only  stayed together long enough to produce one album and one arena tour in 1969. The album's infamous cover, featuring a photograph of Baker's topless prepubescent daughter clutching a toy airplane, was at the time replaced in the U.S. with a photo of the band. The band's name, coined by Eric Clapton, was an ironic commentary on the hype surrounding the "instant supergroup" in the music press.

BLIND MELON A "blind melon" was a term the father of late lead singer Shannon Hoon uses to describe a stupid person.

BLONDIE Blondie formed in New York City in 1974. In *Making Tracks: The Rise of Blondie,* the band's 1982 autobiography by Debbie Harry, Chris Stein, and Victor Bockris, bleached-blond Harry recalls: "Nineteen seventy-four was the nonperiod of punk. Television, the Ramones, and us, either as Angel and the Snake (for two gigs) or with no name, were just playing around. Then we did two or three gigs with a couple of girls, Julie and Jackie, and we all had blond hair, so that's when we started fooling around with the name Blondie. I had always been called 'blondie' by assorted motorists and truck drivers and thought it was a good name, a natural (HA!), so easy to remember."

BLOOD, SWEAT AND TEARS Al Kooper formed Blood, Sweat and Tears in New York City in 1967 as an experimental rock band that would incorporate jazz, blues, folk, and classical elements into its sound. After Kooper left the following year, the band changed direction and had considerable commercial success. Kooper discusses the band's genesis in an interview: **How did you come up with the name?** "I was playing in an all-night jam session, and I had cut my finger and I didn't know it. When they turned the lights on at the end, the organ keyboard was covered with blood. So I called everybody over, and I said, 'Wouldn't this make a great album cover, for a band called Blood, Sweat and Tears?' And so we called it that, except we didn't use that picture because no one had a camera." **Where does the phrase "blood, sweat, and tears" come from?** "It's borrowed from a Winston Churchill speech. That's where it originated." **Were you a fan of Churchill's?** "He was okay.

He was no Magic Johnson . . ." **Are you pleased you took that name, in retrospect?** "Well, actually it's my least favorite credit in my résumé. I left the band and the band got famous doing something that I really wouldn't have done. So people associate me with that, and I don't like to fondly think of it. So I leave it out when I can." **Do you recall any other names that you considered using at the time?** "Oh, sure, Catharsis was one. Herpes Simplex was another. Those were the two working names. We ditched Catharsis because no one could pronounce it, and we ditched Herpes Simplex because they probably wouldn't have let us use it anyway."

BLUE CHEER   The band, best known for their crunching cover of Eddie Cochran's "Summertime Blues," formed in Boston in 1967 and took their name from a particularly high-quality strain of LSD.

BLUE ÖYSTER CULT   Although bands formed by rock critics are usually unlistenable, that's not the case with the Blue Öyster Cult. An early version of the group was launched at the State University of New York at Stony Brook on Long Island, in 1967, by Sandy Pearlman, a writer for the now defunct rock magazine *Crawdaddy. Entertainment Weekly* chronicled the band's birth in an August 1991 issue:

"In 1971, musician and songwriter Sandy Pearlman was trying to devise a new name for his band. Standing on a New York street corner with rock writer Richard Meltzer (who had been in an earlier incarnation of the group), Pearlman glanced into the window of a nearby restaurant and noticed that the menu included Blue Point oysters. 'I said, "Why don't we call it Blue Oyster Cult" he recalls. 'And Richard said, "And we'll add an umlaut over the O!" And I said, "Great" ' . . . [The umlaut] was meant to bring all sorts of ambiguous implications to the name."

THE BONZO DOG BAND   The Bonzo Dog Dada Band, as they were originally called, was formed in 1965 by London art students dedicated to playfully subverting traditional music, primarily the jazz and popular music of the twenties and thirties. Dada came from the Dadaist movement of the late teens and early twenties, which aimed to undermine conventional art and literature in a similarly comic vein. The band named themselves after Bonzo Dog, a British cartoon character popular in the twenties and thirties, because they thought the animal captured the spirit of the period. They changed their name to the Bonzo Dog Doo-Dah Band, reportedly because they grew tired of explaining what Dada was, and ultimately shortened the name to the Bonzo Dog Band.

BOOKER T. AND THE MG'S   Booker T. is Booker T. Jones, a multi-instrumental musical prodigy who in 1960 joined the Stax Records house band as a saxophone player. With the MG's (Memphis Group), he recorded several instrumental hits, including "Green Onions" and "Hang 'Em High," and backed up a variety of Stax and Atlantic performers, including Sam and Dave, Wilson Pickett, and Otis Redding.

BOOMTOWN RATS   Ireland's Boomtown Rats had a minor hit in the U.S. in 1980 with "I Don't Like Mondays," a song based on the case of Brenda Spencer, a seventeen-year-old San Diego woman who shot eleven people and killed two of them on January 29, 1979, because, she told police, "I don't like Mondays." The Rats are better known, however, for the charitable activities of their front man, Bob Geldof, who organized Live Aid in 1985.

In *Is That It?*—his 1986 autobiography—Geldof explains how in September 1985 his then nameless band prepared for their first gig in a classroom at the Bolton Street College of Technology: "We were not sure what was expected of us and so we rehearsed a set which lasted two and a quarter hours. We had plenty of material. What was really bothering us was what name we should choose. We could no longer continue calling ourselves Mark Skid and the Y-Fronts, as we did occasionally. It was too undergraduate and too obvious."

" 'What about Traction?' suggested Gary. " 'Crap, sounds like a heavy metal band. It has to sound dark and brooding. People have to respond to everything, even the name. It must all be exciting.'

" 'What about Nightlife?'

" 'That's not bad. But it needs something more. It needs to be a name like the Rolling Stones that can be shortened to the Stones or whatever. What about Darker Days?'

" 'Sounds like a Doors number. What about the Nightlife Thugs?'

"Nightlife Thugs was written in neat lettering on the blackboard in the classroom at Bolton Street College of Technology. We regarded it with mixed feelings as we entered from the nearby pub where we had spent the last half hour . . ."

After the first set, Geldof had a change of heart:

"The night before I had been reading Woody Guthrie's autobiography, *Bound for Glory*. I had reached the part where, at age of about eleven, oil was discovered in his hometown in Oklahoma. Teams of casual laborers moved in and the place became a boom town. A split had developed between the native kids and the children of the newcomers. Excluded from existing gangs, the new kids formed their own. It was called the Boomtown Rats. Even at that tender age Woody could spot the moral discrepancy and left his old friends to join the new gang. As a result the two gangs eventually merged. Suddenly in the interval during the first gig the aptness of that gesture struck me. I went up to the promoter and said that the band had changed its name. He rubbed out Nightlife Thugs and in its place scrawled the Boomtown Rats.

"The others thought that was a laugh."

BOSTON   Guitarist and keyboard player Tom Scholz formed Boston in 1976. In response to a request for an interview, Scholz designated management representative Jim Collins to respond: **How did the band get its name?** "I spoke to Tom Scholz about it, and he said there are as many different versions of this story as there are original drummers for the band—there're five guys who claim to be the original drummer. He says he doesn't know exactly who thought up the name." **It wasn't Tom?** "It wasn't Tom, and there are about five or six people who claim that they made it up, all of whom would have some varying levels of

37

credibility. He says all that he recalls is that he approved the name. There was a list of about eighty names going around and that was one that he liked, but he was a lot more concerned about the music than he was about the name. He likes it now, though. I was trying to think of some really good story to tell you, like that he wanted to use Chicago but it was already taken. The truth of it is kind of lost in the pages of history, as it were."

DAVID BOWIE   Born David Robert Jones in 1947, he changed his name to Bowie in 1966, after the hunting knife frequently referred to in American films, to avoid confusion with Davy Jones of the Monkees.

BOW WOW WOW   Sex Pistols manager Malcolm McLaren formed Bow Wow Wow in 1980, after pairing Adam Ant's

original backup band with singer Annabella Lwin, a fourteen-year-old native of Burma whom he discovered working at his local dry cleaner. McLaren got the band signed to EMI, the label that had signed and then dumped the Sex Pistols in 1977. He named them Bow Wow Wow in honor of Nipper, the dog who is known to Americans as the trademark of the RCA Corporation, but in England is the mascot of HMV (His Master's Voice) Ltd., the giant retail record-store chain owned by EMI.

THE BOX TOPS   Led by Alex Chilton, the band formed in Memphis, Tennessee, in 1967, and had a series of blue-eyed soul hits, including "The Letter," which went to number one that year. Wayne Carson Thompson, who wrote the song, recalled in *The Billboard Book of Number*

One Hits that the group hadn't decided on a name by the time they recorded it: "One of the guys said, 'Well, let's have a contest and everybody can send in fifty cents and a box top.' Dan [Penn, the song's producer] looked at me and I looked him, and he said, 'Hell, that sounds great,' and named 'em the Box Tops."

BREAD Lite-rock band Bread formed in Los Angeles in 1969 and in three years released eleven Top 40 hits and earned six gold records. Originally called Pleasure Faire, they changed their name to Bread after getting stuck in traffic behind a Wonder Bread truck.

THE BREEDERS Twin sisters Kim and Kelley Deal first formed the Breeders in their native Ohio, before Kim moved to Boston and joined the Pixies in 1986. According to a 4AD record label bio, they chose the name because they liked "the fact that 'Breeders' is both a derogatory term to describe heterosexuals *and* the name of a horror film they've never seen ('because we sound like one')." Kim told *QW* magazine, "My good friend is gay, and we were in a bar together one night. I commented on some guy, and all I remember my friend saying was 'Oh'—in disgust—'He's a *breeder*.' I thought, 'Wow, we're like little rats in the corner copulating.' It was funny, kind of turning the tables. For so long, heterosexuals, especially guys, would say things like 'Homos gross me out, man.' But now it was a homosexual saying 'Oh, well they're *breeders*.' And one of the girls in the band, Josephine Wiggs, is a lesbian, so it's particularly funny in that way." Many music journalists not in on the joke initially took the band's name at face value. "They thought we're like cows," Deal told *QW*. "The Mother Earth–cow crap or something—like we're motherhood. I hope they don't think that anymore."

BROWNSVILLE STATION The band formed in Ann Arbor, Michigan, in the early seventies and had a big hit in 1973 with "Smokin' in the Boys' Room." Guitarist Cub Koda recalls: "It was a week before our very first gig and we still didn't have a name for the band yet. Every guy in the band seemed to want to call it something else. One guy wanted to call it the City. We thought that was too ominous for the style of music that we played. Another guy wanted to name it after that Moby Grape song, 'Omaha.' We nixed that right away. I wanted to call it the Amazing Pelicans, which got vetoed like right quick. Our drummer at the time, T. J. Cronley, was a major league hitchhiker. The guy would hitchhike to gigs and beat us there, and he said, 'Well, y'know, boys, we're playing a lot of Southern rock and roll, rockabilly, that kind of music where it all comes from the South—we should name it after the southernmost city in the United States, which is Brownsville, Texas.' We thought, 'Well—Brownsville? I don't know.' Then it got back to sort of generic names, and someone decided to call it the Station. Then we started thinking that was too bland, it should have more pizzazz to it. What would be like the funkiest place on earth? To which T. J. again said, 'Why that's simple, lads—the Greyhound bus station in Brownsville, Texas. Irresponsible border guards, naked kids running around with flies attached to them, sensational ambiance in the men's room—it's wonderful.' Well, we were all on the floor laughing, and it just seemed obvious. So we said, 'That's it.' We didn't realize that five, six, seven, eight years down the line, with eleven letters in Brownsville, most of our marquee appearances at rock/hippie theaters would have our name reduced down to 'Brown Sta.' "

BUBBLE PUPPY   One-hit wonders Bubble Puppy, who reached number fourteen on the charts in 1969 with "Hot Smoke and Sasafrass," got their start in Austin, Texas, in the late sixties. Originally called the New Seeds, and later Willowdale Handcar, they took their name from Aldous Huxley's novel *Brave New World.*

THE BUCKINGHAMS   Originally called the Pulsations when they formed in Chicago in 1965, the group changed its name after they secured a thirteen-week contract to appear on the variety show "All Time Hits" on the local TV station WGN. When the show's producers requested a British-sounding name, a station security guard reportedly suggested the Buckinghams. Producer James Guercio recalls that the name was inspired by Chicago's Buckingham Fountain.

BUFFALO SPRINGFIELD   Buffalo Springfield helped pioneer country rock during its brief career from 1966 to 1968. Originally called the Herd, the band changed its name after spotting the words Buffalo Springfield on a steamroller. In *Crosby, Stills & Nash: The Authorized Biography* by Dave Zimmer and Henry Diltz, published in 1984, drummer Dewey Martin recalls: "I lugged my drums over to this old house on Fountain Avenue. They were paving the streets, I remember. And there was this steamroller out front with a big sign on the side that read BUFFALO, SPRINGFIELD. When I walked into the house, the guys were already talking about taking that as a group name, and I thought, 'Yeah, what a great name—Buffalo Springfield.' "

THE BUGGLES   Trevor Horn, who is best known for his work as a producer on albums by the Art of Noise, Frankie Goes to Hollywood, and ABC, formed the Buggles in England in the late seventies. In 1979, the band—Horn on vocals and Geoffrey Downes on keyboards—had an international hit with "Video Killed the Radio Star." The video for the song was the first one MTV aired when it launched in August 1981. In the July 1982 issue of England's *The Face,* Horn says: "I know the name's awful, but at the time it was the era of the great punk thing. I'd got fed up of producing people who were generally idiots but called themselves all sorts of clever names like the Unwanted, the Unwashed, the Unheard. . . . When it came to choosing our name, I thought I'd pick the most disgusting name possible. In retrospect I have frequently regretted calling myself Buggles, but in those days I never really thought much about packaging or selling myself. All that really concerned me was the record."

BUSH   The band took their name from the Shepherd's Bush area of London, where they formed in the mid-nineties. That it is also British slang for marijuana was also a factor, as was, perhaps, its reference to the female nether regions. That it is also the name of America's forty-first president is, one can only hope, irrelevant.

THE BUTTHOLE SURFERS   The Butthole Surfers formed in 1980 in San Antonio, Texas. Guitarist Paul Leary recalls: "Well, we started out being called Nine Foot Worm Makes Own Food, and we were like—no, I'm sorry, it gets complicated. We started out as the Dick Clark Five back in San Antonio, Texas. We had this deal about wanting to change the name of the band for every show that we did, so the next show we were the Dick Gas Five, and then we were Nine Foot Worm Makes Own Food. Then we started playing in Austin as that, and then we were the Vodka Family Winstons, and we were Abe Lincoln's Bush. Then we were the Inalienable Right to Eat Fred Astaire's Asshole, and then the next show we were just plain the Right to Eat Fred Astaire's Asshole. Then one night we were playing as something really ridiculous, I think it was Independent Worm Saloon. We had a song that Gibby [Haynes, the singer] wrote called 'Butthole Surfer,' and we were getting ready to play as the Independent Worm Saloon, and some guy got up—I think it might have been Chris Gates from the Big Boys, or somebody, I can't remember who it was that got up—and introduced us as 'the Butthole Surfers.' At the end of that night we got paid a hundred and fifty bucks, so we thought we were going to get rich, and we stuck with that name and, well, here we are." **So it was his idea to name you guys after the song?** "Let me ask Gibby if he remembers who that was . . . Yeah, it was Chris Gates at Dukes's in Austin. When we were getting ready to play, he got up onstage and announced that we were the Butthole Surfers, and we got paid that night. . . ." **So that was a good omen.** "Right. That was the first time we'd ever been paid, so we stuck with the name." **So what was the song about?** "It's on the first EP, and it's just about butthole surfers." **Which are . . . ?** "God, that's kind of a . . . kind of a . . . difficult thing to explain after all these years." **Oh, really?** "There were a lot of wild band names going on in San Antonio at the time. I don't know if you were ever into the 'kung fu' scene in San Antonio back in the early eighties . . ." **I'm not familiar with it.** "There was this place

43

called the Almus Pharmacy that was next door to a hearing-aid store, and on Tuesday nights they'd open up the hearing-aid store and roll away the racks of these hearing aids. They'd have these 'kung fu shows,' they called 'em, with bands like the Ridiculoids, and there were these two bands called the Againsters, and the Againsters—the *Againsters* were against everything, and the *Againsters* were into doing shit over and over. Cleopatra's Vagina was a killer band. Jesus, that was a long time ago . . ." **In retrospect, are you glad that you stuck with the name? Any regrets?** "Oh, no, no regrets at all. My mother even says the name now. It took her ten years, but I've heard her say it now three times about." **Well, I know that in a lot of papers, when they list who's playing where, often they'll abbreviate your name.** "Yeah, but then you get the occasional satisfaction of hearing some guy with a British accent saying it." **Do you still play "Butthole Surfer" in concert?** "We haven't, but you never know. We might just whip that one out. I'd almost forgotten about the song, really."

THE BUZZCOCKS Pete Shelley and Howard Devoto decided to form their band after seeing the Sex Pistols play twice in one weekend in London in February 1976. Here's the story of that turning point, according to the liner notes of the 1989 Restless Records box set *Product:*

" '[Sex Pistols singer Johnny] Rotten was certainly being very abusive and moody,' says Devoto; 'I remember his shoes and his ratty red sweater. We thought they were fantastic: it was, we will go and do something like this in Manchester.' They returned to Manchester with an increased sense of urgency: After we'd seen them the first time, me and Howard were sleeping in the living room,' says Shelley. And as we were going off to sleep, Howard was quizzing me, like if we got our band started, what was my commitment. Would I stick with it, was it a hobby or was I into living the life. And I said: "Yeah, I'm into living the life." '

" 'Identities were changed to seal this pact of transformation. From that weekend in February came the group name from a chance reading of a *Time Out* [a British magazine] review of 'Rock Follies,' [a Seventies TV sitcom about an all-girl rock band] which ends 'get a buzz, cock.' [In American vernacular, this roughly translates to "check it out, dude."] The name hinted at a certain aural and sexual irregularity. Instead of Peter McNeish, there was Pete Shelley, which is what Peter would have been called if he were a girl. Howard Trafford became Devoto: 'I hadn't thought about names until Peter introduced me as Howard Devoto, so I was. Pretentiousness is interesting: your ambition has to outstrip your ability at some point.' "

THE BYRDS   The Byrds were called the Jet Set when they first got together in 1964, named by group leader Roger McGuinn, who was fascinated by airplanes and flight. When they signed to Columbia Records later that year, the band—all hardcore Anglophiles—had become the Beefeaters, after the royal guard in England, in an effort to pass themselves off as British. They renamed themselves the Byrds on Thanksgiving Day that year, misspelling their name like the Beatles, whom they would soon be frequently compared to.

Drummer Michael Clarke recalls: "It was over Thanksgiving dinner, and everything was happening at the moment with the letter B—the Beach Boys, the Beatles. We decided on Birds and then changed the I to a Y." **Why did you decide to do that?** "It gave it a bit of flair, I think." **Who was at this Thanksgiving dinner?** "Well, it was all of us. Me, Gene Clark, David Crosby, Chris Hillman, and Roger McGuinn, Eddie Tickner and Jim Dickson, our managers." **Where were you?** "We were at Jim's house." **Who initially came up with the name?** "I actually don't remember that, but it was by mutual consent."

CABARET VOLTAIRE   Sheffield, England's prolific Cabaret Voltaire took their name in 1973 from the Zurich café that served as headquarters for Swiss dadaists in the years before World War I. It was the band's intention to apply the dadaist aesthetic doctrine of irrational disturbance to music using found sounds and tape manipulations.

CAMPER VAN BEETHOVEN   Former college-radio sweethearts Camper Van Beethoven made their mark in the eighties by combining an absurdist sense of humor and an eclectic musical style. The name was suggested by David McDaniel, one of the band's original guitarists. Lead singer David Lowery told *Rolling Stone* in May 1988:

"McDaniel was into this stuff that would sound like

it made sense, but really it didn't. He'd watch a lot of TV, accept all this mass-media stuff, and spit it out all chopped up."

CAN   The art-rock band formed in Cologne, West Germany, in 1968, first as Inner Space, then the Can, and finally Can. The band allegedly liked the name because it meant different things in a variety of languages: the Turkish word "can," pronounced "chan," means life or soul; the Japanese word "kan" means feeling or emotion; and the Japanese word "chan" means love when used in salutation. Keyboard player Irmin Schmidt has said that the name is an acronym for "Communism, Anarchism, Nihilism."

CANNED HEAT   Canned Heat, formed in Los Angeles in 1966 by Bob "Bear" Hite and Alan "Blind Owl" Johnson, took their name from a song by country blues singer Tommy Johnson. Hite's nickname came from his three-hundred pound frame, and Johnson got his from his fading vision.

CAPTAIN BEEFHEART   When he was thirteen, Don Van Vliet moved with his family from Los Angeles to Lancaster, California. There he met Frank Zappa, a classmate at Antelope Valley High School, who nicknamed him Captain Beefheart because he seemed to have a "beef in his heart" against the world.

THE CARS   The band's name was suggested in 1976 by former Modern Lover David Robinson, after he and Greg Hawkes got together with Elliott Easton, Ric Ocasek, and

Ben Orr, who had all been in a local Boston band called Cap'n Swing. Ocasek liked the name because "it's so easy to spell; it doesn't have a *z* on the end; it's real authentic. It's pop art, in a sense."

THE CAVEDOGS Boston's Cavedogs made their debut in 1990 with *Joyrides for Shut-ins,* an album of hard-rocking pop songs. Bassist Brian Stevens discusses the band's origins: "Todd, our guitar player, was sitting in English class during the late seventies, and the teacher (Steve Ark of Springfield, Ohio) made reference to a woman of questionable physical attributes using the word *cavedog* to describe her. The other students and Todd thought this was funny—this was the seventies. At the same time, Todd's band was looking for a name because they were about to play at the big high school dance—it was the seventies and also Ohio. So like the filament in the glass vacuum for Edison, they called the band the Cavedogs.

"Years later, in the eighties, Todd and I were in a band in Boston going by a name that would embarrass even Sting. Suddenly, as if lightning had struck a second time, the Cavedogs became the only name that we all could agree on. From that day on—the nineties now—we were the Cavedogs, a band of questionable physical attributes."

THE CHAMPS The band formed in Los Angeles in 1957 when the members, working as sessionmen for the Challenge label which was founded by singing cowboy Gene Autry, got together to record instrumental tracks for another artist. Using some leftover studio time, they decided to lay down some additional tracks and release their own single. Needing a group name, someone suggested the Champs in honor of Gene Autry's horse, Champion. "Train to Nowhere" bombed until disc jockeys discovered the B-side, "Tequila," which became a huge hit.

THE CHANTELS   The vocal group met while singing in the school choir at St. Anthony of Padua high school in the Bronx. They took their name from that of a rival school, St. Francis de Chantelle. Their hits included "Maybe" and "Every Night (I Pray)" in 1958, and "Look in My Eyes" and "Well I Told You" in 1962.

THE CHARLANTAS UK   The Charlatans UK formed in Northwich, England, in the late eighties, and picked their name out of a dictionary. The UK was added to distinguish themselves from an American band called the Charlatans formed in San Francisco in 1965.

CHEAP TRICK   The band formed in Rockford, Illinois, in 1974. In a VH1 interview, guitarist Rick Nielsen recalled: "We went under a bunch of different names, 'cause we kept geting fired from every club that we would play at. And finally, [the] one week that we didn't get fired our name was Cheap Trick and so we kept it."

CHICAGO   Originally called the Big Thing in 1967, the band was renamed the Chicago Transit Authority by James Guercio when he took over the band's management in 1967. After the CTA threatened to sue, Guercio shortened the name to Chicago in 1970.

Guercio recalls: "I came up with the name because I

grew up on the northwest side of Chicago and I had a hell of a time getting to school. I used to have to take the bus. It was called the Chicago Transit Authority. *CTA* was what was on the bus that took me to school." **You suggested it and—**"I didn't suggest much, they'll all confirm that. I said 'This is the name, this is what the band'll be called,' and that was it. There wasn't much discussion. Where there was discussion was, after the first album, Mayor Daley and the City of Chicago were threatening litigation." **What was their reason?** "I was not authorized to use the name of the Chicago transit system to name a band, and I hadn't copyrighted it, I hadn't paid them a royalty, so we would've gotten sued if we just used CTA. I don't know where the band was with these issues, but it concerned CBS, and they just kind of turned the Daley dogs on me. The group is not aware of a lot of this because I was in control of all the marketing and was producing the band and managing the band. And I was a little too autocratic. . . . Anyway, I did not want to change the name from the Chicago Transit Authority. And I'll tell you who had the most impact. People were saying, 'It's too long. So you're from Chicago, so you took the bus—nobody's going to remember it. You ought to just shorten it to Chicago.' And I really wasn't responding to the arguments, but I was convinced by David Geffen. David and I were old friends from when he was in the mail room [at the William Morris Agency], and I had helped him with somebody he'd discovered called Laura Nyro. I had worked with Laura, laid out her first album . . . David Geffen talked me into it. He just said, 'Call them Chicago. We can remember Chicago. Why are you hanging on to CTA? You're getting sued.' I've got to give David the credit. I talked to the band and said, 'Boys, we'll shorten the name and call ourselves Chicago.' I had designed all those logos. The minute they fired me, they put their picture on the cover."

THE CHI-LITES An R&B vocal group from Chicago, the Chi-Lites began in 1960 as the Chanteurs, then became Marshall and the Hi-Lites. The group became the Chi-Lites after they were threatened with legal action by another group calling themselves the Hi-Lites. Group leader Marshall Thompson later told an interviewer: "We figured if we added a C to the front of our name, that'd give us an original name and identify us as coming from Chicago." After some soul hits in the sixties, the Chi-Lites broke into the top of the pop charts in the early seventies with "Have You Seen Her" and "Oh Girl."

THE CHIPMUNKS The Chipmunks were created in 1958 by Ross Bagdasarian, who, as David Seville, had a number-one hit earlier that year with "Witch Doctor," a novelty song that featured sped-up voices. Bagdasarian was reportedly driving through Yosemite National Park in California when he came upon a chipmunk who refused to budge from the road. Inspiration struck; the car did not. Bagdasarian recorded "The Chipmunk Song" and named the mythical trio of singing rodents after executives at his record label, Liberty. Alvin was named for company president Al Bennett, Simon for his partner Si Waronker, and Theodore for recording engineer Ted Keep. "The Chipmunk Song" hit number one that year and sold millions.

CHUMBAWAMBA The band formed in Leeds, England, in 1982. In a fax, guitarist Boff explains: "There's a theory that an infinite amount of chimpanzees sitting at an infinite amount of typewriters will eventually, hitting the keys at random, lead to one of them writing the entire works of Shakespeare. Several scientists have tested this logic in order to try to put some kind of context of time and possibility into it. There was an article in something like *The Enquirer* or *The English Observer* in the late seventies which printed a list of words which a chimpanzee had actually typed. Predictably enough none made any sense whatsoever. So in the quest to avoid finding a name which had immediate pigeonhole possibilities, in 1982 Danbert [Nobacon, vocals and keyboards] was blindfolded and placed in front of a typewriter: an Olivetti Dora, in fact, with a green case. He typed a list of words filling an A4 size piece of paper and from that resulting list we found the word chumbawamba. Really. That's it. Sounded good to say, looked weird, so we kept it."

CHUBBY CHECKER Chubby Checker was born Ernest Evans and got the nickname Chubby from a friend at the poultry market where he worked. After he was signed to Philadelphia's Cameo-Parkway label, Dick Clark's wife, Bobbie, suggested he call himself Chubby Checker, a pun on Fats Domino, whom he was adept at impersonating.

CIBO MATTO The name of the New York-based group, formed by Japanese expatriates Miho Hatori and Yuka Honda in the mid-nineties, means "food madness" in Italian.

CINDERELLA Cinderella formed in Philadelphia in 1985 and took their name from a similarly titled soft-porn film that members Tom Kiefer and Eric B. saw on cable TV one night.

THE CIRCLE JERKS Singer Keith Morris formed the band in Los Angeles in 1979 after he left Black Flag. **How did you come up with the name and what were the circumstances?** "Greg [Hetson, the guitarist] and I were over at Raymond Pettibon's house—he's the guy that did all the artwork for Black Flag in the beginning, and he just did the last Sonic Youth album cover. We knew Pettibon because I was in Black Flag for a couple of years. We were over there getting the artwork for some fliers, and we didn't have a name for the band. We were originally going to call ourselves the Plastic Hippies or the Runs, and we decided those names weren't really anything particularly outstanding. Pettibon had an American slang dictionary there. We started flipping through it and I came across *circle jerk*, and I thought, 'Wow, that's kind of interesting.'" **Did you guys decide on it right then and there?** "Yeah, I looked at Greg, and he looked at me, and he kind of said, 'Yeah, this looks like something that we could use, this looks like something that could be permanent.'" **Are you glad you went with it?** "Yeah, I mean, it never bothered me, when I found out what it meant, it was really—it was just a really stupid name. If you look at all these band names, they're just really stupid names, and the more stupid the name, the more outstanding it is, I guess. Or the more memorable." **The reaction to it must have been interesting in various quarters.** "We weren't able to be mentioned in a lot of newspapers, say in the Bible Belt. We were referred to as the

C.J.'s. Just like the Dead Kennedys and the Butthole Surfers. Even the *L.A. Times* won't put Butthole Surfers in the newspaper, it's the B.H. Surfers." **Do you think that hurt you at all, or it didn't really make a difference?** "Y'know, I never really paid that much attention to it, I never really felt it to be that detrimental. It's just like, get on with it—don't be bogged down in all the other bullshit." **I remember reading a press release from somewhere or other, something about Stonehenge—do you recall this? As an explanation for your name, that it was a reference to the druids.** "Oh, yeah, I remember that, that was a press release from about four, five, six years ago." **Did you guys in any regular way make up explanations for those who weren't in on the joke?** "Well, that was one of them, that one of our publicists made up. We really basically, when people asked us what the name meant, we would just steer them towards their local library, and hopefully their local library would have a copy of some kind of an American slang dictionary." **So you wouldn't tell people straight out?** "No, not really. We've told people that it meant like six guys in a van driving around in circle—which happened to us quite a bit. Say like we would pull into a city, say like in Boston, the way the streets are set up, it's very easy to get lost. We just kind of made up things like that." **Any other stories of that nature spring to mind?** "Not really. We had some feminists say that 'well, it's kind of a male kind of thing,' and we said, 'I guess women could do it, too, if you used your imaginations.' "

THE CLASH   The Clash formed in London in 1976. In the liner notes from *The Clash on Broadway* box set, bassist Paul Simonon recalls:

"We had plenty of names that only lasted five minutes before being chucked out the window. There was the Weak Heart Drops, after the Big Youth record, the Outsiders, and Psycho Negatives, and the Mirrors. . . . I was looking through the *Evening Standard* with the idea of names on my mind, and I noticed that the word *clash* appeared a few times. I thought the Clash would be a good name. So I suggested it to the others."

In an interview, guitarist Mick Jones confirmed Simonon's account, adding that "we just picked the word—we weren't aware of any of the connotations until we saw it in adverts and stuff."

THE COASTERS   The Coasters, considered one of the most influential vocal groups of the rock-and-roll era, began as the Robins in Los Angeles in the late forties. In 1955, after two of the Robins left the group, remaining members Carl Gardner and Bobby Nunn were joined by Billy Buy and Leon Hughes, and they changed their name to the Coasters, after their West Coast origins.

COLLECTIVE SOUL   The band formed in Atlanta, Georgia, in the early nineties. In a VH1 interview, singer and guitarist Ed Roland explained: "I was reading the book [*The*] *Fountainhead* by Ayn Rand, and I just came across a part that said 'collective soul.' We were in a little transitional period, trying to rename the band. We were called Marching Two-Step, and everyone thought we were a country act. So we decided to change the name and that's basically the only name we could decide on."

BILL HALEY AND THE COMETS   Bill Haley, best known for the 1955 hit "(We're Gonna) Rock Around the Clock," started a country band called the Down Homers in 1949. They soon changed their name to the Saddlemen, and in 1952 Haley dropped his cowboy image and changed the name of the band to the Comets, a pun on Halley's comet, named for British astronomer Edmund Halley.

COMMANDER CODY AND HIS LOST PLANET AIRMEN George Frayne formed the band in Ann Arbor, Michigan, in 1968. In an interview, he explains how he came up with his name and the band's: "I'm a science fiction nut from way back, and *The Lost Planet Airmen* was the name of a Republic [Pictures] serial made from outtakes and throwaway shit from *Commando Cody, Sky Marshal of the Universe,* which was a Flash Gordon–clone weekly serial that they showed at the movies in 1948. The hero had a black leather jacket on and a rocket on his back that had like two commands—'up/down' and 'fast/slow.' He put it on 'up' and 'fast,' and I went, 'Great, what's this guy's name?' and his name was Commando Cody. So I changed it from Commando to Commander, and the name of the group was the Lost Planet Airmen." **Did the movie studio ever hassle you?** "No, as a matter of fact we had a promotion in L.A. at the Troubador with Tristan Coffin, who was the guy who was the original Commando Cody. We posed for pictures and they published them in *Billboard* and all that usual stupid shit that people do. I really loved that old stuff, that Flash Gordon stuff. I've got a degree in cinematography, so I was doing my own little stuff, having little vacuum tubes fly around on strings and shit."

THE COMMODORES The Commodores began as a funk band in 1970 after meeting at the Tuskegee Institute in

Tuskegee, Alabama, as freshmen. At first called the Jays, they became the Commodores after horns player William King picked the name out of the dictionary. They later joked that they were almost called the Commodes.

THE COMMUNARDS   Formed by ex-Bronski Beat vocalist Jimmy Somerville and multi-instrumentalist Richard Coles in 1986, they named themselves after the French revolutionaries who ruled Paris from March 18 to May 28 in 1871. Their sole U.S. hit was 1987s "Don't Leave Me This Way."

CONCRETE BLONDE   The band originally formed in Los Angeles in 1982 as Dream 6. Singer Johnette Napolitano says of the name Concrete Blonde, "Michael Stipe of R.E.M. came up with the name, and I don't even think he knows what it means. And I've never asked him."

ALICE COOPER   Alice Cooper was born Vincent Damon Furnier, the son of a minister, in Detroit in 1948. He formed a band called the Earwigs in Phoenix in 1965, which he later changed to the Nazz, only to learn that there was another band using the name on the East Coast—Todd Rundgren's group. Although it has been reported that Alice Cooper was allegedly the name of a seventeenth-century witch who, according to a Ouija board, was reincarnated as Furnier, the singer told Headley Gritter the real story in an interview in the 1984 book *Rock 'N' Roll Asylum:* **How did you come up with the name Alice Cooper?** "I have no idea. I

57

really don't. It was one day, just [snaps fingers] boom. We needed a new name and I said, 'Why don't we call ourselves . . .' and I could have said Mary Smith, but I said Alice Cooper. And that was the name." **What drug induced "Alice Cooper"?** "I don't know. It was probably just Phoenix air, you know, Phoenix smog. But think about it— Alice Cooper has the same kind of ring as Lizzie Borden and Baby Jane. 'Alice Cooper.' It's sort of like a little girl with an ax. I kept picturing something in pink and black lace and blood. Meanwhile, people expected a blond folksinger."

CORNERSHOP The Anglo-Asian band formed in London in 1991. Frontman Tjinder Singh, who is of Indian descent, explained their irony-tinged name to Jon Savage in *The Village Voice:* "A lot of people think that all Asians do is run cornershops [convenience stores] and that they're timid and they don't socialize. We want to destroy that stereotype."

ELVIS COSTELLO Born Declan MacManus (not McManus, as often reported) in Liverpool, England, he changed his name at the insistence of manager Jake Riviera when he signed to Riviera's Stiff Records in 1976. He told *Rolling Stone:* "I hadn't picked the name at all. Jake just picked it. It was just a marketing scheme. 'How are we going to separate you from Johnny This and Johnny That?' He said, 'We'll call you Elvis.' I thought he was completely out of his mind." Costello is a family name on his mother's side.

COUNTING CROWS Formed in San Francisco in 1991, the band took their name from a phrase in an old English divination prayer that suggests that life is as pointless as counting crows. Singer Adam Duritz heard the line in the film *Signs of Life*, which starred his former girlfriend Mary-Louise Parker.

COUNTRY JOE AND THE FISH   Formed in San Francisco in 1965, Country Joe and the Fish were one of the most political of the Bay Area psychedelic bands. In an interview, guitarist Joe McDonald explains: **How did you come up with the name Country Joe and the Fish?** "Well, in 1965 I was working on a magazine called *Rag Baby* magazine with a guy named Ed Denson, who owned Takoma Records along with John Fahey. We didn't have any copy for an issue, and so we decided to put out a talking issue of the magazine. Because Ed was in the small-label record business, he knew Chris Strachwitz of Arhoolie Records, and we went up to Chris's house. I had just met Barry Melton, who became the first member of Country Joe and the Fish, and we went up there with a couple of other people to record some songs for this talking issue of the magazine, which was an extended play, the first of the decade, actually, the first self-produced album. It was really kind of an ad hoc thing, y'know, it wasn't that well

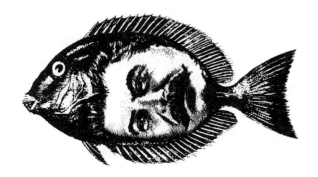

planned. I had written 'Fixing to Die Rag' a little bit earlier, and it was popular, so we decided we would put 'Fixing to Die Rag' on there, and a song, 'Superbird,' and two songs by Peter Krug, one about the Watts riots, which had just happened. So we recorded it all, and it was the first recording of 'Fixing to Die Rag'—skiffle band, kind of washboard, and washtub bass and stuff . . . Afterwards, Ed realized that we had to have some label copy and decided that, because he was into folk music and politics, he would call the group that we had assembled and recorded that day Country Mao and the Fish. I asked him why, and he said, 'Because Mao Tse-Tung had said that the revolutionaries move through the people like the fish through the sea.' And I said, 'Hmmm, wow, that's a little bit . . . dumb.' And he said, 'Well, okay, we'll call it Country Joe and the Fish after Joseph Stalin.' And I had been named after Joseph Stalin coincidentally, and—" **He knew that at the time?** "I didn't consciously know that at the time, and he didn't know that at the time, but I let it go there. I said, 'Okay, well Country Joe and the Fish sounds at least not as dumb as Country Mao and the Fish.' Then it was released, and that was really the beginning of Rag Baby Records, and the beginning of Country Joe and the Fish. I was the only Joe in the group, and I was the lead vocalist, so people began calling me Country Joe." **But that wasn't originally intended, was it?** "It had nothing to do with it at all. Nothing. And I tired of telling people that I wasn't Country Joe. I get a lot of requests for this same story that I'm telling you right now, a lot of requests, and I try to tell people that the story is not as entertaining as the name, and they always insist that I tell them, and then I tell them, and they agree that no, it's really not. But anyway, that's the true story.

There it is." **Where did the "Country" part of Country Mao and the Fish come from?** "Well, like I said, he was into early folk music. There was a folk music revival at that time—delta blues and jug-band music and that kind of stuff, and it was quite common to have Country in front of people's names, like 'Blind' somebody, 'Country' somebody. It wasn't a generic folkband name, but it sounded like one, so that's what it is. Like I said, he was combining folk music and left-wing politics." **Did people suspect the "Fish" was someone in the band?** "Well, ultimately what happened was that people left the group and sold out their interest in the name, and by the end—'69 I believe it was, or '70—we, Barry Melton and myself, finally signed a piece of paper which he interprets as saying that he is the Fish. So when we play together in a week or so, it'll be 'Country Joe' McDonald and Barry 'the Fish' Melton. It's evolved to that. He's become a lawyer, so we don't argue with him anymore."

THE COWBOY JUNKIES The band was formed in Toronto in 1985 by siblings Margo (vocals), Michael (guitar), and Peter Timmins (drums) and bass player Alan Anton. The name was picked because it reflected the band's sound, a mix of country and blues, and was attention getting. Michael Timmins told *Rolling Stone* in March 1989:

"The root of both musics comes from the same American experience. Blues is black, country's white, and yet they come from the same sort of feelings. It's a poor, rural experience."

THE CRAMPS Singer Lux Interior and guitarist Ivy Rorschach met in Cleveland in the mid-seventies. They chose the name, Rorschach explained in an interview, because it sounded like a street gang and had a variety of meanings: "It's an involuntary physical reaction. It's something that your mind can't control. In France, it's a sexual disturbance for men—it's slang for hard-on—so it applies to men and women."

THE CRANBERRIES   The band formed in Limerick, Ireland in the late eighties. Their name was originally the Cranberry Saw Us, with the last two words occasionally hyphenated, a play on "cranberry sauce." It was suggested by the lead singer at the time, who was replaced in 1990 by Dolores O'Riordan. The new lineup eventually shortened their name to the Cranberry by the time they mailed demo tapes to several English record labels. The cassettes were marked The Cranberry's, and when they received their first response, an otherwise encouraging rejection letter from Rough Trade, it was addressed to the Cranberries. The name stuck.

CRASH TEST DUMMIES   The group started in the mid-eighties as a loose circle of friends who gathered at an after-hours club in Winnipeg, Canada, to play what lead singer and songwriter Brad Roberts told *Rolling Stone* was "ridiculous cover tunes, everything from cheesy Irish traditionals to TV theme songs to acoustic versions of Alice Cooper hits." They chose the name Crash Test Dummies as a joke, also considering the Chemotherapists and Skin Graft. "Eventually," Roberts recalled, "the band transformed into something other than just a fuck band on the weekends. But the name stuck, because it had been written down so many times."

CREAM The short-lived supergroup, formed by Eric Clapton, Jack Bruce, and Ginger Baker in 1966, took the name Cream because the trio reportedly considered themselves the cream of the crop of British blues players.

CREEDENCE CLEARWATER REVIVAL The band was formed in El Cerrito, California, in 1959 by guitarist John Fogerty, bassist Stu Cook and drummer Doug Clifford. Clifford explains: "In 1967, we decided not to be a part-time band—everybody was either a student or had a job. We decided that we were going to go for broke and be full-time musicians, so we had to quit everything else we were doing. At that time we also decided to change our name from the Golliwogs, a name that was given to us by our manager. We knew a fellow named Credence Newball and liked his name, but we thought if we had a hit, he'd probably sue us. So that didn't work but we liked the idea of 'credence,' as in truth and justice and all that—we were very young and certainly idealistic. So we added an *E* to Credence to make it totally different, to indicate we were going to do our own thing and we weren't going to play acid rock anymore. Clearwater came from an Olympia beer commercial, and it had a great image—y'know, the stream coming down, and it also had significance in the scheme of things in that it meant we had a clear direction. The revival was a revival of ourselves—we weren't going to wear the uniforms that this manager had for us, we weren't going to do things that we didn't want to do, we were going to take this thing and run with it, so to speak." **And revival didn't have anything to do with a more "rootsy" approach?** "Actually not, not at all, but a lot of people thought that. There were a lot of misconceptions I guess, but that was really it. It was a revival of the four of us, a personal revival if you will." **This book I have here, the *Faber Companion to 20th-Century Popular Music*, says, 'Fantasy's new owner Saul Zaentz encouraged a return to American roots music and gave the band a new name, Creedence Clearwater Revival.''** "No, that's absolutely false." **Maybe he was just trying to take credit.** "I don't know. I don't know what the source of that is, but we named ourselves. It was a laborious task. It took two weeks of purely concentrated effort, and everybody threw in their favorites. Quite honestly, Fantasy was a jazz label and Saul didn't know that much about rock and roll. He knew that we were good at what we did, and he respected what we did, but he didn't tell us what to play or give us our name." **Do you remember some of the other names that you had for a while before you settled on Creedence?** "Initially, we—Stu Cook, John Fogerty, and I—started as an instrumental trio called the Blue Velvets. Then Tom Fogerty [John's older brother] started coming to our gigs, and he used us to back him up on recordings to try and get a record deal for himself as a singer-songwriter. When he was doing that we were Tommy Fogerty and the Blue Velvets. After that, we were the Visions for one week, until we found out that there was another Visions out there, and we didn't want to have problems with them. That's when the manager named us the Golliwogs." **What was his name?** "Max Weiss, former owner of Fantasy records, and we hated it, and he added the little uniforms that we wore and all that stuff." **Were there any other names?** "No. When we changed the name from the Golliwogs, it became Creedence Clearwater Revival and that was it." **It's one of the greats. It's got a nice cadence to it.** "That was part of it, too. It was almost like a musical approach to a name in that sense. In just flowed, and it was fun."

THE CREW CUTS Natives of Toronto, the Canadian quartet began as the Canadaires in 1952. It was Cleveland disc jockey Bill Randle who, in 1954, convinced them to change their name to the Crew Cuts after their hairstyles, which were actually not crew cuts but Chicago box cuts, cropped on top but longer on the sides. But why quibble? Randle helped them get a deal with Mercury and soon they were knocking out the hits, including "Earth Angel," "Ko Ko Mo (I Love You So)," and "Gum Drop."

BUDDY HOLLY AND THE CRICKETS Buddy Holly formed the Crickets in 1957 with Jerry Allison on drums, Niki Sullivan on rhythm guitar, and Joe B. Mauldin on bass. In the biography *Remembering Buddy* by John Goldrosen and John Beecher, Niki Sullivan recalls the origins of the band's name: "We were at Jerry's house, and everything we thought of had been used or didn't fit. So Jerry got an encyclopedia, and somehow we got started on insects. There was a whole page of bugs. We thought about *grass-hopper* and quickly passed that over. And we did consider the name Beetles, but Jerry said, 'Aw, that's just a bug you'd want to step on,' so we immediately dropped that. Then Jerry came up with the idea of the Crickets. He said, 'Well, you know, they make a happy sound, they're a happy type of insect.' I remember him saying, too, 'They make music by rubbing their legs together,' and that cracked us up. So we kept going and tried some other names, but finally we settled on the Crickets. You know, though, we really weren't happy with that name. In fact, at some point, we were laughed at—might have been the Cotton Club, just after our record was released. People kidded us about the name, about how dumb it was."

CROWDED HOUSE The band, originally formed in Melbourne, Australia, in 1985, took their name from the cramped bungalow they shared in Hollywood, where they had come to record their debut album.

THE CRYSTALS The group was formed by five Brooklyn high school girls in 1961, who named themselves after songwriter Larry Bates's daughter, Crystal. They soon became one of Phil Spector's most successful groups, recording such hits as "He's a Rebel," "Da Doo Ron Ron (When He Walked Me Home)," and "Then He Kissed Me."

THE CULT The band began as the Southern Death Cult in 1982, became the Death Cult in 1983, and was finally reduced to the Cult in 1984. Their original name came from a headline singer Ian Astbury spotted in a newspaper.

CULTURE CLUB Culture Club was formed in London in 1981 by singer Boy George, born George O'Dowd. After a very brief stint singing in front of Bow Wow Wow under the name Lieutenant Lush, George formed his own band called In Praise of Lemmings, which evolved into Sex Gang Children. When drummer Jon Moss joined the band, he convinced George to change the name, arguing that it was too negative. The initial suggestion of Caravan Club became Can't Wait Club, and finally Culture Club.

THE CURE   The band, led by singer and guitarist Robert Smith, was formed in Sussex, England, in the midseventies. They performed as Obelisk, Goat Band, and Malice, before becoming Easy Cure in 1977. Smith explains in a band biography: "We decided we needed another name if we were going to start playing again, so one night in the middle of January 1977, we sat around in my kitchen discussing it. One of our songs was called 'Easy Cure,' a song written by Lol [Tolhurst, the band's drummer at the time], and eventually, in desperation we settled on that." A year later, following the departure of original guitarist Porl Thompson, the band decided to change their name again. Smith remembers: "I had always thought Easy Cure was a bit hippyish, a bit American sounding, a bit West Coast, and I hated it, which put Lol's back up as he'd thought of it. Every other group we liked had *the* in front of their name, but the Easy Cure sounded stupid, so we just changed it to the Cure instead. It upset a few old fans but . . . well, there you are . . . I thought the Cure was much more *it*." The story that Smith named the band The Cure because his father was a pharmacist, while perhaps more interesting, is false.

CURVED AIR   The group, which formed in England in 1970 and at one time included future Police drummer Steward Copeland, took its name from *A Rainbow in Curved Air,* avant-garde composer Terry Riley's 1969 album.

D

D GENERATION   The band formed in New York City in 1991. Lead singer Jesse Malin told *Rolling Stone:* "We named ourselves because we felt music and society and everything's degenerated, and we said we're going to be the D Generation. It's a few plays on the words. 'Dad, I'm degenerate. Sorry.' "

THE DAMNED   The seminal British punk band took their name in 1976, inspired by singer Dave Vanian, a grave-digger who often performed in a vampire outfit. They were originally called the Doomed.

DAMN YANKEES   Guitarist Ted Nugent formed Damn Yankees in 1989 with former Styx guitarist Tommy Shaw, ex-Knight Ranger bassist Jack Blades, and drummer Michael Cartellone. Nugent explains: "Tommy Shaw, Jack Blades, Michael Cartellone, and I were in our early hours of discovery, jamming, when I called home to Michigan to see how my hunting buddies were doing. My friend asked what the hell Ted Nugent and Tommy Shaw could possibly sound like together, and I immediately responded that we sounded like a bunch of damn Yankees to me. I felt right away that we all shared a sense of origin, blues and American R&B in our preferred musical attitude, overtly Americana. I had begun to work on my next solo record for Atlantic Records to be titled *Ted Nugent: Damn Yankee!* and I decided that what I played with these boys was just the same as I would play for myself, so I opted to utilize the title then and there. Bingo!"

THE DARLING BUDS   The Welsh quartet, which formed in the late eighties, took their name from Shakespeare's eighteenth sonnet: "Shall I compare thee to a summer's day?/Thou art more lovely and more temperate:/ Rough winds do shake the darling buds of May,/And summer's lease hath all too short a date."

DASH RIP ROCK   Formed in Louisiana in the late eighties, the band named themselves after Elly May's movie-star boyfriend on the sixties TV sitcom "The Beverly Hillbillies."

DAWN   The group, which had a number-one hit in 1971 with "Knock Three Times" and eventually became known as Tony Orlando and Dawn, was named for Stacy Dawn Siegal, daughter of Jay Siegal of the Tokens.

DEACON BLUE   The band formed in Glasgow, Scotland, in 1985, taking its name from the Steely Dan song of the same name.

DEAD CAN DANCE   Brendan Perry and Lisa Gerrard met in Melbourne, Australia, in 1980 and moved to London in 1982. In a Warner Brothers Records press bio, they state, "To understand why we chose the name, think of the transformation on inanimacy to animacy. Think of the processes concerning life from death, and death into life. So many people missed the inherent symbolism, and assumed that we must be 'morbid gothic types,' a mistake we deplored, and deplore."

THE DEAD KENNEDYS The Dead Kennedys formed in San Francisco in the late seventies. In an interview with Peter Belisto in the 1985 book *Notes From the Pop Underground,* singer Jello Biafra recalls: "I thought we should call ourselves Thalidomide, but nobody else really wanted that. [Guitarist East Bay] Ray suggested the Sharks—he was very conscious of wanting to survive and figured a record contract was the way to do it. My second choice for a name was Dead Kennedys. A couple of different people back in Colorado [in Boul-

der, where he lived before moving the San Francisco] came up with that, but didn't have the nerve to use it. That was the one that seemed to provoke the most reaction—positive or negative—so I just began telling people that was the name of the band."

THE DEAD MILKMEN Philadelphia-based wise guys the Dead Milkmen began playing together in 1984. Guitarist Joe Jack Talcum recalls the band's origins in an interview: "I came up with the name when I was writing a parody of a fan club newsletter—like any band's fan club—sort of like the Spinal Tap thing. I needed a name for the fake band, so I came up with Dead Milkmen. It was derived from the Dead Boys, who were a punk band at the time. I wanted it to be like a country or rural folk-punk kind of band, so I thought Milkmen might be appropriate. I put the two words together, and that was it for the name." **Were you in a band at this time?** "No, I was not in a band, I was in high school. I Xeroxed these newsletters to hand to my friends for fun." **And everyone knew it was a gag?** "Yeah, everyone knew it was a gag, that the band didn't exist. Although Rodney [Anonymous, the vocalist], who got the newsletter, got together with me and another friend of mine, who is out in California now, and we started to make tapes, and that's how we started to make the [fictional] band actually become a [real] band." **So when it came time to choose a name, you . . .** "When it came time to choose a name we just used what we already had, because we had already printed twenty-two newsletters by then, twenty-two issues. So in the twenty-third issue, we just made it more truthful." **Is it still being published?** "Yeah." **What are you up to now, what number?** "Fifty-two." **How often does it come out?** "Two times a year, maybe three times a year, but when I was in high school, it would come out about every week. We got through a lot of issues in the early stages." **Did you guys consider any other names?** "Yeah, we had lists and lists of names, and one of the names was Hüsker Dü, that Rodney came up with, from

the game Hüsker Dü. We didn't know about the real band."
Was Hüsker Dü around at the time? "They were around, but
we didn't know of them. But when their record came out,
I bought it, and I liked them. Another name was Orna-
mental Wigwam, which Dave [Blood, the bass player] and
I have performed under, and we released one song on a
compilation. When we don't play with Dean [Clean, the
drummer] or Rodney, we call ourselves that. We had a
whole list of names, actually, but the drummer, Dean, liked
Dead Milkmen the best and thought since we already had
a small mailing list of people who got the newsletter, why
not just incorporate it."

Deee-Lite   The name of the New York-based group,
best known for their 1990 hit "Groove is in the Heart," was
inspired by the song "It's De-Lovely" from the 1936 Cole
Porter musical *Red, Hot, and Blue*.

Deep Blue Something   The band got its start in 1991
at the University of North Texas as Leper Messiah, a name
taken from a line in David Bowie's "Ziggy Stardust." They
decided to change their name because too many people
assumed that they were a heavy metal band. The new
name was coined when lead singer Todd Pipes asked his
bandmates what they should call an instrumental that he
had composed. Drummer John Kirtland recalls, "I said
'Deep Blue Something,' expecting him to fill in the last
word. Instead, he said 'That's pretty cool,' and it became
the name of the band."

Deep Purple   When the band took shape in 1968, they
considered the name Concrete God, but settled on Deep

Purple at the urging of guitarist Ritchie Blackmore's grandmother after her favorite song, "Deep Purple," a number one hit for Nino Tempo and April Stevens in 1963. If this seems like an unlikely inspiration for an act whose trademark was the hard-rocking sound characterized by their 1973 hit "Smoke on the Water," it's worth noting that their first two hits in 1968 were mellow revivals of Joe South's "Hush" and Neil Diamond's "Kentucky Woman." The name is not a reference to hickeys as sometimes rumored.

DEF LEPPARD English heavy metal band Def Leppard formed in Sheffield in 1977. Singer Joe Elliott explains how Def Leppard got its name in a band biography:

"In 1975, when I was idling my time away in art class in school, instead of painting or drawing the obligatory bowl of fruit or vase with a rose in it, I used to design posters for rock bands and concerts, such as Led Zeppelin, the Beatles, the Who, the Rolling Stones. After a while, I ran out of bands, so I started making names up. I invented various names of bands, one of which was Deaf Leopard.

"When I left school, I took my art folder home, and somehow the badly put together poster for the mythical band Deaf Leopard ended up on my bedroom wall. So when we all got together in my room to discuss the forming of a band and what we could call it, it was suggested, I think by Sav [bassist Rick Savage], 'Why don't we call our band Deaf Leopard?' He had seen the poster and I had told him that they didn't exist, it was just a bad, school-drawn, shitty poster. We all decided then and there—the majority of us; I don't think [guitarist] Pete Willis was too keen on it—that we thought it sounded good.

"Once we got into our little rehearsal space and were

firing up, learning our new songs, the original drummer for the band, Tony Kenning, suggested that we change the spelling of the name Deaf Leopard to Def Leppard because it didn't look good as it was. It was a little too 'punky' looking. There were a lot of punk bands out at the time with animals in their names—Boomtown Rats, Flying Lizards, Slaughter and the Dogs—and we didn't want 'spikies' showing up at our gigs. So Tony crossed the *A* out of Deaf with a pen and stuck a stick on the *O* to make a *P*. But it wasn't until we rewrote the name without the *A* that someone pointed out that it looked a bit like Led Zeppelin, but we couldn't be bothered with changing it by then. We'd rather be linked to Led Zeppelin than to Slaughter and the Dogs or the Flying Lizards.

"So we stuck with it. Any relevance to similarities between Def Leppard and Led Zeppelin are absolutely, 100 percent coincidence, even though we really are big fans of theirs."

THE DEL FUEGOS   The band formed in Boston in 1980. Singer and guitarist Dan Zanes named the band after Tierra del Fuego, the southernmost point in the world before Antarctica. Says Zanes, "We were looking for something as low down as you can get. Del Fuegos sort of said it all."

THE DEL-LORDS   See **The Dictators**

DEPECHE MODE   In 1980, vocalist David Gahan joined synthesizer players Vince Clarke, Martin Gore, and Andy Fletcher, who were performing as Composition of Sound, to form a new band. Gahan remembers: "We were rehearsing for gigs in the spring of 1980, but were yet to agree on a name. I was attending Southend Technical College at the time, studying fashion, and I would sometimes refer to fashion magazines for ideas. One of these magazines was a French publication called *Dépêche Mode* [which means 'fast fashion'] and the name just kind of stood out. I took a copy along to the next rehearsal, and the other three agreed that we should take the name."

DEREK AND THE DOMINOES Eric Clapton's band made its debut at the Lyceum in London in June 1970. In *Eric Clapton in His Own Words* by Marc Roberty, Clapton remembers: "Tony Ashton [of the group Ashton, Gardiner & Dyke] suggested we call ourselves Del and the Dominoes because he always used to call me Del. So it became Derek and the Dominoes. It was the last minute in the dressing room before we went on stage at the Lyceum. We didn't have a name up to that point. You don't think of that when you're forming a group. In fact, when someone suggests to you that you get a band title, that's when you really start to worry about whether you should have a band at all, because you realize so much hinges on the name and you've blown the whole gig no matter what the gig is like."

DEVO Devo got their start in Akron, Ohio, in 1972, and were named after the band's philosophy of "de-evolution."

In a V-H1 interview, bassist and vocalist Jerry Casale explained: "We thought that there wasn't progress, there was regression, and that things were falling apart. We called it 'de-evolution' and took the name and contracted it to Devo since it was more catchy."

THE DICTATORS The Dictators formed in New York City in the early seventies, and after they broke up, singer Handsome Dick Manitoba (born Richard Blum) and guitarist Scott "Top Ten" Kempner formed the Del-Lords in 1982. Kempner discusses the origins of both bands in an interview: "Before the Dictators, [keyboard player] Andy Shernoff, who was our main songwriter, he had one of the first fanzines in America. It was a fanzine sort of based on rock and roll and sort of based on his friends, and it was called *The Teenage Wasteland Gazette*. He would write these articles, and some of them would be factual and some of them he would just completely make up. One time he made up a story about a fake rock festival, and he made up all these names for bands, like Beat the Meatles. Our road manager was Steve Shanks, and there was a band called Shanks' Mother. There was Tommy the Truck, Fabulous Moola—named after the female wrestling champion—the greatest sports dynasty of all time, she was champ for like twenty-seven years—and the Dictators. And when Sandy Pearlman, who became our first manager and producer, came to hear the band, and we didn't have a name, and he loved the band, he asked, 'Well, what's the name of the band?' At that point the Dictators was the best of the ones we had, so we said, 'How about the Dictators?' and that was it. This is '72, '73. We knew each other from New York City, but Andy was going to school up in New Paltz."

Tell me about the Del-Lords. "I came up with the name the Del-Lords. It was meant to have a fifties kind of rock band connotation, and also a street gang. Where I grew up in the South Bronx, there were a couple of bands who used the 'Del' prefix. There were the Del Bombers and the Del Diamonds, and I always thought that was the coolest thing in the world. I always thought that there was a real connection between a street gang and a rock and roll band, at least the way I play it. So there were all these things floating around, and one night, me and a friend of mine, my ex-brother-in-law actually, were sitting around watching TV, smoking a bunch of pot, eating Häagen-Dazs, and watching the Three Stooges. I always say it was like in *West Side Story* when Tony sees Maria, how the whole room goes dark and there's a spotlight—this episode was produced, written, and directed by Del Lord. And that was just too much. It's like, what does God have to do, actually come down and deliver the pizza himself, y'know? This was good, I was struck. The first bunch of guys I tried it on, they didn't like it. They thought it sounded too much like a street gang. I was like, well, yeah, exactly. So it was rejected, it was too intense for them. When [guitarist] Eric Ambel joined the band from Joan Jett and the Blackhearts, the name we were using at the time was the Cheatin' Hearts, after the Hank Williams song. Eric felt like he was walking into this joke. He split with Joan Jett on bad terms, they had really kind of screwed him, and he felt sort of like going from the Blackhearts to the Cheatin' Hearts was too much. So I said, 'Hey, I got this other name. How about the Del-Lords?' And these guys go, 'Yeah, man, that sounds like a street gang!' And that was it." **How did the whole "Del" phenomenon start?** "I don't know, but somebody must have taken it from the Spanish, meaning 'of the' something. Some moron from the Bronx, probably from my neighborhood, said, 'Yeah, man, that's fuckin' cool—Del. Del-Lords!' He just applied it without knowing anything about it. I think it's just a misinterpretation of something that became part of our lingo, our rock lingo."

DIE KREUZEN From an interview with guitarist Dan Kubinski: **How did you guys end up choosing your name?** "The four of us were living in a one-bedroom apartment with this girl, and she was always talking about how she was going to get a band together and she was going to call it Die Kreuzen. She had found this name in some kind of a German Bible, some sort of church manual or something, I can't remember what it was. She had this book, and she was always talking about, 'I'm going to call it Die Kreuzen, I'm going to call it Die Kreuzen.' She never did, and we liked the way it looked, we liked the way it sounded, so we were like, 'That's us—that's what we need.' So that's the story." **Do most people know what it means?** "Well, a lot of people ask what it means, and a lot of people tell us what it means, and it's all different. When we played in Germany, the people over there would ask, 'Well, what does this mean?' We were like, 'Well, you tell us!' " **So what were some of the different things you've heard from people who claim to—** "People who come up and are authoritative and claim to know exactly what it means because their German teacher told them?" **Yeah.** "It means to cross the street, or it means 'the crossing,' like when you cross yourself in church—y'know, 'Father, Son, Holy Spirit,' whatever. I've even heard things like 'two people meeting and talking and crossing in front of a church.' Just all kinds of weird shit." **And what does it mean to you?** "What it actually means, the two words are used incorrectly together, I guess. If it was supposed to be 'the cross,' it would be *Der Kreuz,* not *Die Kreuzen.* What it meant to us—it didn't mean anything to us, it was just something to call ourselves. It wasn't like the Splatterheads, or the Scumbuckets from Hell, because you know what kind of music that's going to be when you hear the name. We wanted something that you couldn't pigeonhole, and we thought that was a good thing. That's what it meant to us." **Are you glad you picked it?** "Yeah, I think we have the most misspelled name in rock, but . . ." **I think Procul Harum is up there.** "They probably are, you're right." **What happened to the girl you were living with who was going to start this band?** "I'm not sure what happened to her—she moved out to California and we never heard from her again." **Did she know that you were appropriating her name?** "Yeah, we were still living with her at the time, and we just said, well, we're taking it." **I heard that when you'd play out in L.A., you would occasionally get low-riders showing up at your shows.** "Yeah, they thought we were a low-rider band, they thought we were Die Cruisin'."

THE DILS   The pioneering American punk band the Dils was formed by brothers Tony and Chip Kinman in the late seventies. In an interview, Tony explains the band's origins: **How did you guys come up with the Dils?** "The Dils started as a band that Chip and I put together right out of high school. The name was based on a poem about a band I'd written in

school. The Dils was a contraction of the name of that band. Later, a lot of people thought it meant different things, but it didn't really mean anything specific. It was just like a nonsense syllable." **What was it a contraction of?** "The band in the poem had been called the Cosmic Dilrod Troubadours. To us, that name—the D-I-L-S, those four letters—just stood for the band. When the Dils moved up to San Francisco and became part of a punk scene there, a lot of people thought it stood for different things—dildos; dill pickles; a contraction of Dylan, as in Bob, even though the spelling was wrong; or Dillinger, one of the reggae deejays. It really more or less came just to stand for us rather than anything else."

DINOSAUR, JR. From an interview with guitarist J Mascis: **How did you choose that name of all names?** "I don't really remember, to tell you the truth. We just kind of thought it was cool." **Was it your idea?** "Yeah." **Was it a reference to "dinosaur rock" or anything of that nature?** "Not really, no." **Were you guys actually sued by the band the Dinosaurs from the West Coast, or did they simply threaten you?** "Yeah, they just, y'know, sent a certified letter, a cease-and-desist kind of thing. They just wanted us to change our name, so their hippie buddies wouldn't go see us and think it was them. The guy, the Fish, Barry Melton [of Country Joe and the Fish], he's the lawyer, and his office is on Haight Street, so I guess that he became a lawyer after he became the Fish . . . So we just thought of some stuff and came up with *junior,* and that was okay with them." **Did you guys have any other names that you considered at the time before going with Dinosaur?** "We were Mogo at first. We had a singer who was in the band I was in before, Deep Wound. We played one show and got rid of him." **Mogo—what was that from?** "This book, *Mogo's Flute,* that was in my basement." **What was that about?** "I don't know—some kid's book." **Do you have a particular fondness for dinosaurs?** "No . . ." **It just popped into your head?** "Yeah. Now I get tons of dinosaur paraphernalia from my relatives, though I keep telling them no." **What do you do with it all?** "Lose it . . . My sister gave my dad a sweatshirt she made for his birthday that said 'Dinosaur Sr.'" **Are you pleased you went with the name?** "I don't think about it. I mean, it bummed us out at the time, to have to change it, everyone hated the *junior* part. I wanted to change it." **Everyone in the band?** "All our friends and stuff." **Why?** "I don't know, it just sounds . . . They'd all go, [sing-song] 'Junior, junior' . . . make fun of us . . . thought it was lame. Some people still won't even say that." **What, "junior"?** "Yeah, it bothers them." **Does it bother you?** "I don't think about it."

DIRE STRAITS Guitarist Mark Knopfler launched Dire Straits in London in 1977, originally calling the band the Cafe Racers. Under that name, the band debuted at a festival headlined by Squeeze. A friend of drummer Pick Withers observed their sorry financial condition and suggested they call themselves Dire Straits, which they did for their second gig.

DR. FEELGOOD John "Wilko" Johnson formed the band in 1971 in Canvey Island, England, taking its name from the 1962 song "Doctor Feel-Good" by bluesman Willie "Piano Red" Perryman, which was recorded under the name Dr. Feelgood and the Interns. The band did not take its name from a song by Johnny Kidd and the Pirates, as has been reported.

Dr. Hook   The band was formed in Union City, New Jersey, in 1968 by front men Ray Sawyer and Dennis Locorriere. The group played the bar circuit as the Chocolate Papers, among other names, until lead guitarist George Cummings renamed them Dr. Hook and the Medicine Show in 1969. Dr. Hook became associated with lead singer Ron Sawyer, who had lost his right eye in a car crash and wore an eye patch, giving him a piratical appearance. The band's hits included the satirical "Sylvia's Mother" and "The Cover of 'Rolling Stone.' "

Dog's Eye View   Singer Peter Stuart explains, "I lived in a basement apartment in Chicago and all I could see were fire hydrants and feet walking by . . . so I decided that I had a dog's eye view of the world."

The Doobie Brothers   The Doobie Brothers formed in 1970 in San Jose, California. Drummer John Hartman discusses the band's beginnings in an interview: **How did you guys choose that name?** "Well, we were all living in a house on Twelfth Street in San Jose, and we were sharing the rent because it was cheaper that way. We put this thing together at the time, it was like a three-piece, and I guess we were trying to figure out the name. Actually, I think we were moving from a three-piece to a four-piece." **Who was in the band at that point?** "I'm trying to think—it was Tommy [Johnston, guitar] and myself, that's for sure, and Dave Shogren on bass, and I think Pat [Simmons, guitar] was getting into it. I'm pretty sure we were going in that direction, and we needed some sort of name. We were calling ourselves all kinds of things, but we needed some sort of name to continue on. There was a guy, Dyno Rosen, who was living there—Keith was his real first name. He was a real madman who was doing his own little pottery thing in the backyard. He was kind of an all-around artist. One day, we were at the table, Tommy and myself, and Dyno's sitting there eating Cheerios, and he's got milk in his mustache. Tommy and I are talking about a name. Prior to this, we were looking at dictionaries and encyclopedias, wondering, 'What are we going to name this stupid thing?' Dyno is sitting there eating his Cheerios, and boom! He says, 'Why don't you guys call yourselves the Doobie Brothers?' We looked at each other and went, 'What? What are you talking about? What's that?' I didn't know what it meant. Tommy was kind of in a daze, going, 'What?' And Dyno says, 'Yeah, call yourselves the Doobie Brothers, huh, huh, huh, huh, huh.' So I went, 'Yeah, right,' and Tommy went, 'Sure, yeah, we'll think about it.' And what had happened was, we had a show to do, we got a job I think a couple of days later, and the guy wanted to know, 'Well, what do you guys call yourselves?' And we didn't have a name except for, y'know, that morning when Dyno said, 'Why don't you call yourselves the Doobie Brothers?' So we used the name and we just stuck with it." **Was Dyno a big smoker of doobies [marijuana]?** "Yeah, I'd say he was moderate. He got into that stuff, he got into the lifestyle. He was out of the Navy, and he was

'doing his own thing,' as it were. You remember those days. He was trying to get into the crafts. He was trying to make his own pottery. I think that was his major thing, making pots from scratch." **So the name stuck.** "Yeah, it stuck for a couple of months. Then we got a shot at doing an audition with this little production company down in San Mateo, and that mushroomed into a contract with Warner Brothers. When Warner picked us up, there was no turning back. We were an underground band—we looked really freaky, and I use that word in the context of that period. We had long hair, we wore the Levi's, and we had lived in a single house—they called it a commune, it was not a commune, it was just a rental share." **Who's "they," the publicists?** "Yeah, the publicists. We made the mistake of telling them that we did these shows from time to time and bikers would show up, so the publicists said, 'Oh, it's a biker band,' and blew everything out of proportion." **I read in a bio in one of these rock encyclopedias that you guys would perform regularly for the Hell's Angels.** "Well, we never did." **What about the Doobie name? Did everyone understand what it was a reference to? Have you ever caught any flak for it?** "Oh, yeah. Well, I was stupid, first of all. I was from the East Coast and I never really got into the culture. I've got to be honest with you—Tommy and myself were kind of rednecks in a lot of ways, we weren't into that whole hippie culture. We went into it, but we did it on our own terms. We weren't like, 'Free love, baby.' We really never did that. We were into the peace thing and the freedom aspect, and the cultural thing, but we never grasped the whole thing. So I didn't know what doobie meant, until I read the article. Dyno had been reading *Rolling Stone* and pointed out this paragraph: 'as they were smoking a doobie.' I said, 'Rosen, what does this mean?' and he said, 'You idiot! It's a joint!' " **Was Warner Bros. at all nervous about the reference? Did they know what it meant right off the bat?** "Sure, they knew. I don't know if they were worried about it. I don't think so, a large company like that, even in those days. They had gone through the Hendrix period and Joplin and all of that, and I think their main concern was how we could perform and were we going to make money for them, and so on. We had the problem of dealing with it on the road. We had the problem at radio stations, where they'd go, 'Doobie? What does that mean?' And we'd have to tell them. And a lot of times in the first few years, we'd say, 'Uh, it's a French family name.' We went so far, seriously, as to go to a radio station that was square and straight and go, 'Doobie? Haven't you heard of *Romper Room*?" **And they bought it?** "They bought it. To tell how trite that is, you had to get by that hurdle for them to talk to you. If it related to a drug, it didn't matter if you did it or not, as soon as *doobie* meant marijuana, that meant you did it. You were a long-haired hippie commie pinko and you were off the station, and they'd never play you. And it happened to us. A couple of stations pulled our stuff when they found out what it meant. And hell, we were sitting, going, 'Who cares? It's a name.' We were going to call ourselves the Red Devils, y'know, because of the meat product, but we figured the Christian element down in Oklahoma wouldn't take that too well." **You've got to look at things from every angle, I guess.** "Well, it's unfortunate, because when we first got into this, we tried to second-guess everything. You had to've been there, but we were pretty bad off. We were trying to work and nobody would hire us. We were scraping for dough just to make rent, let alone food." **In retrospect, are you pleased you went with it?** "I don't think we could've come up with a better name. I can recall the feeling of 'Gee, these names aren't going anywhere, and Doobies is just as bad as the rest of them.' " **I read somewhere that at first you called yourselves Pud.** "That was before Doobies, yeah. And of course, you can't use that name, so we had to change. People were getting pretty hip to that. We only used that for a very short time."

THE DOORS   The name the Doors grew out of conversations Jim Morrison had with his roommate Dennis Jakob at UCLA. Discussing names for an imaginary rock band, they agreed that a good choice would be the Doors, which came from a poem by William Blake: "There are things that are known and things that are unknown, in between the doors." Aldous Huxley used the line for the title of his book on mescaline experimentation, *The Doors of Perception.*

DRAMARAMA   The band formed in New Jersey in the early eighties. Bass player Chris Carter remembers: "I believe it was a girl in a bar who we knew from high school or something who came up with the name. She said it to our lead singer when we were trying to come up with names. Apparently it's a slang term for theater people who take their roles home with them. 'I'm a pharmacist,' y'know, like all day long—someone who just gets too involved with their role and just becomes that person. It was funny because it was like 1981 and Bananarama just came out or was about to come out, or something. But we liked it and didn't think there were too many people who would confuse *drama* and *banana*." **Did you guys ever**

have that problem? "Not really, because I don't think anyone ever really heard of us on a wider scale until '86 or '87 and by then they were kind of over. We had more of a problem with the name in that people thought we were a different kind of band. They thought, 'Oh, they're a gothic band,' or, 'They're some electronic band.' We almost called our last album *Too Late to Change Our Name.*"

THE DREAM SYNDICATE   The Dream Syndicate formed in Los Angeles in the early eighties. Singer and guitarist Steve Wynn says of their name: "Well, like most everything else, we stole it. It's kind of funny actually. We got the name from a Tony Conrad record. He was in Faust. He had a solo record called *Outside the Dream Syndicate,* and we just went through every name in the world, and our drummer, Dennis Duck, said, 'Well, how about the Dream Syndicate?' At that point we were so exasperated with trying to pick a name that we said, 'Fine, that's great, steal it, great.' The postscript to the story is that we were playing a show in Buffalo, on our first tour, and this guy walks up to us after the set and says, 'Hi, I'm Tony Conrad.' And we said, 'Uh-oh. Are we in big trouble?' And he said, 'No, I love you guys, you guys are great, you can keep the name.' That was wonderful. The final postscript is that we spent the first several years of our existence being endlessly compared to the Velvet Underground, and being told we were nothing but a Velvet Underground rip-off and all that kind of stuff, and then we found out later on that the Dream Syndicate was stolen by Tony Conrad from a band in the late sixties, an avant-garde noise band." [Conrad was actually in the band, which formed in 1964.]" **That LaMonte Young was in?** "Yeah, and John Cale [later of the Velvet

Underground]. So everything came around again. We has no idea about that whole thing, but we did know about the Tony Conrad record. **After you learned of the Velvets connection, did you regret choosing the name, after being compared to them so relentlessly?** "I hated the name at first. Every name you make for a band you hate, and then eventually you grow into it. As time went on, I really grew to like the name a lot. In fact, the hardest thing for me about breaking up the band was I really loved the name."

THE DRIFTERS When they formed in New York City in 1953, the name the Drifters was selected because until that point all of the members—Clyde McPhatter, Gerhard Thrasher, Andrew Thrasher, and Willie Ferbee, who was quickly replaced by Bill Pinkney—had "drifted" from one group to another. Today, over three dozen people can legitimately claim to have been full-fledged members of the Drifters at one time, and most of them have performed in bogus touring versions of the group.

DRIVIN' AND CRYIN' Like the Cowboy Junkies, the name is an allusion to the two types of music they cross-pollinate, rock (drivin') and cryin' (country).

DURAN DURAN Duran Duran formed in Birmingham, England, in 1978. Bassist John Taylor named the band after a villain played by Milo O'Shea in Roger Vadim's 1967 science-fiction spoof *Barbarella* starring Jane Fonda. Taylor recalls: "I remember sitting at home one night watching *Barbarella* on BBC TV. I'd always liked the film, thinking it was *so* sexy, but this time was struck more by the words Duran Duran, which kept getting repeated. A man's name, in fact, was what it was. Sample dialogue: 'Barbarella . . .

You must go to the planet Earth and find Duran Duran.' Well, I had a little combo of extrovert nature happening at the time centered at our Birmingham City Art School. There was myself, Nick, Steven Duffy (later Tin Tin, much later Lilac Time), and a forgotten clarinetist [Simon Colley]. The sounds we were making were quite out of the way and required an out-of-the-way moniker. After some small deliberations, the shoe fit."

DURUTTI COLUMN   Durutti Column was formed in Manchester, England, in the late seventies. Guitarist Vini Reilly named the band after an anarchist brigade in the Spanish Civil War.

BOB DYLAN   Born Robert Allen Zimmerman in Duluth, Minnesota, in 1941, Dylan changed his name in 1962. When asked by a reporter from the *Chicago Daily News* in November 1965 whether he changed his name from Zimmerman to Dylan because he admired the poetry of Dylan Thomas, as was popularly believed, he replied: "No, God, no. I took the name Dylan because I have an uncle named Dillion. I changed the spelling, but only because it looked better. I've read some of Dylan Thomas's stuff, and it's not the same as mine." This myth persisted, prompting Dylan to ask Robert Shelton, author of the biography *No Direction Home: The Life and Music of Bob Dylan,* to "straighten out in your book that I did not take my name from Dylan Thomas."

THE EAGLES The Eagles began as Linda Ronstadt's backing band in 1971. Drummer Don Henley recalls in an interview: **How did you guys settle on the Eagles?** "Well, first of all, I think the guy you need to talk to is Glenn Frey. This was more or less his idea. I think he was the one who came up with the name, for a number of reasons. I think we all agreed that we wanted a name that wouldn't go out of date, like we didn't want Strawberry something or other. We wanted something that was all-American and would be sort of timeless, and not be subject to the fads and fashions and whimsies of the day. We were all very interested in Indian lore and Indian mythology and Indian religion at the time, and the eagle was a sacred symbol in the Native American world. It was the animal that flew closest to the sun and carried the prayers of people on the ground up to the gods according to Indian legend. We had a habit of going out to the southern California desert and doing various kinds of ceremonies that were associated with the Native Americans. We'd go out as a band with a friend of ours who was sort of our teacher; he's dead now, but his name was John Barrick. We did the peyote rituals and threw up a lot. Glenn was and is a very big sports buff, and the Eagles also sounded like a sports team. In fact, we've been confused with the Philadelphia Eagles several times. That's really all I remember." **A lot of the doo-wop groups in the late fifties and early sixties had bird names. Was that a—** "Well, there were the Byrds, who were obviously a big influence on us. I don't know if that came into play or not." **I'm also thinking of the Orioles, and—** "We didn't think about that, that was not a consideration. It was more that we just wanted something all-American, something that wouldn't go out of fashion, something that was easy to remember, and something that had a very broad connotation." **Did you perform under any other names before you were the Eagles?** "No, I don't think we did. We came up with it before we did any kind of performing in public." **Are you pleased you went with it looking back now?** "Yeah, well, it's always really hard picking a name, it's really difficult. But in retrospect I guess it sort of stuck. I guess the band makes the name. I mean, just looking at Beatles without attaching it to that group, it's kind of a silly name. I guess you sort of make the name, whatever it is, so that's what happened. It turned out to be okay. I mean, you're always apprehensive when you pick a name. You go, 'Oh God, is this ridiculous? Or is it cool?' "

In an interview, Glenn Frey confirmed Henley's story: "That's essentially what happened. We had this sort of name meeting over at Henley's apartment on Camrose in Hollywood, and as I recall, we were all sitting around trying to talk about names and stuff. There was a time, when J. D. Souther and I were together as Longbranch Pennywhistle, we thought about calling ourselves Double Eagle. Part of it was that we are both Scorpios, and Scorpio evolves from the spider to the lizard to the eagle." **According to what?** "Just some astrological mumbo jumbo. So that word was around. The thing that clicked for us, about the Eagles, was that it was a simple name, it did relate to Native American mythology, it did also sound like a car club, a sports team, things of that nature. It was on the dollar bill, and every country has an eagle—the German eagle, there's an eagle on the flag of Mexico, every nation has one. Also, it's the only bird of prey that does not prey on other birds. It had all of that. It seemed to be a sort of a 'cover all the bases' kind of name. It could mean what

you wanted, you could take it any way, there was a lot of latitude for interpretation. That's really how it came to be, and everybody thought it was a good name. We've been stuck with it ever since." **What were the circumstances where you guys were confused with the Philadelphia Eagles?** "That would just happen when I would introduce myself, 'Hi, I'm Glenn Frey from the Eagles,' and they would just look at me like, 'Well, you must be the place-kicker, because you're not big enough to play football.' "

EARTH, WIND & FIRE   The band began as the Salty Peppers in Chicago in 1969, lead by Maurice White, who had recently left the Ramsey Lewis Trio. White had developed an interest in astrology and Egyptology while touring the world with that group, and this fascination inspired him to rename his band Earth, Wind & Fire the following year after the three elements in his astrological chart.

ECHO AND THE BUNNYMEN   The band grew out of the Liverpool postpunk scene in the early eighties that also gave rise to the Teardrop Explodes and Big in Japan. The band made its debut in November 1978 as a trio—vocalist Ian McCulloch, guitarist Will Sergaent, and bassist Les Pattinson—plus a drum machine. The name was coined by McCulloch's roommate, Paul "Smelly Elly" Ellenbach, whose initial suggestions included Glycerol and the Fan Extractors and Mona Lisa and the Grease Skins. Echo referred to the band's beat box, in addition to the Liverpool evening newspaper. In September 1979, Echo the beat box was replaced by flesh-and-blood drummer Pete de Freitas.

McCulloch has said that they chose the name to make sure they'd never take themselves too seriously. Co-manager Martin Kirkup told *Rolling Stone* in December 1987 that he thought the name had limited their exposure on U.S. radio: "Program directors have said they don't want to play a band named Echo and the Bunnymen. They think the name is silly or something. They deliberately ignore them."

EINSTÜRZENDE NEUBAUTEN   The industrial rock band's name means "collapsing new buildings" in German, chosen because it conveyed their desire to make music from the sounds of destruction.

ELECTRIC FLAG   Michael Bloomfield started the band in San Francisco in 1967. In the liner notes for *The Best of*

Electric Flag, bassist Harvey Brooks states, "The name of the band came up when we played a high school and they had an electric flag there. It had a base with a pipe sticking out of it and then a motor that would blow wind out of the holes, making the flag wave. It seemed symbolic."

THE ELEGANTS   Formed in New York City in 1957, the five-man vocal group took their name from a billboard advertising Schenley's Whiskey, which claimed it was the "liquor of elegance." They had a hit with "Little Star," which topped the charts in 1958.

EMF   The group formed in Cinderford, England, in 1989 and had an international hit in 1991 with "Unbelievable." They claim their name stands for "Epson Mad Funkers," supposedly a contingent of New Order groupies, and not "Ecstacy Mother Fuckers," a reference to the drug ecstacy popular at raves, as is often reported.

THE EMOTIONS   Sisters, Sheila, Wanda, and Pam Hutchinson, who topped the charts in 1977 with the disco hit "Best of My Love," got their start as a gospel group. First simply called the Huntchinsons when they began singing in their native Chicago in the fifties, they eventually became the Heavenly Sunbeams. In the late sixties, they marked their transformation into a secular group by changing their name to the Emotions, inspired by a friend's comment to their father that their voices elicited an emotional response in the form of spinal chills.

THE ENGLISH BEAT   The English Beat formed in Birmingham, England, in 1979. After the Beat broke up, guitarist Dave Wakeling and singer Ranking Roger formed General

Public in 1982. Wakeling recalls how both bands got their names, beginning with the Beat: "I was looking in the music section of *Roget's Thesaurus,* and I think there there's a part that had harmony on one side and discord on the other. This was 1979, so there was lots of discord in punk music. I noticed the word *clash,* then I noticed the word *slam,* but at first look I thought it said *sham,* and I was like, 'My God, all the groups get their names out of here!' So looking over from the discord side, I thought, 'Well, I wonder what there is in the harmony side. That would be nice.' Because we were going for a kind of harmony— musical, racial, social, etc. And more or less the first thing I saw was *beat,* and I just thought, 'Of course!' I just wandered around for a few days saying to people, 'What about the Beat?' And they all said, 'Of course! Why hasn't anybody done it?' I suppose because of the Beatles everybody had kept away from it for a little while, the Merseybeat and that sort of thing. So that was that." **There was an American band called the Beat, right?** "Yeah, that's right, there was." **How soon after naming yourselves the Beat did you discover that?** "About four months, I think. We'd done quite a lot of shows. We got a phone call, I think from Bill Graham's management company, that said—I think they'd seen us in the *New Musical Express* or something—they wanted us to be aware that they had a group called the Beat. Then we got another message saying that if we'd like to consider Bill Graham Management as representation for the band, we could probably call ourselves the Beat, which was a nice introduction to the music industry. We said no. We wanted to call ourselves the Beat Brothers first. We thought that was—well, we'd never been to America, but we thought that sounded very American. And then somebody said no, the people who owned the name the Blues Brothers would object, they found it too similar to them. So by that time we'd realized that people in America for some reason seem to love the word *English*. They didn't really like the words *British* or *UK* that much, but something about *English* was kind of cute—muffins or something. So we decided on the English Beat. So that was how that turned up." **And how about General Public? How did that come about?** "I'm a bit more vague about that. I do remember a time when I just kept seeing TV newspeople interviewing politicians, and every time politicians lied, they'd always make out they'd got a mandate: 'The general public has made it quite clear . . .' That sort of thing. So it seemed to be [invoked in] the name of crimes done by politicians in the name of people who didn't vote anyway. So I thought that was interesting. Then I thought it sounded kind of good because it was *1984*-ish, and I thought of General Public as a sort of big brother figure, as if he was some sort of military dictator. Then I just kept seeing the phrase on TV news shows all the time, and I thought it was great—we'd just be advertised all the time on the evening news. Of course, now that the group's finished, it works on me as well. I go, 'Oh, my God, I thought they were talking about the group!' " **Do you recall any other names for the Beat or General Public that you almost went with and then abandoned?** "Everett [Morton], the drummer of the Beat, was championing the idea of the group being called Skin Deep. He thought that was quite good, but that was because he was a drummer, I think, and he thought it was clever, because of drums/skins, I suppose, and having a multiracial lineup. That's the only one I remember. In that same section in the thesaurus I saw *discharge,* which I thought was kind of funny, but then another group used that some months afterwards anyway, and I was kind of glad. It's always been a good joke."

EUGENIUS   Singer and guitarist Eugene Kelly formed the band in Glasgow, Scotland, in the early nineties. Originally called Captain America, the group, under threat of a lawsuit from Marvel Comics, switched to Kelly's nickname.

EURYTHMICS   Annie Lennox and Dave Stewart, ex-lovers and former members of the Tourists, formed the Eurythmics in December 1980. The name is defined by the *American Heritage Dictionary* as "the choreographic art of interpreting musical composition by a rhythmical, free-style graceful movement of the body in response to the rhythm of the music."

EVERCLEAR   Led by Art Alexakis, Everclear formed in Portland, Oregon, in the early nineties. In an interview, Alexakis explains the origins of the name: "I had the band name before I had the band. . . . I always thought the name Everclear would be a great name for a really intense rock band. Because I really got sick on it. The dichotomy of it is so funny. It looks like water, but it's pure spirit. . . . So I thought it would be a good name for a rock band and open ended, so the band could change within it." **It didn't proscribe your sound.** "No. It would be intense. I knew all my music was going to be intense whether lyrically or musically. But other than that, it was pretty open ended." **I'm not actually familiar with Everclear. What is it exactly?** "Everclear is pure corn alcohol." **Is it a brand name?** "Yes it is." **Have you ever heard from the makers?** "We called them a long time ago. The guy just asked me not to do anything with any other alcohol company and he didn't mind. Then I found out about a year after I took the name that about the same time American Music Club had a record called *Everclear.* A lot of people tried to read into that. But I had the name way before they did on their album."

EVERYTHING BUT THE GIRL   Tracey Thorn and Ben Watt met in 1982 while studying at Hull University in England. In a VH1 interview, Thorn recalled: "We were living in a town in the north of England called Hull, and they had a furniture shop called Turner's Furniture Store, and they had a big slogan along the front of the shop which basically said that they could sell you everything but the girl, you know, to make your home complete. And when Ben and I got together we really thought we'd just be making one single or something and we chose this throwaway, disposable name, and . . . were stuck with it." Watt added: "It was really kind of cheap and vulgar and pop. I think people at the beginning were really intrigued, and I think they still are. There was a lot of questions in the early days about 'Is there a girl? Isn't there a girl?' It came out of that period in the early eighties when a lot of bands had slightly sort of obscurist names like Echo and the Bunnymen, and the Teardrop Explodes, you know, Orchestral Manoeuvres, all these kinds of things. It was just that sort of period."

EXTREME   Drummer Paul Geary explains, "The group name has a lot to do with our sound. From Prince to Led Zeppelin, we have a wide range of influences."

FAITH NO MORE   Asked today, the band usually says that Faith No More was the name of either a greyhound or a thoroughbred that won the boys a lot of money at the racetrack, enabling them by buy equipment and live happily ever after. When asked to confirm this, Chuck Mosley, lead singer on the group's first two albums, laughed and gave his account of their formative years: "Me and [bassist] Billy [Gould] played together like in '70—shit, I don't know. But our first band together was the Animated. Then Billy moved up to Berkeley and got this band together with [keyboardist] Roddy [Bottum] and some other guys called Sharp Young Men. I guess that's when he met [drummer] Mike [Bordin] and that other singer. From what I remember, they changed it to Faith No Man, and then, after Billy, Roddy, and Mike ditched the other singer, they called themselves Faith No More—as a joke on the guy." Mosley was booted from the band in 1988 and replaced by Mike Patton.

THE FALL   Formed in Manchester, England, in 1977 and led by caustic front man Mark E. Smith, the prolific, influential Fall took their name from the novel of the same name by Albert Camus.

FASTBALL   The band formed in Austin, Texas, in the mid-nineties and had a breakthrough hit in 1998 with "The Way." They claim that they took their name from title of a baseball-themed porn movie.

FASTER PUSSYCAT   Glam metal band Faster Pussycat formed in Los Angeles in the late eighties. They took their name from the 1966 camp film classic *Faster Pussycat! Kill! Kill!* by Russ Meyer, who returned the compliment by directing their first video. In an Elektra Records press release, the band members discuss their inspiration: "The Russ Meyer films," explains guitarist Brent Muscat, "all have extremely beautiful women that are smart and powerful and really cool." "And have big boobs," adds singer/lyricist Taime Downe. "I just loved that movie—it was so psychotic and goofy, and I loved that name. I said, 'I gotta have a band called that.' "

THE FEELIES   The Feelies formed in New Jersey in 1977. Although *Time* magazine reported in a September 1988 story that guitarist Bill Million "may have got the name 'subliminally' from a long-ago child's game: put yourself inside a covered box and guess what's inside," it actually comes from what Alduous Huxley called the futuristic movies in his classic novel *Brave New World*.

54-40   The band got its start in Vancouver, Canada, in 1981 and took its name from the campaign slogan of James K. Polk, the United States' eleventh president, "Fifty-Four Forty or Fight," which sought to expand the U.S. border northward.

FINE YOUNG CANNIBALS   The band was formed in 1984 by bassist David Steele and guitarist Andy Cox following the breakup of the English Beat. After recruiting singer Roland Gift, they took their name from the 1960 film *All the Fine Young Cannibals* that starred Natalie Wood and Robert Wagner, which none of them had seen at the time. According to *Halliwell's Film Guide,* they were fortunate: "The glum joys of sex and dope in the big city are revealed in this boring rather than daring farrago, which is not even unintentionally funny."

FIREHOSE   Following the 1985 death of Minutemen guitarist D. Boon in an automobile accident, bassist Mike Watt and drummer George Hurley added Ed Crawford to the lineup and changed the band's name to fIREHOSE. Watt says the name was inspired by the 1966 documentary *Don't Look Back,* in which Bob Dylan flashes a placard that says "fIREHOSE" to accompany the line "Carry 'round a firehose" from the song "Subterranean Homesick Blues."

THE FIXX   The band was briefly called Jungle Bunny and the Banana Boat Boys until, as drummer Adam Woods told *Rolling Stone* in November 1984, "we realized some people were insulted." Their choice of  the Fix, a drug reference, was amended to the Fixx to placate their record label.

THE FLAMING LIPS   Wayne Coyne, lead singer and guitarist for the Oklahoma City-based band, told *Rolling Stone,* "It's such a dumb name that it doesn't matter. There are some great band names out there, like Fugazi, where you get an idea what's it about, but still it's mysterious enough to make you wonder. But the Flaming Lips? It's just fucking silly."

FLEETWOOD MAC   In 1967, bassist John McVie, drummer Mick Fleetwood, and guitarist Peter Green, all veterans of John Mayall's Bluesbreakers, formed Peter Green's Fleetwood Mac. Green got top billing because of his fame as an extraordinary blues guitarist, second in England only to Eric Clapton. The band released three albums before Green left in 1969 to record a solo album and then disappeared. According to *The Faber Companion to 20th-Century Popular Music,* "he spent much of the seventies absorbed in what was variously described as fundamentalist religion or mental breakdown."

THE FLEETWOODS   The vocal trio of Barbara Ellis, Gretchen Christopher, and Gary Troxel had several hits in the late fifties and early sixties. They formed the group while still in high school in Olympia, Washington, in 1958. Originally called Two Girls and a Guy, they changed their name to the Fleetwoods at the suggestion of producer Bob Reisdorff, who noted that the three members had the same telephone exchange, FLeetwood.

FLESH FOR LULU   From an interview with singer Del: "Basically, the name came from Lulu the Scottish singer— she was in a film called *To Sir With Love* with Sidney

Poitier. She was a little schoolgirl and a little rock singer, and she had a hit with a cover of 'Shout.' All the band is vegetarian, and we saw her buying a [burger at] McDonald's one day, and we just thought, 'Flesh for Lulu,' and that was it." **You're vegetarians? What were you doing in McDonald's?** "Victoria Station is a big open-plan station, and McDonald's actually doesn't have a wall outside it. You can just see in and people walk in and out really quickly—the fast-food thing." **Were you fans of Lulu's?** "No, no, she's really rubbish now, she sells clothes in mail-order catalogs, that's about her only claim to fame now."

FLIPPER The San Francisco punk band formed in the early 1980s. In a roundabout way, their name is a reference to the television adventure series starring Flipper, the dolphin that aired on NBC from 1964 through 1967. In a 1992 interview for this book, singer and bassist Bruce Lose elaborates: "I left to go to Portland for a couple of months, and they got this other singer, this guy Rick Williams, who sang with the Sleepers, and he had come up with the name Flipper or suggested it, and then everybody had their own variations on the reasons for [using] it. He did it because it was the only thing he could remember from having pets and stuff like that named by the same name. There'd be like a dog that had three legs, or a turtle with a couple of fins missing, or something like that, and he called them all 'Flipper.' Then Ted and his reasoning, from thalidomide babies, and with girls, if you flip her over they're all the same—things like that. In Europe, they liked it because it was always on pinball machines, it always says 'flipper.' It's really strange. They'd send us Xeroxes of pinball machines and things that said 'flipper' on them."

THE FLYING BURRITO BROTHERS   Led by Gram Parsons, the band formed in Los Angeles in 1968. Co-founder Chris Hillman discussed the band's name in an interview: **Tell me about The Flying Burrito Brothers.** "You know Gram Parsons . . . When Gram was going to Harvard for ten minutes . . . he was playing in all these bands and met these people. At some point in time they came up with this funny name, The Flying Burrito Brothers. When Gram came out to L.A. in '67, he worked with me in the Byrds for a few months. We wanted to get a band going. We had two names. We had The Flying Burrito Brothers, and he explained to me that this was a name that Barry [Tashian] and he had come up with a year or two earlier and never done anything with, or we were going to use the name the Alabama Shieks, which I sort of liked. It ended up The Flying Burrito Brothers. It was Gram, I've got to tell you, as sometimes aggravating as he was, I loved him dearly. He had this wonderful sense of humor and wonderful. . . .It was like, he would come up with these ideas, like The Flying Burrito Brothers, and he would go design a rhinestone nudie suit with marijuana plants on it. And here it is, we were trying to play country music in the sixties. . . . Plus, the name the Flying Burrito Brothers and that's it, we're acrobats. That's where that came from. In fact, we [the Byrds] borrowed it! I had met Gram—and gosh! I must have heard that name before we really got close, because we borrowed that concept and we put *The Notorious Byrd Brothers* album out. And six months later I'm in a group: The Flying Burrito Brothers."

FOGHAT   Foghat formed in London in 1971. Singer and guitarist "Lonesome" Dave Peverett recalls: "The name originates from when I was a kid. My brother and I, long before I was in music, were playing this word game, kind of like Scrabble. It had tiles in it—it wasn't actually Scrabble, but it was that kind of game. We were making up silly words, and *foghat* was one of them. We thought it was hilarious. We used to laugh about this sort of nonsensical word. Years later, we tried to use it in one of the early blues bands I was in. We tried to get the singer, Chris Jordan, who was in Savoy Brown with me later on, to change his name to Luther Foghat, and he wouldn't do that. Then, when we formed the band [that would become] Foghat, and we had the album finished and we had the artwork done, we were going to be called Brandywine, which is a horrible name for a band. At the last minute, I suggested the name Foghat. I did a drawing of a guy in a hat with fog coming out of it and brought it up to the artist that was doing the album cover. The label said, 'All right, that's fine,' and the band agreed to it and said, 'At least we've got a logo.' So that's it—no real deep meaning to it. It was just kind of a nonsensical word. We liked it because it had no meaning really, it was just a name, and it didn't tie the band to anything. We liked that because at that time we weren't really sure what the direction of the band was going to be, although the first album kind of set the mold for it really." **Are you glad you chose it?** "Yeah, because it's become what it is. I mean, you say the word *Foghat* and there's only one meaning for that really. I think it's worked."

FOO FIGHTERS Former Nirvana drummer Dave Grohl formed the band in 1994. The name, as explained in an official band biography, stems from his interest in unexplained phenomena: "Toward the end of the Second World War, U.S. Air Force flyers patrolling the German skies would encounter a number of strange aerial phenomena in the area between Hagenau in Alsace-Lorraine and Neustadt an der Weinstrasse in the Rhine Valley. Similar to modern reports of UFOs, or so-called 'flying saucers,' these objects would come to be referred to as 'Foo Fighters' ('Foo' being slang for the French *feu,* fire) or, by those who believed the highly maneuverable balls of light to be a newly developed German weapon, 'Kraut Balls.' One incident reported on November 23, 1944 had Foo Fighters tailing an American plane over the Rhine Valley for some 18 miles. Four days later, two pilots logged an encounter with a large, glowing, orange mass moving approximately 250 mph. They followed it briefly before sudden, inexplicable radar malfunctions forced their return to base. Naturally, pilots who made official reports regarding Foo Fighters were subject to skepticism if not outright ridicule. An imposed silence ensued, only to be broken a month later by two flyers from the 415th Squadron who reported a December 22 pursuit by two Foo Fighters. Two nights later the same pilots were 'attacked' by a glowing red object while flying over the Rhine. Disturbed by the frequent and vivid nature of these reports, authorities attempted to dismiss them as St. Elmo's Fire, a naturally occuring byproduct of mutual electrostatic induction caused by the very planes being 'attacked.' Theoretically, the immaterial nature of St. Elmo's Fire would account for its radar invisibility, while the charges present in these energy bodies could explain interference in the planes' radar functions. Yet reports of Foo Fighters persisted, climaxing in May 1945 with the sighting of five orange balls traveling in a triangular formation near the eastern edge of the Pfazerwald. With the conclusion of the war, however, decreased air activity in this region logically led to fewer sightings of Foo Fighters. Eventually, they would be forgotten until their reemergence in 1950, heralding the modern age of UFO sightings." Grohl's own label, Roswell Records, is named for the town in New Mexico where some allege an alien craft crash-landed in the fifties.

FOREIGNER The band was formed in New York in 1976 by guitarist Mick Jones after he left the Leslie West Band. The band was originally called Trigger, but when it was discovered that another band was using the name, Jones chose Foreigner because of the dual nationality of the original lineup: he, Dennis Elliot, and Ian McDonald were British, and Lou Gramm, Ed Gagliardi, and Al Greenwood were American.

THE FOUR SEASONS Frankie Valli began his career as a solo singer in 1952 and then joined the Variatones, which renamed themselves the Four Lovers. The group went through several name changes during the next decade, recording as Frank Valle & the Romans, the Village Voices, and Billy Dixon & the Topics. In 1962, their recording of "Bermuda" was released by Gone Records under the name the Four Seasons, after the landmark restaurant on East Fifty-second Street in Manhattan opposite the label's offices.

THE FOUR TOPS The group formed in Detroit in 1954 as the Four Aims. To avoid confusion with the Ames Brothers, they changed their name to the Four Tops because they were "aiming for the top."

FRANKIE GOES TO HOLLYWOOD The band formed in Liverpool, England, in 1980, taking their name from a newspaper headline referring to the film plans of the young Frank Sinatra. Singer Holly Johnson, born William Johnson, took his name from a character in Lou Reed's "Walk on the Wild Side."

FREE The name was suggested by Alexis Korner, an influential figure on the British rhythm and blues scene in the sixties, after his own group Free At Last. In addition to serving as a mentor for Free founder Paul Kossoff, Korner had a hand in the formation of Led Zeppelin. His pioneering Blues Incorporated group included the founders of the Rolling Stones and Cream.

FUGAZI Ian MacKaye named the band after army slang for "fucked up situation." He found it in *Nam,* a collection of Vietnam veterans' war stories.

THE FUGS The satirical Fugs formed in New York City in 1965, led by poets Ed Sanders and Tuli Kupferberg. In an interview, Kupferberg explained the band's name: "Well, it  was Ed's idea to form the band because we thought we would raise the level of rock lyrics. I think we did a little. I picked the name from Norman Mailer's *The Naked and the Dead.* He used it as a disguise for the word *fuck.* There's a

story—it may be apocryphal—that when Dorothy Parker was introduced to Norman Mailer at a party, she said, 'So you're the young man who doesn't know how to spell *fuck*.' So that's about it, I guess."

GALAXIE 500   The band, which formed in Boston in the mid-eighties, took its name from a sixties Ford muscle car.

GANG OF FOUR   The Gang of Four's careening funk-rock and politically incisive lyrics made them one of the most exciting postpunk bands of the late seventies and early eighties. The significance of their name was dissected in a 1982 profile in *Musician* magazine by J. D. Considine: "Even the band's name has political overtones, deriving as it does from the tag given to the widow of Mao Tse-tung and three other Chinese-government officials accused of counterrevoluntionary activities by Hua Kuo-feng and the post-Mao government. The question is, though, just how deep do the Gang's politics

run? 'I don't know that much about maoism,' [singer Jon] King admitted. 'I know that it's a branch of Chinese communism. . . .'

"As it turns out, the name was chosen as much for laughs as anything else. 'We knew exactly who they were,' King said, 'but it was suggested because it was a good name for a band.'

" 'Obviously, it was chosen in the first place because it was naming what we were,' said [guitarist Andy] Gill, 'and in the second place because it had associations with a radical group. It was a joke in a sense and serious in a sense.'

" 'The irony of it now,' added King, 'is that in England, the people who are called the Gang of Four in the papers are the Social Democrats, the right-wing pull-offs from the Labour Party. So now we're asked, 'Did you name yourself after the Social Democratic Party?' "

THE GAP BAND The Gap Band, one of the most successful funk bands in the eighties, was formed in the early seventies by brothers Ronnie, Charlie, and Robert Wilson, cousins of Parliament Funkadelic's Bootsy Collins. They named the band using the first initials of three streets in the Tulsa, Oklahoma, neighborhood where they grew up: Greenwood, Archer, and Pine.

GARBAGE Drummer Butch Vig, bassist Steve Marker, and guitarist Duke Erikson played together in the bands Spooner and Firetown before forming Garbage with Scottish vocalist Shirley Manson in Madison, Wisconsin, in the mid-nineties. The name was suggested by Pauli Ryan, a local musician, upon seeing the mess of tape from some of the band's early recording sessions.

GENE LOVES JEZEBEL   Twin brothers Jay and Michael Aston formed the band in London in the early eighties. Jay discusses the band's name in an interview: **So, how did you guys come up with the name?** "Oh, it's fairly long-winded, do you mind that? . . . . Okay. It was late 1981. Mike and I were in Wales, and there wasn't much of a scene down there, so we basically hitched up to London. And as you do when you move to a new city, you just check out the whole scene. We ended up going to clubs every night and going to see bands. We noticed that *all* the bands around that time—there was Bauhaus, Killing Joke, Southern Death Cult, Sex Gang Children—were very black. There was a whole 'gothic' scene, as it got called later. We just wanted to kick against that. We wanted something that was Technicolor and three-dimensional. I was working down at the Institute for Contemporary Art in London and was hanging out with a lot of young filmmakers, and Mike was in art school at St. Martin's. We were making little films with these people, super-8 stuff. One of the films that I was in they called *Jezebel*.

My brother Mike had been called Gene after Gene Vincent. Mike was a brilliant soccer player, and some of the other team went out to get him and managed to break his leg. He was limping around like Gene Vincent when we first started singing together, so we used to call him Gene. We were looking for a name that would make people want to come and see us, and we thought, 'Let's make it very theatrical. Let's have two characters.' Gene Loves Jezebel was just a statement of the fact of our relationship. It was masculine/feminine, black/white, yin/yang, whatever it was, y'know? We were young, we were naive. Our heads were full of the wildest ideas, and we chased our dreams, had a lot of fun, and it worked very well for us. We signed a record contract within probably two months of being in London. I thought it was a good thing in the long run, though I might've much rather developed the act first. We kind of sounded like the Stone Roses with a much more violent vocal section. It was very pretentious, very much performance kind of art, but we were teenagers. That was basically it. It was a kick against the scene, and we never thought anyone would put Gene Loves Jezebel on their leather jackets, which was the fashion at the time, but we were wrong. They did that, too." **Have you ever regretted the choice?** "No, in some ways, being ahead of our time is like being on the beach before the sun comes up or something." **Back in Wales, did you have any other names?** "We had a Welsh name for a while. We called ourselves Slav Aryan. It means 'good money' in Welsh."

GENERAL PUBLIC   See **The English Beat**

GENERATION X   The pioneering punk band, fronted by Billy Idol (born William Michael Albert Broad), took its name from a pop sociology paperback that examined the behavior of English teenagers in the sixties, specifically the Mods and Rockers.

GENESIS   Genesis formed at the Charterhouse School in England where the original members were students in the mid-sixties. Peter Gabriel, Tony Banks, and Chris Stewart called themselves the Garden Wall, and Mike Rutherford and Anthony Phillips were in a band with several others called the Anon. In 1966, the two bands merged and recorded a demo tape, which they gave to Charterhouse alumnus Jonathan King, who signed them to Decca Records in 1967. It was King, today a legendary producer and label executive, who named the band, as he did 10cc. In an interview, King recalls the genesis of Genesis: **How did you end up naming Genesis?** "Well, Genesis came to me because it was right at the start of my career in the business. I'd just written and recorded a record called 'Everyone's Gone to the Moon' that went to number one. I was up at Cambridge University at the time and had decided to go back to my old school, Charterhouse, as a sort of old boy for the Old Boys Day, as you can imagine, rather triumphantly returning to my old school, sort of flaunting the fact around that I'd been number one in the charts. And I was approached by this kid who had a cassette of his band who didn't have a name or anything, but were the local school band. And as of course they were a year or so younger than me at school—I'm sure you realize that somehow at school you never talk or even become aware of people either a year younger or a year older than you—I didn't actually know them as people, but I listened to the tape and liked it, decided to record them, and gave them the name Genesis because it was sort of the beginning of my production career. I had actually produced a couple of hits before—I produced a record called 'It's Good News Week' that I also wrote, by a band called Hedgehoppers Anonymous. But since this was the first band I felt was a serious band, I wanted to call them Genesis, as the beginning of my production career. So Genesis was the name they got, and we immediately discovered that there was a soul band in America called Genesis, and the American record company wanted us to change the name, and I refused to do so. So we put the first album out without an artist name, just calling it *From Genesis to Revelation.* Then the soul band folded or something, so we managed to keep the name and the name stuck with them."

THE GERMS The band formed in Los Angeles in 1977. Guitarist Pat Smear, in a 1992 interview for this book, recalled: "Well, Darby [singer Darby Crash, who died of a drug overdose in 1980] came up with it. We originally called ourselves Sophistafuck and the Revlon Spam Queens, and there were a couple of others. But he liked the Germs. He was always thinking about the future. He liked the Germs because it was like, 'Well, this is the start of something new.' Y'know, the germ of an idea or something like that, and I just liked it because it was silly. **Any regrets you chose it?** "Well . . . now. But not then." **Why now?** "Well, just 'cause I'm thirty-two years old and I'm remembered for a band called the Germs." **Were you already playing when you picked the name, or did you pick the name before you started?** "Well, we considered ourselves a band, but we hadn't played anything—we hadn't gotten the instruments or even the songs, for that matter. But we considered ourselves a band. We picked the name and immediately went out and had T-shirts made at the iron-on lettering T-shirt place and strutted around a couple of months saying we were a band. We would go to record stores, in-store appearances and stuff, and just cause trouble and make a mess and get all drunk and screw with people while we were wearing our T-shirts and say, 'We're the Germs, we're the Germs.' And someone finally said, 'There's a show, why don't you play?' We were drunk enough to do it, and we went and played. We didn't have any songs or know how to play our instruments or anything like that. We just went and made a bunch of noise, and they threw us off after five minutes."

GIANT SAND Originally called Giant Sandworms, the band is named after the creatures in the classic sci-fi novel *Dune*.

GIN BLOSSOMS The band was formed in Tempe, Arizona, in the early eighties by guitarist Doug Hopkins and bassist Bill Leen. The band's name is a deceptively pretty term to describe an ugly condition: capillary damage caused by excessive drinking. Robin Wilson, the Gin Blossoms' lead singer, who joined the band in 1988, told VH1: "It's those things when old men drink too much, they have a sugar disorder and their nose, the capillaries on their nose explode—they get a big, red nose. . . . It's a great name. We're very fortunate. I like the fact that it's got this really twisted duality to it. It sounds really pretty, and what it represents is something really quite ugly and sort of disgusting. What a Gin Blossoms is literally—what is symbolizes, I suppose, is loss of control." Ironically, it was founder Doug Hopkins's excessive drinking that got him kicked out of the band in 1992. He killed himself in 1993 at age thirty-two.

THE GO-BETWEENS Formed in Brisbane, Australia, in 1977, the band took their name from the 1970 film *The Go-Between* starring Alan Bates and Julie Christie.

THE GODFATHERS Originally called the Sid Presley Experience, in 1985 the band renamed themselves after the Francis Ford Coppola film after looking through a copy of *Halliwell's Film Guide*. Peter Coyne, the band's lead singer, told *Rolling Stone* in June 1988: "The Godfather seemed to sort of jump out."

GOLDEN EARRING The band formed in 1964 in The Hague, Netherlands. In an interview, singer Barry Hay, who joined in 1968, explains: "They were first called the Tornados or some stupid name, and then they found out that there were at least five other bands called the Tornados. They played instrumental music then, like the Shadows and the Ventures and that sort of stuff, and they played this  song called 'Golden Earrings' that was from the sound track of a film that Marlene Dietrich starred in. It's sort of a gypsy song. It's a gypsy film. She plays this typical Marlene Dietrich character, driving all the men mad, y'know. It turned out to be the band's favorite song, and they'd start their shows with it. When they had to change their name, they decided to name themselves after the song. It's that simple."

GOO GOO DOLLS The band formed in Buffalo, New York, in the mid-eighties and took their name from an ad in the back of a comic book for a baby doll.

GRAHAM CENTRAL STATION The name of the seventies funk group, launched by former Sly and the Family Stone bassist Larry Graham, is a pun on New York's Grand Central Station, which, to be precise, is actually called Grand Central Terminal.

GRAND FUNK RAILROAD The band, which formed in Flint, Michigan, began as Terry Knight & the Pack and released a single called "I (Who Have Nothing)" that almost reached the U.S. Top 40 in 1967. The following year, Knight stepped down to become the group's manager and renamed them Grand Funk Railroad, after Canada's Grand Trunk Railroad. The band fired Knight in 1972, which led to a series of bitter, multimillion-dollar lawsuits.

THE GRATEFUL DEAD From an interview with the Dead's official publicist, Dennis McNally: "The Grateful Dead were called the Warlocks, and in November 1965 they were sitting around [bassist] Phil Lesh's apartment, in Palo Alto, California, considering the fact that there was apparently some other band called the Warlocks and they'd have to come up with a new name. They came up with various ideas, all of which got sillier and sillier, and in the end, literally, God's truth, they picked up the dictionary that was lying there, which was a Funk and Wagnalls dictionary, opened it up, and Jerry Garcia stabbed a finger in and it landed, honest to God, on 'grateful dead.' The entry was a reference to a motif in folklore specifically explored by Francis Childs, a turn-of-the-century British ethnomusicologist who classified ballads. You know, those sort of English folk ballads. There was this kind of ballad, that kind of ballad, and there was a grateful dead ballad. In the grateful dead motif, a traveler is going along the road, finds a body that's not being given a proper burial, usually because it owes money, resolves the debts of the body, and puts its spirit to rest, as it were. The body is then given a decent burial and the guy goes along his way. Usually he then encounters a representation of that spirit, usually in the form of an animal, which helps him in his own quest. The whole meaning, of course, is the notion of the resolved spirit of the dead and the whole idea of good karma and a cycle— death and life and rebirth and all that good stuff." **That was all in the dictionary?** "I think the dictionary definition may have been something as short as 'a type of myth in folklore.' Expanded, that's what it is. They found it, and they looked at each other, from all accounts, and at least three band members said, 'No, that's too intense, that's too heavy, I don't like it.' But it's also one of these things that once you get it, how can you not go with it? And it has obviously served them well. A punch line to this story is that the first time they played, their first significant gig, was for Bill Graham at the Fillmore Auditorium on December 10, 1965, and Bill loathed the name. He thought it was a terrible name that would drive people off. It was a benefit for the San Francisco Mime Troupe and Bill's first show at the Fillmore. There were many acts, so they had a little easel at the side of the stage with placards with the name of each act. And Bill was so mad about the name change he put 'The Grateful Dead, formerly the Warlocks' up on the sign. But obviously he came to appreciate the name."

GREEN DAY   Guitarist Billie Joe Armstrong and bassist Mike Dirnt (born Michael Pritchard) formed the band Sweet Children in their hometown of Rodeo, California, in the late eighties. They renamed themselves Green Day after one of their own songs, an ode to hanging out and smoking pot.

THE GUESS WHO   The band formed in Winnipeg, Canada, in the early sixties. Guitarist Randy Bachman explains how the Guess Who, and Bachman-Turner Over-drive, which he formed in 1972, got their names: **The story I heard was that your record company called you "Guess Who?" as some kind of promotional stunt.** "Yes, at the time we were called Chad Allen and the Expressions. We were a Canadian band in Winnipeg, having no success getting airplay. This was in the early sixties, and there was no Canadian music scene or anything. We were trying to write our own material, and it wasn't that great. Y'know, nothing is that great when you're writing your first songs. We'd go to rerecord old American songs and they'd get redone by the Beatles or the Searchers or the Seekers—y'know, 'Slow Down,' 'Dizzy Miss Lizzy.' All these British groups were doing old American songs, and we didn't know what to record. No one was doing old British songs. So I had this idea: 'Let's go and get some old British songs.' So we went and got this song called 'Shakin' All Over' by Johnny Kidd and the Pirates that had been number one in England in '61 or '62. We copied it, did it in our own style, sent it in to the record label, and they said 'This sounds fantastic, it sounds like a hit. But it won't get any airplay because you're a Canadian band from Winnipeg. Now let's pretend you're from England. Let's put "Guess Who?" on there. We want you guys to get a really great name. Chad Allen and the Expressions is an old-sounding name. Why don't you get a new name like the Seekers or the Searchers, y'know, the Stones, the Beatles. We want a name that has one or two syllables.' So we said okay.

"So they basically had this contest where they put 'Guess Who?' on the record label. I still have it; it was just a white label and all it said was 'Guess Who?' on it and then 'Shakin' All Over.' In the meantime, we were supposed to get a new name. Then we were going to tell everyone, 'Oh, guess who we are, we are this new name.' Before we knew it, that song had rocketed to number one in Canada. Suddenly, the radio stations were saying, 'Here they are, Guess Who.' When we went to the record label and said, 'Well, we have a new name'—I don't even remember what the name was—they said, 'No, no. You guys are called Guess Who.' I thought that was totally ridiculous as a name. It was like Abbott and Costello: 'Who's on first?' And then the Who were just coming out, and we said there was going to be confusion, and they said, 'No, the radio is calling you Guess Who.' We said, 'Well, can we at least put *the* in front of it, and be *the* Guess Who?' They said okay. So then the song got released in the States, and I think probably late '63 it was released on Scepter Records. It went to Top 20 in *Billboard,* and there we were called 'the Guess Who.' We didn't like it. It's like if I came up to you and said, 'By the way, you don't look like your name, you look like a Sherman.' And then you said, 'I don't want to be called Sherman, it's a weird name.' Well, you can imagine being four, five guys in a band, and somebody's saying, 'By the way, you're not called this anymore, you're called that.' " **You can't remember the name that you guys wanted to be called instead?** "No, we hadn't really settled on it. I think we had five or six. Y'know, you tend to go to a library, get books on butterflies and ornithology. Y'know, birds, butterflies, airplanes. Names like the Spitfires, Johnny and the Hurricanes, names that stand out. We might've had five or six and said to the label, 'Now you pick the one you want from these.' And they said, 'No, you already have a name, you're called Guess Who.' So we put *the* in front of it and endured. We went to England in '67, saw the Who

playing at the Marquee club, and we went up to them and said, 'We want to talk to you about the name. We're the Guess Who and you're the Who, and one of us has got to drop this, 'cause it's leading to mass confusion.' Everywhere we went, people asked us to play 'My Generation.' We were on tour then because of 'Shakin' All Over.' We were on the Kingsmen's 'Louie, Louie' tour. We were on these big caravan bus tours with Dick Clark, and the Turtles, Sam the Sham, Dion and the Belmonts. It was really great, but everywhere we went, people would ask for 'Shakin' All Over' and 'My Generation.' I said to John Entwhistle, 'We got to work this out.' He said, Aw, piss off.' That ended that. He said, 'Look, there's the Byrds and the Yard-birds, there's the Who and the Guess Who—that's it. We're not changing. Are you going to change?' We said, 'No, we were hoping you would.' He said, 'Aw, piss off.' We were kind of friends after that. But then they came to tour here, with Herman's Hermits or something, and everyone asked them to play 'Shakin' All Over.' Then they ended up putting it into their show, and they recorded it many years later on their *Live at Leeds* album. So we both got stuck with each other's name association. Then, you'd say to some-one, 'the Who,' they'd say 'My Generation'; you'd say 'the Guess Who,' they'd say 'Shakin' All Over,' 'cause that's all we had. Then in '69 we had our string of hits with 'These Eyes,' 'No Time' 'Undun,' 'American Woman,' and that kind of set us apart from the Who, 'cause they then went on with 'Pinball Wizard' and a zillion other things. So that's how we got that name." **When did you make the transition from the Guess Who to BTO?** "Well, I left in 1970, almost

121

1971, and I started a new band with my brothers and Fred Turner, and we were originally called Brave Belt, which is the name of a brave's belt that he puts his scalps on. Neil Young got us a deal at Reprise—he was there with his own solo album in between Buffalo Springfield and Crosby, Stills and Nash—and Brave Belt went nowhere. People kept saying, 'What does it mean?' I'd say, 'Well, it's the scalp belt a brave hangs his scalps on.' People said, 'That's stupid. Why don't you call yourselves "Something your name" that people will recognize from the Guess Who? Use Bachman because they know you've written the songs.' So there were me and my two other brothers, and there we took care of the Bachmans, and then there was Fred Turner. So for about six months we were called Bachman Turner. But that was the era of Seals and Crofts, and Brewer and Shipley, and we would show up and people would think we were a two-guy acoustic folk act, and we'd blow the back wall out of these little coffee houses we were booked in. We needed something in our name to show we played heavy rock music.

"So late one night in Windsor, Ontario, we were crossing the border to go into Detroit after a gig. We were in a Husky gas station or something, and at the cash register I saw a magazine called *Overdrive*. I said to Turner, 'Isn't that a great name for an album,' 'cause then you had really great album names and great group names, you hardly couldn't even tell which was the name of the group and which was the name of the album. I said, 'Isn't *Overdrive* a great album name?' And he said, 'No, that should be our group name. Overdrive, it means like "get in high gear."' So I wrote it down. Our record label had said, 'Look, get a new name. Brave Belt stinks, get a new name, and use your name in the title.' So I wrote it down on a napkin, which, as you know, are long in restaurants. They come in those chrome things. So I wrote Bachman first. There wasn't much room to put it sideways, so I put the napkin longways. Under that I wrote Turner, under that Overdrive. I called the record label the next day and said, 'We've got a new name. It's fantastic: Bachman-Turner Overdrive.' They said, Are you kidding? It's so long, no one will ever remember it!' I looked at the napkin and there was BTO, so I said, 'How about BTO? We'll have a long name and a short name.' Crosby, Stills and Nash were using CSA, and Chicago Transit Authority—this is before they were just Chicago—were using CTA. They said, 'Oh, that's cool, a long name and a short name, great, go for it.' So that was our name. Then when we were having our first album's pictures taken, we were in a great big field, which was on a hill, and the photographer said, 'Back up, crowd in a little closer together.' The grass was kind of knee-high, and as he's saying, 'Move over, back up,' as he's trying to get us in line with his camera, I tripped. I tripped over something, and I went and lifted it up and it was a great big wooden gear, eight feet around—some logging thing that they'd used up here in British Columbia. We lifted this up, and we stood all holding this gear, and that's on the back of the first BTO album." **And that became kind of a logo for the band.** "Fred Turner looked at it, and he said, 'Y'know, that kind of looks like a Ferrari overdrive gear.' And we're going, 'Wow, lightning bolts! The gods of rock and roll have given us this name, Overdrive, and now we trip over a gear that looks like a Ferrari overdrive gear except it's eight feet tall and wood.' So we lifted it up, and it's on the back of the first BTO album, then we replicated it on the front with a couple other gears and put the BTO in the middle, and voilà, a worldwide trademark and symbol out of nowhere."

GUNS N' ROSES   Axl Rose grew up in Lafayette, Indiana, as Bill Bailey, the son of L. Stephen and Sharon Bailey. When he was seventeen, he learned that his real surname was Rose; his natural father, William Rose, had skipped town when he was a baby. He began calling himself W. Rose, then added Axl, the name of a local band that he was in at the time with future Guns n' Roses guitarist Izzy Stradlin. He told *Musician* magazine in June 1992: "That was the name of a band I had with Izzy, and at one point he said, 'You live, breath, eat, sleep, walk, and talk Axl. Why don't you just be Axl?'" Later, he had his name legally changed to W. Axl Rose and says his initials—W.A.R.—were not meant to signify anything.

When the band formed in L.A. in 1985, they considered a variety of names, including Heads of Amazon and AIDS. Guns n' Roses was chosen by combining the names of two bands that the members had played in, L.A. Guns and Hollywood Rose.

GWAR   While they say they're the evil spawn of visitors from Uranus who were stranded in Antarctica, the theatrical shock-rock group GWAR actually consists of musicians, dancers, and artists who met at Virginia Commonwealth University in Richmond in 1985. Their name is reportedly an acronym for "God What an Awful Racket," although band members have also said that it came from a comic book titled "Gay Women Against Rape."

THE HAPPY MONDAYS   Formed in Manchester, England, in 1981, the Happy Mondays were one of the pioneers of that city's influential rave scene. Guitarist Mark Day dubbed the band Happy Mondays in 1983 after the New Order hit "Blue Monday," a song reportedly inspired by the 1980 suicide of Joy Division vocalist Ian Curtis.

HAWKWIND   Hawkwind formed in London in 1969. Bassist Lemmy (born Ian Kilmister) joined the band in 1971. After he was thrown out of Hawkwind in 1975 following an arrest in Canada on drug charges, he formed Motörhead. In an interview, Lemmy explains how both bands got their names: "The reason for Hawkwind was that [sax and flute player] Nick Turner had a big nose and he farted all the time. He had a fuckin' nose like a beak and he farted all the time, so we called it Hawkwind." **I heard it had something to do with Hawkwind Zoo. Was that the original name?** "Yeah, that was the original name, but it was the same reason—a nose like a hawk's beak and he farted all the time." **Is there a place called Hawkwind Zoo in London?** "No." **There's no such place.** "Well, there might be now, but there wasn't then." **Why did you add on the Zoo at first?** "I wasn't with them then. But believe me, it fitted. Believe me." **Wasn't "Motorhead" the name of a Hawkwind song?** "I wrote it when I was with Hawkwind. It was the B side of the last single I did with them, 'Kings of Speed.' It had a violin solo in it." **Why exactly did you come up with that name, and what did it mean?** "It's old American slang for speed freak. James 'Motorhead' Sherwood of the Mothers of Invention. It's also like motorin', motormouth, moving fast—y'know, runnin' along there." **When you're all sped up?** "Sort of like that, yeah. Even when you're not, y'know, people drive cars fast and people call them motorheads. It fitted rather well, I thought." **Is that how you are in that sense? Are you a bit of a—** "I was then, I'm gettin' on a bit now. Silver threads amongst the gold now, ain't I?" **Were there any other names you contemplated before settling on Motörhead?** "Yeah, Bastard I was going to call us. My manager pointed out to me that we probably wouldn't get too much prime-time TV. Not really getting any anyway. There was another name floating around we thought of for a while, but I can't remember what it was. It can't have been very good. Not as good as Bastard, anyway. I still think that would've been a good name, and the funny thing is, when Wurzel joined the band, he'd just come from a band called Bastard." **There seems to be a lot of overlap. A lot of guys come up with the same ideas.** " 'Cause we're all fuckin' stupid, y'know."

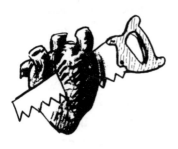

THE HEARTBREAKERS Guitarist Johnny Thunders [born John Genzale] and drummer Jerry Nolan formed the Heartbreakers in New York City after leaving the New York Dolls in 1975. In an interview, ex-bandmate Sylvain Sylvain claims credit for the name: "Just before the Dolls broke up in 1975, we were with [manager] Malcolm McLaren in the car—this was in Florida—and 'Heartbreak Hotel' came on the radio. We were all sitting together in the car, driving from Tampa to who knows where, y'know, and I turned around to Johnny and Jerry, and I said, 'Wow, that would be a great name for a band, the Heartbreakers.' "

HEAVEN 17 The band was formed in 1980 after synthesizer players Ian Craig Marsh and Martyn Ware left the Human League to establish the British Electric Foundation. The B.E.F. was a production unit whose first project was Heaven 17, for which they recruited vocalist Glenn Gregory. The name came from a group in the Anthony Burgess novel *A Clockwork Orange*.

HELMET Described as "thinking man's metal," Helmet formed in New York City in the late eighties. The name was inspired by the suggestion of a friend of singer and guitarist Page Hamilton, who recalls: "Reyne was fascinated with the whole German thing. Especially the fact that I'd lived in Germany for a while. She said to me one day, 'You should call the band Helmut.' On our first demo we actually put an umlaut over the *M* as a sort of German gag."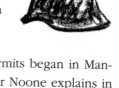

HERMAN'S HERMITS Herman's Hermits began in Manchester, England, in 1963. Vocalist Peter Noone explains in an interview: "We were originally called Pete Novak and the Heartbeats, and I was Pete Novak and wore this silver lamé suit, which I bought from another guy in another band in town. It didn't really fit, but it was cheap. We won this competition and I became 'the Crown Prince of the Twist.' But by 1963, it was getting a bit tired—you know, even my mum could do the twist by now, and I was never going to be chubby. So we were looking for another name and we used to have meetings, like those fifteen-year-old-boy-serious meetings: 'Let's call a meeting.' We used to rehearse in this place called—I can't remember the name of the place, like the Golden Garter or something, in Manchester. We were rehearsing there and *The Bullwinkle Show* came on. It was a bar and it was closed. The pubs were always closed. We used to offer to play one free date a week to get free rehearsals there. I went to school so we rehearsed from four to five-thirty for free. In the bar was a television, and the *Bullwinkle Show* was on at four-thirty every day. It was sort of going on in the background and we were very amused by it—it was so way ahead of its time. And there was a guy in it that we thought was named Herman. And I said, 'Herman—that would be great!' I had seen an American cartoon with this really wimpy-looking guy with glasses. I borrowed the guitar player's glasses and I looked like Buddy Holly when I wore these glasses. I said, 'Great! We can do Buddy Holly songs and I'll call myself Herman.' You know, it was so sort of anti-rock and roll, so sort of anti-Elvis Presley. 'Cause everybody was being called George and Paul suddenly, and Fred. Nobody in England was called Herman in those days, nobody. We'd never, ever heard of anyone named Herman, so it was totally unique. So we were all excited about me being Herman and we were looking for a name to go with it, and the barman says, 'Call yourselves Herman and the bloody Hermits.' We said, 'Hey, Herman and the Hermits. Brilliant.' The drummer's mother made us some sackclothes so we'd look like hermits. But I wouldn't wear mine because it was abrasive, you know. We did an afternoon show at the Plaza Ballroom in Manchester, and the guys walked onstage in these sackclothes. I had on this blue suit. My manager took me and bought me a suit on credit—I wouldn't wear the sackclothes. Everybody laughed in the audience and that was the one and only time we wore them." **Do you remember any of the other names that you considered at the time?** "Herman and the Supermen was one of them. Herman and the Supermen would have been a disaster, especially for four white, wimpy English guys. Then we thought to call ourselves Watkins and the Dominators because we had an amplifier which was a Watkins Dominator. So we thought 'Watkins and the Dominators!' Then we thought Dominator sounded like something in a book with men with whips and men in leather underwear, you know. So we dropped that one. Herman's Hermits was the perfect name for our band. Couldn't have been a better name. It was totally different. And for years everybody called me Herman. I remember John Lennon always used to call me Herman and it amused me." **When did you realize that the character was actually called Sherman, not Herman?** "We told my sister that we were calling ourselves after the guy on *The Bullwinkle Show* and she said, 'Well, his name is Sherman.' But we stuck with it. We had already printed the cards. In those days every band had a card. You know: 'The Beatles: weddings, bar mitzvahs, anything, money, call us.' We'd done the cards. It was like nine pounds for a thousand cards, which we'd give to anybody, even other guys in school."

HOLE   Hole was formed in Los Angeles in 1990. Singer
Courtney Love, who was married to the late Kurt Cobain of
Nirvana, named the band after a line in
the play *Medea* by Euripides:

"There's a hole burning deep
inside me." She says she chose it
because "I knew it would confuse people."

THE HOLLIES   The Hollies formed in Manchester, England, in 1962. Although it has been reported that they were
named after the Christmas decoration, in *Crosby Stills & Nash:
The Authorized Biography,* for which
he wrote the foreward in 1984, original guitarist Graham Nash states, "We
were Buddy Holly crazy. So that's
how our name came about."

THE HOLLYWOOD ARGYLES   When the number-one song
"Alley-Oop" was first recorded by Gary Paxton in 1960, the
Hollywood Argyles didn't exist. Paxton, who had a couple of
hits as the latter half of Skip and Flip, was under the impression that he was still under contract to his old record label
when he came to Los Angeles and recorded the song. To
avoid legal complications, instead of releasing the single
under his own name, as he had wanted, he credited the
song to the fictional Hollywood Argyles, named after Argyle
Street, adjacent to the Hollywood studio on Sunset Boulevard where he recorded. When Paxton learned that he was
in fact no longer under contract to his old label, it was too
late. The single was a hit, and Paxton eventually hired a full

band to perform with him as the Hollywood Argyles, although they forever remained a one-hit wonder.

HOODOO GURUS The Hoodoo Gurus began in Sydney, Australia, in the early eighties. In an interview, guitarist Brad Shepherd explains the origins of their name: "It's quite simple, really. I'd always wanted to call a band the Gurus, and it didn't seem to be quite enough. The Hoodoo part came along because it sounded like it rhymed. The Hoodoo comes from the voudoun religion from, I think, West Africa. It was transplanted to the Southern states of the U.S. with the slaves, and also to parts of the Caribbean, and became voodoo and hoodoo. We were interested in that. I thought it was a curious religion and sounds kind of fun. It also counteracted the whole thing of the Gurus— with this sort of sixties, sort of Maharishi thing, sort of ethereal and mystical. We thought it was more carnal. Light and darkness. It added to the balance. When we first started, for about eleven months we called ourselves Le Hoodoo Gurus because we wanted to emphasize the French nature of the voodoo aspect. "No one could spell our name correctly. Every time we played we had a different spelling. I think the worst one was Two Loose Zulus that  someone put in the newspaper listings. The words are so obvious in themselves; it's when you put them together it seems to stymie people." **Any regrets?** "It could be worse. We could be called Deep Purple."

THE HOOTERS   The Hooters were formed in Philadelphia in the early eighties by Rob Hyman and Eric Bazilian, who helped arrange and performed on Cyndi Lauper's best-selling debut album. In an interview, Hyman explained how they chose their often-maligned name: "Actually, we have a good story, despite everyone else's opinions and rumors of the derivation. Officially, when we first started playing in the early eighties, we had this old warehouse in a kind of run-down part of Philly where we practiced that we called the Ranch. It was definitely not a ranch. One of the first projects we did, just like any band, was make a home demo, actually just to get work. We were making a tape of about ten songs to play for club owners, and since it was mostly all original stuff, it was not easy in the begin-

ning. Anyway, a friend of ours was engineer-ing. His name was John Senior and he had a small sound company. We were just doing a live tape and were running down the levels of all the instruments. At that point we had adopted the Hohner melodica as our trademark. We had a little picture of that as our logo. It was just an instrument that a friend of ours had lent us. In the early days we played a lot of ska and reggae when all the two-tone bands were around. The engineer had no idea what the instrument was, and we were running down a song called 'Man in the Street,' which is an old reggae song by Don Drummond, actually a ska instrumental. We were getting levels of the instruments, and he said, 'Play on that hooter thing. Play the hooter.' None of us had any idea what he was talking about. He said, 'Y'know, that hooter thing, that kind of hoots.' I was like, 'Oh, the melodica-hooter, okay.' So that became our name for the instrument. We were looking for a band name at the time, and of course, like any band, we went through a zillion names, and it seemed like that was *the* name—Hooter. We liked the name the Wailers—instead of wailing, we were hooting. The rest of the guys were kind of wondering what the name of the band was going to be and we had this light bulb of an idea. When Eric Bazilian and I—we formed the band and wrote the songs together—told David, the drummer, he said, 'No way—you can't call the band that.' So then we knew we had a good name, when he said that. Basically, it's a musical term." **But the *rumors*, however . . .** "We have traveled around and we have heard every reference that there is. Sexual, drug-related—I've heard connotations and meanings for that word that I could never have imagined." **Hooters in some parts are slang for a woman's breasts. What's the drug reference—pot?** "I think pipe, hash pipes—I don't really know." **Did you regret taking the name at that point?** "Oh, no, we love the name. Partly because it was our own creation. In fact, we ended up getting an endorsement from the Hohner Company. They've been custom-making the instruments for us—we go through a lot of them—and they started calling it the Hooter, the 'Hohner Hooter.' For us, it's a musical term."

HOOTIE AND THE BLOWFISH The name was inspired by nicknames lead singer and guitarist Darius Rucker had given two members of his college choir. Hootie was wide-eyed like an owl, and the Blowfish had puffy cheeks, like a blowfish.

HOT TUNA   Jorma Kaukonen and Jack Casady formed a splinter group from the Jefferson Airplane in 1968, originally calling the band Hot Shit before renaming it Hot Tuna at their record label's insistence.

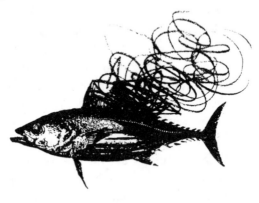

THE HUES CORPORATION   The disco-soul group got its start in Los Angeles in 1969 and had a hit in 1974 with "Rock the Boat." Group leader Wally Holmes recalled in *The Billboard Book of Number One Hits,* "I wanted to call the group the Children of Howard Hughes, because I knew Hughes was single and he represented a conservative element. I was kind of wild in those days and I thought a fanstastic thing would be to take a black group and call them the Children of Howard Hughes." To avoid legal complications, Holmes "came up with the idea of the Hues Corporation," a veiled reference to Hughes and, perhaps, the group's racial identity, as in hues of skin tone.

THE HUMAN LEAGUE   The Human League formed in Sheffield, England, in 1977, and took their name from "Starforce," a science fiction game. Synthesizer players Martyn

Ware and Ian Craig Marsh left the band in 1980 to form Heaven 17. Vocalist and synth player Phil Oakey and Adrian Wright, who handled "stage visuals," recruited new members and had several hits, including "Don't You Want Me" in 1982 and "(Keep Feeling) Fascination" in 1983.

HUMBLE PIE After he left the Small Faces in 1968, guitarist Steve Marriott formed Humble Pie in Essex, England, with ex-Herd guitarist Peter Frampton. Frampton recalls: **How did Humble Pie become Humble Pie?** "Well, when we all got together and rehearsed, we didn't have a name, so one night we decided we'd all go home and think about it and call each other on the phone. And we did, and the one that we went for was one that Steve had thought of, which was Humble Pie. That was it. He was very, very clever with words and names in general." **Do you know what the appeal of that was?** "I think the fact that we knew that we were already being called a supergroup because Steve was from the Small Faces and I was from the Herd. I think that the term 'you eat humble pie,' it was sort of a reverse on the way people were thinking of us, so it was sort of downplaying the supergroup image." **And that's why everyone liked it?** "Yeah, because it had a nice meaning for us. The only thing was, the first time we did *Top of the Pops,* the big English TV show—you always used to go to the BBC photographer's room either before or after the show because they take a picture of you to put on the credits for next week. If your song went up in the charts, they played the video again of what you just did. We walked into his dressing room, which he'd made into his little photographic studio, and there were four plates and a big pie. You can imagine where the pie ended up—on the photographer and on the wall. We weren't about to—that really wasn't what Humble Pie was about." **In retrospect, are you pleased you went with it?** "Oh, it's a classic name, a wonderful name really." **Where did the Herd get its name?** "That was before I joined the band. I don't know. I used to go and watch the Herd. They were one of the biggest bands in London. I've no idea." **I wonder if it was a pun—you know, "Have you heard the Herd?"** "Well, that's how we advertised it when we had our first single out. Big teasers, 'Have you heard the Herd?' But that wasn't the reason, no. It was probably more like Woody Herman's Herd than anything else—Woody Herman, the great jazz band leader."

HÜSKER DÜ   The influential Minneapolis trio formed in the early eighties and took its name from a board game popular in the fifties, which means "Do you remember?" in Swedish. It was chosen so the band wouldn't be easily categorized. Guitarist Bob Mould noted, "Back in '79 there were a lot of bands picking really punky and power pop names. We wanted to grab hold of a name that was timeless, ambiguous, and that would not label us."

ICEHOUSE Guitarist and vocalist Iva Davies formed the band in Sydney, Australia, in 1980, as Flowers, but changed the name to Icehouse to avoid conflict with a Scottish band called the Flowers. *Icehouse* was the name of their debut album and is Australian slang for an insane asylum. Icehouse had hits in the U.S. with "Crazy" in 1987 and "Electric Blue" in 1988.

THE ICICLE WORKS The band formed in Liverpool, England, in the early eighties and took its name from a science-fiction story by Frederick Pohl called "The Day the Icicle Works Closed." "It's a futuristic Humphrey Bogart detective story," Ian McNabb, the band's singer, told *Rolling Stone* in March 1984. "We chose the name because we thought it was imaginative." The band had a hit in the U.S. in 1984 with "Whisper to a Scream [Birds Fly]."

INXS The band formed in Sydney, Australia, in 1979. Drummer Jon Farriss recalls how they got their name: "We would like to say that INXS thought of its own name. But we didn't. In fact, a roadie who was working with us for a short while during a tour of Australia in 1979 came up with the idea. One of our first managers suggested that we use it and adopt a mysterious 'inaccessible' type of image. We played behind a wall of lights in Devo-style clothing without saying anything except 'Ours' before playing one of our own songs. Cool idea and it worked for a while, but we outgrew it pretty quickly.

"Inaccessible and INXS (In Excess) was a mild contradiction of terms, as well as the fact that we didn't enjoy being inaccessible! Excessiveness, well, we preferred that. We chose the name INXS simply because we loved it. It had an interesting twist, four letters, in-your-face type of attraction to it."

IRON BUTTERFLY   Iron Butterfly formed in San Diego, California, in 1966. Their biggest hit, 1968's "In-a-Gadda-Da-Vida"—an edited version of the seventeen-minute album track that featured a two-and-a-half-minute drum solo—was allegedly a play on the phrase *in the Garden of Eden.* Lead singer and keyboard player Doug Ingle told Irwin Stambler in *The Encyclopedia of Pop, Rock and Soul:* "I wanted a name we could live up to. We wanted to be good. Good consists of being heavy, tight; together, not only musically, but as people. It also means being light, dynamic, versatile, and original. I added all those qualities together and it boiled down to heavy and pretty. At the time, insect names seemed to be the big thing, so we became Iron Butterfly."

IRON MAIDEN   Bassist Steve Harris launched Iron Maiden in 1976 in London, naming the band after a medieval torture device referred to in *The Man in the Iron Mask.*

THE JAM   The band took shape in 1975 in Woking, England, where singer and bassist Paul Weller and drummer Rick Buckler began jamming together during lunch hour in their school music room. These jams inspired the band's name, not a favorite breakfast jelly, as sometimes reported.

JAMIROQUAI   The name of the British group is a hybrid of the words "jam"—as in a musical jam—and "Iroquai," a variation of Iroquois, the name of the American Indian tribe with whom frontman Jason Kay was enamored.

JANE'S ADDICTION   Lollapalooza founder Perry Farrell formed Jane's Addiction in Los Angeles in 1986, following the break-up of his first band, Psi Com, which he started in 1981. After Jane's Addiction folded in 1991, he launched Porno for Pyros the following year. Farrell discusses his band's names in an interview: **Let's start with Jane's Addiction. How did that come about?** "Jane's Addiction came about through . . . well, my friend Jane, who was my roommate. We lived in a house that was very busy, socially, a lot of musicians living there. And Jane was like this *femme fatale* that I loved very much, and I named it in her honor." **What was the addiction?** "Well, the addiction. Let's keep the addiction broad. Addiction is addiction in every case.

It's the same thing, just with a different format. You know what I mean. It doesn't matter if it's coffee. It doesn't matter if it's drugs. It doesn't matter if it's religion. It doesn't matter. You know what I mean. It doesn't matter if it's lifting weights. Addiction is addiction." **I heard a rumor that it had something to do with "Sweet Jane"—you know, Lou Reed?** "No. It's Jane." **Another story was that Jane was a hooker through whom the band met.** "No, that's not true. We had a woman that was a prostitute who was managing us." **But she was not Jane?** "No."

JAPAN Japan formed in London in 1977 and was one of the leaders of the New Romantic movement. The name was chosen, singer and guitarist David Sylvain noted in Arthur Pitt's 1982 book *A Tourist's Guide to Japan,* "to get away from that rubbishy idea that a band's name has to give an idea of its music; our music had nothing to do with our name." But Sylvain, who was born David Batt and renamed himself after Sylvain Sylvain of the New York Dolls, did

 admire the country and its culture: "To me, Japan is the most ideal country. There's a lot of things about it that you could call unhealthy—it's an almost uniform country, a lot of people there think the same way—but they're completely open-minded about what's going on."

THE JEFFERSON AIRPLANE Jefferson Airplane was formed in San Francisco, California, in 1965, by singer Marty Balin, whose first recruit was guitarist Paul Kantner. In an interview, Kantner recalls the band's genesis: **Who thought of the name and how'd it come about?** "We just had

a lot of boring names swirling about." **Do you remember some of them?** "No, they were so boring, nothing comes to mind. Jorma [Kaukonen] brought the name to us, actually. He was hanging out with a lot of white blues players, white college kids who learned blues licks, some of them real good. They would immerse themselves in the blues legend, somewhat sarcastically, not disrespectfully, but just in sort of an educated-white-boy snide way, pleasant, fun. One of the blues players had this dog that was called Blind Thomas Jefferson Airplane, sort of like Blind Lemon Jefferson with a twist. And Jorma suggested the Jefferson Airplane, the name surfaced somehow. So we took that name as sort of our temporary name—just a name we could use until we chose a real name, a respectable name that looked like it could be on the charts or something. Actually, we weren't thinking of charts in those days, but we were thinking of a respectable name. By the time our band opened, which was on Friday the thirteenth in 1965 in August, nobody had thought of a better name, so we had to sort of go with that, and it worked out okay."

In a separate interview, Marty Balin echoed Kantner's story: **How did you guys come up with Jefferson Airplane?** "Jorma came up with it, our guitar player. He had a friend who had a little dog named Thomas Jefferson Airplane. One day we were trying to think of a name and he said, 'Why don't we call ourselves Jefferson Airplane?' We all laughed and thought it was pretty funny and didn't take it seriously, but we tried all these names out on our friends and they didn't like any of them, but when we said 'Jefferson Airplane' they all laughed and cracked up. So when we got back together, we all said, 'Y'know, all my friends, they kind of liked that Jefferson Airplane.' Everybody had the same reaction, so we said, 'Yeah, let's call ourselves that,' because that's the reaction that we were trying to get from people." **What, a smile or a laugh?** "Yeah, smile and crack them up. That was the spirit of the band, and so we kept that name."

In 1974, Jefferson Airplane officially became Jefferson Starship. Kantner explains the name change: "Jefferson Starship—that's when the band went their separate directions. Jorma and Jeff went off into Hot Tuna, and I, being a science fiction freak, took that particular bent, of just going one step up the evolutionary ladder as it were, from airplane to starship. It's just a science fiction thrust, and remains so to this day."

It has been reported, most notably in the *Billboard* book *Rock Movers & Shakers* and in *Entertainment Weekly,* that the band was named after a kind of roach clip made by splitting a paper match at one end. Kantner explains: "It was the other way around. That came around in the early seventies, if I'm not mistaken. It's something we used, we just never called it a Jefferson Airplane."

Balin concurs: "That came after our name. They named that after us. It was kind of a thing that we used to crack up at, y'know. It was kind of nice that people named their roach clip after us."

THE JESUS AND MARY CHAIN Brothers William and Jim Reid formed the band in 1983, performing their first gig in Glasgow, Scotland, the following year. In an interview, William Reid explains how he chose the name: **How did you guys settle on the Jesus and Mary Chain, which is certainly a distinctive name?** "To be honest, I don't think there's any story to it. I just made it up one day." **What**

were the circumstances? "The circumstances were that we had a gig coming up, our very first gig, and we needed a name, within two weeks basically. So I made up the name, there and then." **On the spot?** "Yeah." **Were you jotting names down and you combined Jesus and Mary with Chain?** "No. I'd always liked the word Jesus, and I had an idea that when we needed a name that I would somehow get Jesus into it, but then I just said 'Jesus and Mary Chain,' and Douglas and Jim, who are in the band, said, 'Yeah, that's good enough, that'll do.' And that was it. Over the years people have asked me, 'How did you get the name?' and I've told people countless lies. Like I told people that I got it from a Bing Crosby film, and I told other people that I got it on the back of a corn flakes packet, just to make it sound interesting. But let's face it—the real story is pretty mundane, really." **Any regrets, or are you glad you went with it?** "I've always thought it was a brilliant name. The only regret really, is that the world is so conservative, and I think it's probably done our career damage having that name." **Because people assume it's something blasphemous?** "Yeah. To me it doesn't have any blasphemous connotations at all. It just states 'the Jesus and Mary Chain.' It doesn't say that Jesus is a junkie or whatever. There's no disrespect to anybody in the name. I think the names Jesus and Mary are sacred and a lot of people don't allow you to use them. I know it's harmed our career. I know that in the States lots of radio stations don't play our records because of the name. I know that if U2 were called the Jesus and Mary Chain, they wouldn't be playing stadiums because they wouldn't have got past a certain level that we find hard to get past. AOR radio stations are kind of nervous about the name. Some of them, when they do play our records, they don't say the Jesus and Mary Chain, they just say 'the Mary Chain.' It's kind of annoying—it's not what we're called." **Is there such a thing as a Jesus and Mary Chain? Is that a reference to anything at all?** "I don't think so. I don't think I've ever heard that." **It's not some biblical thing?** "I've no idea. The words just popped into my head. They sounded good, and we needed a name for the band quick, and that was that." **Were there any other names you considered at the time and didn't go with?** "Yeah, the Daisy Chain was one." **When I heard of the Jesus and Mary Chain and wondered what the chain referred to, I thought it might be that.** "Well, that probably came from that. Because . . . motherlove. I suppose motherlove has Mary connected to it." **So these were all thoughts that were swimming around in your head?** "These were names that I had already made up, not that same day but in the weeks before that, and nobody really liked them." **You were the one who came up with the name?** "I was the one who came up with all the names, actually. There were about ten of them before that, and none of them were suitable. But the Jesus and Mary Chain one, I never even thought about it. I suppose if I'd have thought about it, there may have been a reason, but it just sprung out. And what happened over the years is that people in interviews have asked me about it, and you tend to try to have a theory, you force yourself to have a theory, and I don't think it works. I always disappoint people when they ask. That's why the corn flakes and Bing Crosby things came about. I disavowed the Bing Crosby thing because it got on my nerves. People were asking, 'Well, what was the name of that Bing Crosby film?' And I was saying, 'It doesn't exist.' "

JESUS JONES   The English band, which had a Top 10 hit in the U.S. in 1991 with "Right Here, Right Now," formed in 1988. Louise Allen, a spokesperson at their management company in London, explains: "Jesus Jones started out inauspiciously on a beach in Spain. Originally they got together in the summer of 1988. Mike, Jerry, and Gen were on holiday, just sitting on a beach. They were all in bands that weren't getting anywhere, and they just decided to come back and try something else. The three of them were sitting on this beach surrounded by all these Spanish people, most of whom seemed to be called Jesus. The name Jesus Jones just seemed like a nice juxtaposition."

JETHRO TULL   According to the liner notes to the *Jethro Tull* box set, in 1963 Ian Anderson, Jeffrey Hammond, and John Evans played their first gig as the Blades, named after the club in James Bond books. By 1966, however, they had changed their name to the John Evan Smash and finally the John Evan Band, Evans taking the *S* off his last name because Hammond "thought it sounded better." After two years of struggling, the seven-piece soul revue was whittled down to a blues quartet, and "for the next couple of months they played under a variety of names: Navy Blue, Bag of Blues, Ian Henderson's Bag of Blues, the frequent name changes allegedly the only way they could play a club a second time." Eventually the band hooked up with producer Derek Lawrence, who "wanted to call the group Candy Coloured Rain, but luckily a booker at the Chrysalis booking agency who had studied history suggested Jethro Tull, the name of an eighteenth-century agriculturalist who invented the seed drill. The [band's first] single was released on the MGM label miscredited to Jethro Toe and was greeted with total indifference by the record-buying public."

ELTON JOHN   Born in London in 1947, Reginald Kenneth Dwight joined the local soul band Bluesology when he was fourteen. In 1966, Bluesology became the backing band for

blues singer Long John Baldry and was rechristened the John Baldry Show. The following year, Reg Dwight changed his name to Elton John, borrowing the first names of Baldry and saxophonist Elton Dean.

JO JO GUNNE   Vocalist and keyboard player Jay Furguson and bassist Mark Andes started the band in Los Angeles in 1971 after leaving Free. They took their name from a Chuck Berry song.

JOURNEY   Journey began as the Golden Gate Rhythm Section in San Francisco in 1973, after Santana's production manager Walter "Herbie" Herbert encouraged Santana guitarist Neal Schon to form his own band. Herbert, who became the band's manager, explained in an interview how Journey got its name: "The name Journey was created by a gentleman named John Villanueva, who worked with me during the Santana days, was actually with Santana before I got there, and helped put together Journey in the first place. We had this contest that we ran on KSAN radio to name the band and got all these lame suggestions. He came up with the name Journey, we all liked it, and then we said, 'Jeez, he's part of the organization—that kind of screws up our contest. We're going to have to say that someone else actually came up with the name Journey.' And so we said at the time that it was a gentleman named

Toby Pratt [who won the contest] and that he got a lifetime pass to Journey shows. Then years and years later we admitted that there was no such person as Toby Pratt, that it was really John Villanueva who named the band." **What was Villanueva's relationship to the band? Was he in Santana?** "No, he was the percussion roadie, and I was the production manager. He and I are best friends, and he still works here with me and with my production company, Nocturn. Throughout the Journey era, he did their promotion. Sandy Einstein did east of the Rockies and Europe, and John did west of the Rockies and the Orient, and did all their promotional activity. He continues doing that." **So you guys contacted the radio station and said, "Hey, we need a new name, can you set it up for us?"** "Yeah. I think at the time it was Tom Donohue at KSAN, and they put together a contest, and there were lots and lots of postcards, maybe a couple thousand. It was a mail-in thing." **What were some of the names?** "Rumpled Foreskin, Peter Beater and the Mound Pounders, just stuff like that. A lot of wiseass stuff. Some of it was okay, but it was John who came up with Journey."

JOY DIVISION Joy Division began in Manchester, England, in late 1976 as the Stiff Kittens, changing their name the following year to Warsaw, after a song on David Bowie's *Low* album. Later that year, they dropped the name to avoid confusion with the London punk band Warsaw Pakt. They adopted their new moniker from the book *House of Dolls,* a novel of sadomasochism set in a Nazi concentration camp in which the "joy division" was the barracks where prostitutes and other prisoners were kept alive to service the guards.

JUDAS PRIEST   Judas Priest began in Birmingham, England, in 1969. While it has been reported that the name came from the Bob Dylan song "The Ballad of Frankie Lee and Judas Priest," founding bassist Ian Hill recalls: "There was another band called Judas Priest, which had disbanded before the one started by K.K. [Downing, the original guitarist] and myself back in 1969–1970. The vocalist from that band, Alan Atkins, joined with K.K., myself, and John Ellis, our drummer at the time, after seeing us rehearse. We tried to think of a name for our new band but drew a blank. It may have been K.K. who suggested that we use the name Judas Priest. In any case, we all thought it was an excellent idea, as the name seemed to fit perfectly, and the original band already had a good following locally before they split. Aside from these considerations, the phrase 'Judas Priest' was also familiar to Americans, as it was used as a substitute for the exclamation 'Jesus Christ' in early, overcensored movies. So, after phone calls had been made to the other members of the original band, the name was officially used by us. Who in the first band thought up Judas Priest, why and where it came from, I don't know. We probably never will."

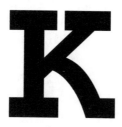

KAJAGOOGOO   Originally called Art Nouveau and later the Handstands, the synth-pop band got their start in Leighton Buzzard, England, in the early eighties and had a hit with "Too Shy" in 1983. As for their name, bassist Nick Beggs told *Record:* "It's like something a child would say. When people say it they can't quite pronounce it, but once they know it they can never forget it."

KANSAS   Kansas evolved from a band formed by guitarist Kerry Livgren, bassist Dave Hope, and drummer Phil Ehart, all native Kansans and classmates at West Topeka High School, in 1970. In 1972, the band changed its name from White Clover to Kansas at Livgren's suggestion.

KING CRIMSON   King Crimson was formed as Giles, Giles & Fripp in Bournemouth, England, in 1967, by Giles brothers Pete [bass] and Mike [drums and vocals], and guitarist Robert Fripp. After some personnel changes, the band became King Crimson in 1969, the name suggested by Peter Sinfield, the group's lyricist. In the *Essential King Crimson* box set, released by Virgin E.G. in 1991, Fripp notes: "The name King Crimson is a synonym for Beelzebub,

which is an anglicized form of the Arabic phrase B'il Sabah. This means 'the man with an aim' and is the recognizable quality of King Crimson."

KING MISSILE   The band was formed in New York City in the mid-eighties by singer John S. Hall and guitarist Dogbowl. Hall discusses the band's name: **Tell me how you came up with the name King Missile, and what its significance is, if any.** "It was this guy named David Sparks who came up with the name. I was going around at the time asking people what the name of the band should be, and he said, 'It should be King Missile.' And I said, 'That's it, that's a great name, what is it?' And he said, 'It's a Japanese comic book character.'" **Had you seen the comic book?** "I saw it a few years later. The character had a lot of powers but lacked the self-confidence to use the powers until his friends rallied behind him and gave him confidence." **Did Sparks explain that at the time and that was part of the appeal?** "No." **Do you recall any other names that you went by or considered before going with King Missile?** "I used to have a band called You Suck, but that was a different band." **Are you pleased with that selection?** "It's kind of an alternative to—the joke I used to tell was that we wanted a name that was an alternative to the usual patriarchal phallic stuff."

THE KINGSMEN   The band, best known for the 1963 hit "Louie Louie," began in Portland, Oregon, in 1958. That year, the parents of saxophonist Lynn Easton arranged for the acquisition of the name the Kingsmen from another local band that had recently broken up.

THE KINKS   The Kinks began as the Ravens in London in 1963, a band that was formed by Dave Davies and then joined by his older brother Ray. They were renamed by manager Larry Page. Kinky was a word in vogue in London at the time and was applied to everything from sex to fashion.

KISS   Kiss was formed in New York City in 1972. Singer and guitarist Paul Stanley recalls how they got their name in an interview: "We were at the point where we were already rehearsing songs, and very clear on what the band was about and who we were. That's the point where you have to come up with a name to kind of reflect that. I was driving my '63 Plymouth Grand Fury on the Long Island Expressway, and the name suddenly came to me. I remember thinking to myself, 'God, I know this is the right name, I hope I don't get any grief from the other guys.' I told them I thought the band should be called Kiss and I held my breath, waiting for some sort of response, and everybody went, 'Yeah, that sounds pretty good.' So there you have it." **What inspired you? Did you hear a song on the radio?** "I think Kiss just conjured up so many different images. It's a word that I felt, no matter where you went in the world, people were going to recognize it. It's just a universal word, even where, obviously, they don't speak the language. It's also short, and it looks great, and not much more than that. It can be a kiss of death, or it can be real soft. In that way, without having the kind of contrast, it has the same stuff to me as Led Zeppelin, Iron Butterfly, those kind of things, where it's light and heavy, or dark and light, but it's all in one word. Kiss has all those connotations."

Did you guys ever play under another name? "Never, although, of course, those are stories that look great in print." **What are some of the stories that have gotten back to you guys? I remember something about Kids in Satan's Service.** "Right. There was Knights in Satan's Service, or Keep It Simple Stupid. Then somebody was saying that we were thinking of calling ourselves Fuck—it just never happened. It's kind of an honor and a compliment to have rumors and myths written and spoken about you, 'cause I guess it means in some way you have some sort of importance. But none of those stories are really true." **I think there are more stories about Kiss than most other bands.** "And some of the best ones are unknown to the public." **Are you pleased you went with it?** "No complaints so far."

THE KLF The English group, formed by Bill Drummond and Jimmy Cauty in 1987, had a handful of hits in the early nineties, including "3 A.M. Eternal" and "Justified and Ancient." KLF reportedly stands for "Kopyright Liberation Front."

KMFDM This German industrial group stands for Kein Mehrheit Führ Die Mitleid, which roughly translates to "No pity for the majority," not "Kill Mother Fucking Depeche Mode," as has been rumored.

THE KNACK The Knack formed in Los Angeles in 1978, and had a huge hit the following year with the single "My Sharona" and the album *Get the Knack*. Vocalist and guitarist Doug Fieger explains in an interview: "We were originally called 20/20. I had sent a demo tape to this guy named Ken Barnes, who had a local magazine called *Bomp*—he was the editor—hoping to get some publicity for the band. We didn't hear anything from him, and about two, maybe three months later I was looking through the new copy of that magazine and I saw an article about a band named 20/20—and it wasn't us. And as it turned out, he managed this band, so I always suspected that he got our tape and photo, liked the name of the band, and took it. I don't know that for sure, but that was my suspicion.

"It forced us to come up with another name. The day I discovered this picture in that magazine I started looking through the dictionary, and when I got to *knack* in the *K* section, I stopped. It was short, it was to the point, it had a neat sound, it started and ended with a *K,* which I thought was nice, it kind of reminded me of the Kinks. It had a meaning that could be applied to a band—having the knack, having a special ability, which is what the dictionary definition is. More than anything though, it was short. I didn't want to have one of those long, descriptive names, with some fruit or color in it. The funny thing is, there was a band called the Knack in the sixties. They were a local Los Angeles band and were also on Capitol Records, coincidentally. They put out a single, which I think is the only record they ever released, and it wasn't a hit. I grew up in Detroit, so I had never even heard of them. And [guitarist] Berton [Averre], who grew up out here [in L.A.], had never heard of them. When we got signed to Capitol, nobody who was there had been around back in the sixties. But somebody in the art department was going through the art archives and came up with the picture sleeve of the single cover, which they used to do pretty regularly back in the sixties. He brought it in and said, 'Did you know that there was a band on the label called Knack?' and nobody did.

"As a matter of fact, I heard some rumor at the time—it might not have been a rumor, it might have been real—that these people were contemplating suing us. I had done a trademark search on the name and there had been nothing with that name, so we didn't have any problem there."

THE KNICKERBOCKERS Originally called the Castle Kings, the Knickerbockers had a hit in 1966 with the Beatlesque rave-up "Lies." They took their name from Knickerbocker Avenue in their hometown of Bergenfield, New Jersey, where they got their start in 1964.

KRAFTWERK The synthesizer band Kraftwerk was formed in Düsseldorf, Germany, in 1970 by keyboard players Ralf Hutter and Florian Schneider-Esleben. *Kraftwerk* is German for power plant." Hutter told *Sounds* magazine: "'*Kraftwerk* basically means "power plant." We plug our machines into the electrical system and create transformed energy. The Human Machine (Die Mensche Machine in German—one of the group's nicknames for itself, another being Klangchemiker, or Sound Chemists) means that we plug ourselves into the machines also. We play with our brains, our hands, our mouths, our feet, and sometimes we use contact microphones, which pick up the sounds of the clothes we are wearing or how much my beard is growing that day. We play the machines, but the machines also play us. This we don't deny like they do in conventional music. There the man is always considered superior to his machine, but this is not so. The machine should not do only slave work. We try to treat them as colleagues so they exchange energies with us.'"

L

LED ZEPPELIN   Guitarist Jimmy Page formed Led Zeppelin after the breakup of the Yardbirds in 1968 and originally called the band the New Yardbirds. Although Keith Moon, the drummer for the Who, is usually credited with suggesting the name, Richard Cole, Led Zeppelin's longtime tour manager, shed some new light on the matter in an interview: "What happened was Keith Moon, John Entwhistle, and I were in New York at a club called the Salvation. At the time I was with the Yardbirds, so that would have been around May of '68. Now Keith and John were always going through things about leaving the Who, and they were talking about forming a new band. They were gonna try to get Jimmy Page on guitar, Stevie Winwood on vocals, and then they came up with this name in the club. I have a feeling it was Entwhistle—I'm not sure, most people say it was Moon—and he said, 'Oh, that's good, I've got the name for it—we'll call it Lead Zeppelin, 'cause it will go down like a lead balloon.' So that's where it came from. It originally started out as a new name for Keith and John."

According to the Led Zeppelin biography *Hammer of the Gods* by Stephen Davis,

Page misspelled *lead* "so the thick Americans wouldn't mispronounce it 'leed.' "

LET'S ACTIVE   After producing albums for a variety of artists, including R.E.M. and the dBs, in a studio built in his parents' garage, guitarist Mitch Easter launched Let's Active in 1981 in North Carolina. In an interview, he explains the origins of the band's name: "The October '81 issue of *Atlantic* magazine, I think, had this article about the Japanese use of English. In Japan, there's a lot of clubs with English names and stuff, and a lot of store banners in English, and apparently they're monumentally creative in their syntax to this day. And they had a lot of examples, and that was just one of them. I think the person [who wrote the article] had seen it on somebody's jacket or something.

"You know how when you're starting a new band you sort of make these lists of names and you think they're all real clever. So that was on our list, and I think the first show we had was coming up right around the time we were putting the list together. I think we gave a couple of names to R.E.M.'s manager Jefferson [Holt]—we were opening for them—and said, 'Yeah, we're not sure what our name's gonna be, it's gonna be one of these, so you can put one on the poster.' I'm not sure if he put it on there or if we decided and told him to put Let's Active on there or not. But anyway, we were gonna get something that made sense, but we never got around to it.

"Needless to say, we were really sorry right away. We got billed as Les Active—with one and two *S*'s, both of which have their own [connotation]—and way other more forgettable variants on that happened, too. And of course, as people'd say, 'What's your name?' we'd have to say it like eighteen times and tell them the whole story. But nevertheless, there were people who right away thought it was really great: 'No, you can't change it, it's great.' So we didn't. It was like life itself, part regret, part joy."

THE LEMONHEADS "A lemonhead is a Midwestern candy—yellow spheres that are sweet on the outside and really sour on the inside," band founder Evan Dando told *Details* magazine. When asked if the name was a musical metaphor, he replied: "I'm not quite sure. Our friend Ivan suggested the name when we were in high school. We had pages and pages of really bad names, but we decided we'd rather pick someone else's bad names than one of our own."

LEVEL 42 The band formed in London in 1980 and took its name from the novel *The Hitchhiker's Guide to the Galaxy* by Douglas Adams, in which "42" is the answer to the question, "What is the meaning of life?"

THE LEVELLERS The band formed in Brighton, England, in 1988. Guitarist Simon Friend explained in a record label press release, "There used to be a political party at the time of the English Civil War called the Levellers. They were against the church, for freedom of speech . . . the first people-power party in Europe. A leveller is somebody who makes all things equal. That's what we are."

L7 The all-female band formed in Los Angeles in the late eighties. Guitarist Suzi Gardner explains: "We didn't really want a gender reference in our name, and so we were just coming up with words or phrases. Nobody liked anybody else's suggestions, so I just said, 'Well, what about L7?' I wasn't crazy about it, thinking nobody else would be either, but when I threw it out, everybody went, 'That's okay.' They didn't jump up and down or anything. They just went, 'Ah, it's all right, it's okay, we've got a show coming up, we need a name. We agree.'" **Did they all know the meaning of it then, that in the fifties it meant "square?"** "Suzy knew what it meant. Rene, our bass player at the time, knew what it meant. Roy, our drummer, wasn't even there—he was probably vomiting on himself at that

 point, after a case of beer." **You guys, I assume, didn't grow up in the fifties, so how did you originally come up with it?** "I thought it was common knowledge what that meant. I learned it from *The Flintstones*. On one show, Fred became a rock star, and Wilma was trying to blow his cover by spreading the rumor that he was 'L7' to all the kids because she wanted him at home. That's how I heard about it. It's also in 'Wooly Bully,' and it's in a Sex Pistols song. People weren't saying it around my neighborhood or anything, but it's something that I grew up with. We lie to the press all the time. If they don't know what it means, we assume they are L7, and we bullshit them." **What are some of the things that you say?** "We say it's Lesbian Seven. We say it's a level of consciousness that you attain when you get to level seven in meditation. We say it's lubrication, a love jelly called L7. There's actually a guitar amp called L7, made by someone like Ampeg—some weird, offbeat company." **Do any of you guys use those amps?** "No, but we saw them. We were like, 'Oh, wow.' We didn't even know

that they existed. There's also a panty size L7—large seven—very appropo for this band." **So the name wasn't a deliberate attempt to be "anti-hip?"** "We really just wanted a name that was easy to remember, that was brief like Black Flag. We didn't want a long name, like Men Without Hats. We wanted a short, to-the-point name, 'cause really, after your band gets going, it doesn't matter what the fuck your name is. The Pixies don't sound anything like the name the Pixies, and Nirvana sounds like they'd be a hippie band, like Jethro Tull, but Nirvana kicks ass. It doesn't really matter what your name is." **What were some of the other names that you were bandying about?** "Noooo!" **You knew I was going to ask that.** "I wanted to call us Keg o' Slaw. At Long John Silver's, that's what they call their coleslaw, 'keg o' slaw.' I just loved that name. Everybody went, 'Beep! Next.' Nobody else like it. I also suggested Captain's Log."

THE LIGHTNING SEEDS   The Lightning Seeds is a band of one: Ian Broudie, a veteran of the Liverpool music scene of the early eighties and an original member of Big in Japan, a band that included Holly Johnson, later of Frankie Goes to Hollywood, and Budgie, future Siouxsie and the Banshees. "Prince sang this line, 'The thunder drowns out what the lightning sees,' " Broudie told *Rolling Stone* in September 1990, "but I heard it as 'the lightning seeds,' and it seemed like a good image."

LIPPS, INC.   Multi-instrumentalist Steven Greenberg and vocalist Cynthia Johnson came together in Minneapolis, Minnesota, and had a number-one hit in 1980 with "Funkytown." The name is a pun on "lip synch."

2ft.

LITTLE FEAT   Little Feat was formed by singer and guitarist Lowell George after leaving Frank Zappa's Mothers of Invention. The name was inspired by Mothers drummer Jimmy Carl Black, who used to tease George about his "little feet."

THE LITTLE RIVER BAND   The band began in Melbourne, Australia, in 1975, having evolved from a London-based band called Mississippi. Criticized for using an American name, they rechristened themselves the Little River Band after a resort town near Melbourne.

LIVING COLOUR   Vernon Reid formed Living Colour in New York City in 1984. He says of the name: "It was inspired by the intro to the old Walt Disney show. ['The following program is brought to you in living color.']" **Why the British spelling?** "I thought the word *colour* was more interesting to look at when spelled with a U." **Do you recall any other names that you considered at the time?** "I *briefly* considered two other names: Point of View and Dangerous Vision."

LOOP   Formed in Croydon, England, in the mid-eighties, Loop took their name from an obscure Velvet Underground track that appeared on a flexi-disc in an issue of *Aspen* magazine.

LOS LOBOS   In an interview, bassist Conrad Lozano recalled: "Let's see, about 1973, when the band first started, we were just basically hanging out learning how to play Mexican folk music. All of us, being rock and roll musi-

cians at that time, . . . we were just trying to learn other music, you know? Because of the cultural awareness thing going on, we thought we would learn a little bit about our culture through the music. And so we started listening to some of the stuff that was coming out of Mexico, the traditional folk stuff. And we would sit around, drink a few beers and learn to play the music. And, of course, using instruments that were not really native to the area. Like say we were doing a song that came from Veracruz—well, we didn't have a harp which is native of that music, or native of that area. . . . So we would maybe use mandolins in place of a harp. We had been doing this for a month, month and a half. Somebody came over and said, 'Hey man, would you guys like to play for this little thing. You can play a half an hour, forty-five minutes or whatever. Just to, you know, just to do it.' So here we go, we have our first gig. And we don't have a name. So we used to make fun of all these different Mexican bands, bubblegum bands that had all these funny names. And there was this one band called Los Lobos del Norte, which meant 'The Wolves of the North.' This is a Mexican band, from Mexico. And we thought they were pretty funny because they, you know, they were sort of a bubblegum kind of band. So anyway, we thought it was funny. So we thought, 'Let's call ourselves Los Lobos del Este de Los Angeles.' which means 'The Wolves of the East of L.A.' And that's where that idea came from. I don't know who it was that yelled it out. It could have been Cesar [Rosas, guitarist.] I'll give Cesar

161

the credit. Maybe. Or it could have been another member of the band that was with us for the first two years of the band's existence, a guy named Frank Gonzalez. But somebody yelled that out. And we thought, 'Wow! That was funny.' We all laughed and thought, 'Well, hey, that's kind of cool. Let's do it.' So as the years went on the name sort of stuck. Around 1980–81, when we decided to go back into rock and roll, we cut the tail end and just called ourselves Los Lobos. And that's the name that we kept." **Did you ever hear from that other band?** "Oh, no." **I'm sure they're long gone.** "I would imagine so. I really don't know." **And now that you've used the name for so long, are you happy with it?** "Oh yeah! I mean, it's part of our culture, so to speak. The wolf is a very important animal in Mexico, and here, in the States. And it's part of a cultural thing. It really is." **Did you ever consider changing your name?** "Never. You know, that's the funniest thing. After that first gig, we sort of liked the name and we just kept it."

LOVE BATTERY   Formed in Seattle, Washington in the late eighties, the band named themselves after a song on the Buzzcocks' second album, *Love Bites,* released in 1978.

LOVE AND ROCKETS   Following the breakup of Bauhaus in 1983, and after a brief incarnation as Tones on Tail, guitarist Daniel Ash, bassist David Jay, and drummer Kevin Haskins formed Love and Rockets. They named themselves after the underground comic book by the Hernandez Brothers.

LOVERBOY   Loverboy formed in Calgary, Canada, in 1979. In an interview, lead guitarist Paul Dean explains how he chose the name: "I was in a band before Loverboy called Streetheart. And the one thing that I liked about the name was that it had some irony to it. It showed some toughness and some vulnerability. So I was on a name-finding mission for the band, and I was looking through my girlfriend's magazines—*Cosmo,* and all these girl magazines. And I just happened to notice that all the covers had cover girls on them. So I figured, 'Coverboy—now there's a pretty good irony to that.' I don't know how I figured it at the time, but that was my thinking: Coverboy. Then the next logical step was Loverboy, and I just went, 'Hmmm, this is going to get a reaction.' Mike [Reno, the band's lead singer] and I were going to call it the Mike Reno-Paul Dean Project or something. People asked me, 'So what are you doing? What's the name of your band going to be?' and I'd tell them, 'The Paul Dean Band.' They'd go, 'Yeah . . . okay.' So I figured with a name like Loverboy, at least we're going to get a reaction. Whether good or bad, these people are going to notice it, it's going to stand out, y'know? So we tried it, and we got a lot of name-calling from it, but we said what the hell, we're going to go with it anyway because at least it creates some kind of shit in the industry, not just another bland name." **So you knew you were going to got some heat.** "Better than nothing, better than no heat. I think the second week we were called homos or something, and people in Japan and Germany really had a problem with the name, they couldn't figure it out, they figured it was a gearbox name. You get the idea of what I'm saying." **Were there any other names that you worked under?** "No, that was the first thing that we made public when we came out. We never played with another name, but considered a couple of other ones. A couple of them have been done since. There's a couple that I've heard but can't remember them offhand." **Now that you look back, are you glad you did it?** "Glad we called it Loverboy? Not really." **Why's that?** "It's a pretty hard thing to live up to when you're forty-six."

THE LOVIN' SPOONFUL Singer John Sebastian and guitarist Zal Yanovsky, who had previously played together in an electric folk band called the Mugwumps with future Mamas and Papas Cass Elliot and Denny Doherty, formed the Lovin' Spoonful in New York City in 1963. In an interview, Sebastian explains the meaning of the band's often misunderstood name: "The Spoonful was already starting its early rehearsals, and we were still looking for a name. I, by chance, ran the idea of a rock and roll band past Fritz Richmond, who was the jug player with the Kweskin Jug Band. And I said, 'Gee, Fritz, this thing is going to be sort of a cross between Chuck Berry and Mississippi John Hurt.' And he said, 'Oh, why don't you call it the Lovin' Spoonful.' That fast. I had been playing nightly with Mississippi John and had not thought of this idea. But the credit goes to Fritz Richmond—who, as I mentioned, was the jug player for the Kweskin Band and was also the engineer on most of the Doors records, all of the Elektra Janis Joplin, and all of my output on Warner Brothers." **So he said "Lovin' Spoonful," and your reaction was . . . ?** "I immediately took the name home and started trying it out on people. At that particular moment in time, you have to remember, people were called the Dovells and the Chantays and things like that, and I came along with this idea and everybody said, 'Gee, it makes me feel ninny to say it.' " **Okay, now tell me—what exactly is it a reference to?** "Okay, it is a reference to cunnilingus. It comes from a song by Mississippi John Hurt called 'Coffee Blues.' And that's it." **Did everyone know right away that that's what it was a reference to?** "No. Most people thought it was a drug reference. And in fact, in our first year of interviews people would ask whether we were alluding to narcotics." **And that would be a spoonful of what—heroin? Is that what they were assuming?** "Well, I guess that would be what they were assuming, yeah." **When they said they were uncomfortable saying it, was it those who knew what it meant or simply those who didn't like its ring?** "No, it was not the reference part of it, it was just that it was kind of awfully all warm and fuzzy for the era. People wanted to be tough, so this really flew in the face of all of that." **So when Fritz immediately said "Lovin' Spoonful," what appealed to him about the reference, and what appealed to you that led you to use it? Was it the reference, or was it the fact that it was warm and fuzzy when everyone else wanted to be hard?** "The answer to the first part is that Fritz was simply reacting to me saying 'a combination of Chuck Berry and Mississippi John Hurt.' I think that he probably, being knowledgeable about all of this music—remember, his background was learning all these thirties and forties tunes, and he knew all of Mississippi John Hurt's repertoire long before Mississippi John was even rediscovered—he was reacting to that. I immediately liked the name because it had a little mystery, and it also had this kind of in-your-face warm, fuzzy feeling that was so unfashionable that it was going to work." **Was this one of Hurt's more famous songs?** "Yes, it was a big crowd-pleaser because of his particularly innocent delivery and his guileless way of presenting it. His audience was frequently filled with beautiful college women—he always had appeal for the women in the audience. He would usually start by taking a sip from a coffee cup that was onstage. It was usually on a little stool by his chair, and he'd sip from the cup and say, 'I always have my cup of Maxwell House coffee, 'cause it's good to the very last drop.' And then he'd drink, and you knew instantly it was scotch. Then he'd resume playing, and with great innocence play this song that would go, 'I love my baby by the lovin' spoonful.' And as he began to sing about it, by the third or fourth time, when he'd come to the words 'the lovin' spoonful,' everybody would know what he was referring to. It was a set piece for him, and that's why it was memorable." **When people would ask you if this was a drug reference, what would you tell them?** "We would tell them, 'No, it's a cunnilingus reference.' " **So you were pretty blunt about it.** "Yes, as a matter of fact it was always hilarious, because we didn't ask this question, after all—we were just answering the question. I remember several occasions when it would be a deejay who would get us on the air and go, 'Hey, fellas! We got the Lovin' Spoonful here! Hey, guys, we want to know, what's that name about anyway, guys?' And we would just answer, very deadpan, 'It's about cunnilingus.' Or we'd say, 'It's about oral sex.' And there would always be this wonderful pause, this dead air space as the guy digested it and realized that he asked the question, and then he would just take a left: 'What colors do you like, Joe?' " **Looking back now, are you pleased with your choice of name?** "Oh, absolutely."

LUSCIOUS JACKSON   The band named themselves after basketball player Lucious Jackson, whose name was misspelled in a sports record book.

Lynyrd Skynyrd   The band formed in high school in Jacksonville, Florida, in 1965 as the Backyard, later changing their name to Lynyrd Skynyrd after Leonard Skinner, a gym teacher known for his hostility toward long-haired students. Later on, when the band had become famous and Skinner was working in real estate, everyone let bygones be bygones and Skinner introduced the group at a hometown concert.

M   Under the name M, Paris-based British pop musician Robin Scott topped the charts in 1979 with the song "Pop Muzik." Scott recalled in *The Billboard Book of Number One Hits:* "At the time when I was putting the [record] sleeve together in Paris, I was thinking that I really needed a pseudonym which would create sufficient interest. I was looking out of the window and I saw this large M, which you see all around Paris for the Metro, and I thought, 'Perfect. I'll take that. And the more people read into it, so much the better.' I should have never told anybody who I was."

Madness   The band formed in London in 1976 as the Invaders. In 1979, the band changed its name to Madness after the 1963 ska hit by Prince Buster, the Jamaican recording star who was one of their major influences.

THE MAMAS AND THE PAPAS   Denny Doherty and husband and wife John and Michelle Phillips formed the New Journeymen in St. Thomas in the Virgin Islands in 1964. Joined by Cass Elliot the following year, they moved to Los Angeles and changed their name to the Mamas and the Papas. In her 1986 autobiography, *California Dreamin'*, Michelle Phillips recalls: "During the early period we lived first communally, on Franklin Avenue [in Los Angeles] and then on Flores . . . It was soon after we moved into the house on Flores and during the early stages of the first album that we had a Great Revelation. We did not really have a name. New Journeymen wouldn't do at all. We were sitting around thinking about it, smoking pot and watching the Les Crane show, a real hard-nosed talk show. Sonny Barger of the San Francisco Hell's Angels was on this particular night, and we were half listening and half trying out names. Magic Circle was a sort of favorite, but it sounded pretentious, and though we were trying for something mystical, we knew that was really the wrong approach.

"Les Crane was sticking it to Barger, very aggressively, and it struck us as odd that he should have him on the show at all. Crane began to talk about the Hell's Angels women, suggesting they were sluts.

"Barger straightened up in his chair. 'Some people call our women cheap. But we just call them our mamas.'

"It was at that point that Cass jumped up and said, 'Ah! We are Mamas. I don't know who you guys are, but Michelle and I are the Mamas.'

"I joined in. 'Yes, We are the Mamas.'

"John looked very thoughtful and sat for a minute or two before saying, 'Mmmm . . . yes. The Papas and the Mamas. That sounds pretty good.'"

" 'You asshole!' shouted Cass. 'You don't say "the Papas and the Mamas." You say "the Mamas and the Papas"!'

"We went to Lou Adler and Bobby Roberts and Andy Wickham [at Dunhill Records] with this idea, and they were ecstatic. They loved the name. Later, of course, John made up a story, a whole tale of how we were in the islands and we got the name . . . 'The Papas used to do this and that, and the Mamas used to get the wood and cook the food,' he'd say to interviewers. A whole lot of bullshit. We got our name from Sonny Barger and Les Crane.

"So . . . the Mamas and the Papas we were, and we finished the album, and the name went up there on the cover in big letters: 'The Mama's and the Papa's,' apostrophes and all."

In his 1986 autobiography, John Phillips's version of this pivotal moment in their career is less detailed, and gone are any references to the islands: "We didn't even have a name yet. We solved that problem while watching a TV interview with the Hell's Angels one night as one of their bikers was explaining how they called their women 'mamas.' Our newest member, Cass, was on a sassy roll, mouthing off to the TV. 'Well,' she said, 'we've got mamas in our gang and we've got papas, too. You can call us the Mamas and the Papas.' "

THE MANHATTANS Formed in Jersey City, New Jersey, in the early sixties as the Dulcets, they had a number-one hit in 1976 with "Kiss and Say Goodbye." Bass vocalist Winfred "Blue" Lovett explained why they changed their name in the book *The Top Ten:* "It didn't sound that exciting. Dulcets means 'melodic tones,' but how could you explain that to the public? We needed a catchy name that would last. So, with the cocktail theme in mind—not the borough of Manhattan—we picked the name Manhattans."

THE MARCELS   Formed in Pittsburgh, Pennsylvania, in 1960, the multiracial vocal group took their name from the wavy "marcelled" hairstyle worn by several members. They had a big hit in 1961 with "Blue Moon."

MARILLION   The band began in Aylesbury, England, in 1978 as Silmarillion, named after *The Silmarillion* by J. R. R. Tolkien.

MARILYN MANSON   Brian Warner placed himself firmly in rock & roll history when he chose his yin-yang stage name, which combines the glamour of Marilyn Monroe with the horror of Charles Manson, and neatly evokes his musical sensibilty and carefully crafted image. Most of his bandmates have similar stage names, including Twiggy Ramirez, named for the sixties British fashion model Twiggy and the California serial killer Richard Ramirez.

THE MARSHALL TUCKER BAND   There was nobody named Marshall Tucker in the Marshall Tucker Band, which formed in Spartanburg, South Carolina, in 1971, and sold more than 10 million records between 1973 and 1984. Originally called the Toy Factory, after founder Toy Caldwell, the band changed their name to the Marshall Tucker Band after the blind piano tuner who had previously used their rehearsal space to restore and tune old pianos. According to the most frequently told story, one of the band members found an old key ring with Tucker's name on it on the floor. "Some people have said it was a business card," Tucker told the *Spartanburg Herald-Journal*, "others said a sign over the door, and others have told the story of the key ring. Choose the one you like best." The band never met Tucker, and once, when they appeared on *The Merv Griffin Show,* said that they believed he was dead. The comment triggered a torrent of calls to the Tucker residence from concerned friends and relatives. "I had my nephew, who is a lawyer, write them a letter," Tucker recalled, and for the next several weeks the credits at the end of *The Merv Griffin Show* included the line "Marshall Tucker is alive." "It never bothered me that they used my name," he noted. "I never made one penny off it, but I'm not bitter about it. I didn't want any. I'm just glad they made good."

MARTHA AND THE VANDELLAS   The Detroit vocal trio of Martha Reeves, Annette Sterling, and Rosalind Ashford were signed to Motown Records in 1962. Reeves changed their name from the Del-Phis to Martha and the Vandellas, inspired by Detroit's Van Dyke Street and Della Reese, her favorite singer.

MATCHBOX 20   "People would ask, 'What's the name of your band?,'" singer Rob Thomas told Edna Gunderson in *USA Today,* "and I'd say 'Larry.' We went through entire books of names." After burning through a variety of short-lived monikers, including Big Shoe Spider, Tindersockets, and Joanie Loves Chachi, the Florida-based band took their name from the number "20" and a patch that read "Matchbox" on a softball jersey. "The two parts weren't even related," Thomas recalled. "Matchbox 20 was the stupidest name we had ever heard. But a couple months later, it was the only name that stuck in our heads."

THE McCOYS   Best known for the 1965 number one hit "Hang on Sloopy," the band was formed by high school classmates in Union City, Indiana, in 1962. They took their name from the Ventures' instrumental "The McCoy," the B-side to the 1960 hit "Walk Don't Run."

THE MC5   Formed in 1967, the highly political MC5 were originally called the Motor City Five, after their hometown of Detroit.

MC 900 FT. JESUS   Dallas, Texas, native Mark Griffin took his stage name from television evangelist Oral Roberts' claim that a "900-foot Jesus" appeared before him one day in a vision.

MEAT LOAF   Born in Dallas, Texas, in 1948, burly Marvin Lee Aday was nicknamed Meatloaf by his high school football coach.

THE MEAT PUPPETS   The Meat Puppets formed in Phoenix, Arizona, in the early eighties. The band's name

 was inspired by their sense that sometimes the music seems to play them, not the other way around; the music becomes the master and they are but mere puppets. Singer and guitarist Curt Kirkman explains in an interview: "After careful and prolonged deliberation, we chose that one because we had a song that was named 'Meat Puppets,' and it was named after our style that we were pursuing, which was more or

less the reason that we got together and have stayed together this long. It related to whenever the three of us played together, it would be like there was something else, the actual thing that was being created by the three parts, the whole of it not only seemed greater, it actually seemed to reverse roles. It seemed to be responsible for us rather than vice versa, and that's how we got it."

MEGADETH   Guitarist Dave Mustaine formed Megadeth after he was kicked out of Metallica in 1983. "The band's name means the act of dying," he explains, "but like really mega! To be more specific, one million deaths, or the hypothetical body count of a nuclear fallout."

THE MEKONS   The Mekons formed in Leeds, England, in the late seventies. Founding guitarist John Langford told *Rolling Stone* in February 1990: "A Mekon was a tyrannical space alien that terrorized earth in a 1950s English comic called 'Dan Dare.' "

MEN AT WORK   Men at Work formed in Melbourne, Australia, in 1979. In an interview, singer Colin Hay recalls: "I was driving in the country in Australia, years ago with my girlfriend, and at that time there were all these signs everywhere. They have them here as well, or they used to have them here—they might've changed them to 'Persons at Work,' I don't know. There were signs on the side of the road saying 'Men at Work' everywhere, and we drove past one of these signs and there were about ten guys digging a trench. One of them was

actually digging the trench and the nine others were watching, as is usually the case. That struck me as being amusing and it struck me as being somewhat indicative of—it was kind of humorous, more than anything else. My girlfriend turned to me at the time—we both kind of looked at each other—and said, 'That'd be a great name for a band.' And I said, 'Yes, it would,' so that's where it came from. I suggested the name to the other guys in the band, and we had like a lot of different names and so forth that'd been come up with. I came in and said, 'Men at Work,' and everyone went, 'Yeah, y'know, well, kind of.' Then we had to start playing at this hotel, but we hadn't settled on a name. The owner of the hotel finally called up and said, 'Look, we've got to put something at the front telling people who you are, y'know.' So the guitarist, Ron Strykert, came in and he said, 'I think we should go with Men at Work.' So we did that. And they used to have this blackboard outside this pub where we played that had 'Men at Work' on it every Thursday night, and it was funny because a lot of people used to go in and apply for jobs. They used to drive past and think, 'Oh, they need people to work.' There was something underdoggy about the name as well that I quite liked. It kind of always struck me as coming up from underneath or something. So that was where it came from." **Are you glad you went with that?** "Absolutely! It was great because, y'know, you see it everywhere on the side of the road. You know what it's like—when you actually settle on a name, all of a sudden it fits."

METALLICA Metallica formed in Los Angeles in 1981. *Circus* magazine reported on the origin of the band's name in June 1992: "According to [singer and guitarist James] Hetfield, 'Lars [Ulrich, the drummer] stole it from a friend of ours, Ron Quintana.' As Hetfield tells it, Quintana had a list of proposed names for a fanzine, 'and Metallica was one of them.' He chuckles as he recalls the titles Quintana tossed around. 'What were the other ones? Oh, yeah, Ripshifta with a *T-A,* not a *T-E-R.* It was either that or Blitzer.' A pause. 'The other one that wouldn't quite have made it was Thunderfuck.' Quintana ended up choosing the title Metal Mania for his 'zine, and Metallica was left by itself. 'So we kind of adopted it.' "

MFSB   The name of the group, a rotating crew of more than thirty studio musicians who played on the majority of the records released by Philadelphia International Records in the early 1970s, has been widely reported to stand for "Mothers, Fathers, Sisters, Brothers." The truth, as Wayne Jancik notes in *The Billboard Book of One-Hit Wonders,* is a bit different: "To those in the know, like Philly arranger Bobby Martin, MFSB stood for 'Mother F***in' Son of a B****.' But if you asked any one of the group's members what the initials stood for, he or she would look you straight in the eye and reply 'Mothers, Fathers, Sisters, Brothers.' Cute."

MIDNIGHT OIL   The band was named by a keyboard player who was only briefly in the band. It's from the expression "burning the midnight oil."

MILLI VANILLI   The group was formed by producer Frankie Farian in Munich, Germany in 1988. The name has been described as an homage to the group Scritti Politti, the name of a Berlin discotheque, and a Turkish phrase meaning "positive energy."

WAYNE FONTANA AND THE MINDBENDERS   Originally formed in Manchester, England, in 1961 as the Jets, they changed their name to the Mindbenders the following year after *The Mind Benders,* a film starring Dirk Bogarde that was playing at the local movie house. Lead singer Fontana, born Glyn Geoffrey Ellis, rechristened himself in honor of the label that signed the band, Fontana Records. Their hits in the U.S. included "Game of Love" in 1965 and "A Groovy Kind of Love" in 1966.

MINISTRY   Singer Al Jourgensen formed Ministry in Chicago in the early eighties. He explains: "I was at home writing my first song on a four-track. I had no name for my band or the song, and as I finished the song, I looked up at the TV screen; there was a movie on called *Ministry of Fear,* with Ray Milland. I thought, 'Wow, groovy name for a band.' After that, it was changed to Ministry of Truth, then we changed it to Ministry of Canned Peaches, then finally Ministry."

MINUTEMEN   The band formed in San Pedro, California, in the late seventies as the Reactionaries, changing their name in 1980 to the Minutemen because their fast and furious songs typically clocked in under sixty seconds.

THE MIRACLES   The group was originally called the Matadors, but changed their name following the recording session for the group's first single, "Got a job," in 1957. In his 1989 autobiography, *Smokey,* Smokey Robinson explains how the name the Miracles was selected: " 'You gonna have to change your name,' [Motown records honcho Berry Gordy] said afterwards. 'The Matadors sounds a little jive.'

"Everyone thought of a name, scribbled it on a piece of paper, and threw it in a hat. By chance we picked my choice.

" 'Miracles,' said Berry, mulling it over. 'I like the sound of that. I like the attitude. Yeah, y'all are Miracles.' "

MR. BIG   The hard-rock band formed in Los Angeles in 1988 and had a number-one hit in 1991 with the romantic ballad "To Be With You." Vocalist Eric Martin told Fred Bronson in *The Billboard Book of Number One Hits:* "We had all kinds of weird names like 'Mars Needs Women,' 'The Evil Stepsisters'—we were gonna open for Cinderella. But our drummer Pat [Torpey] was looking through a bunch of rock-and-roll records and listening to the bands that we wanted to have the spirit of, like Free." Torpey came upon upon the Free song "Mr. Big" and the band decided to make it their name. "It was a coincidence, because Billy [Sheehan, the bassist] said when he was in the band Palace he used to do a bass solo with that song."

MOBY GRAPE   Moby Grape formed in San Francisco, California, in 1966. In an interview, guitarist Jerry Miller recalled how they chose their name: **How did you guys come up with Moby Grape?** "Well, we were all hanging out in the studio in San Francisco, and [bassist] Bob Mosley and Skippy [Alexander Spence, lead singer and guitarist] went out to have a little lunch, and they came back laughing like crazy with a name for the band. They were thinking of this joke, y'know: 'What's purple and swims in the ocean?' So they came back in and said, 'Moby Grape, we'll just be Moby Grape.' So that's how it happened." **Right on the spot you guys said all right?** "Yeah, we all got along with that pretty good. We all laughed, and whatever makes you laugh is good." **Were there any other names that you were considering at the time?** "There was one that our manager wanted—he liked Bentley Escort. It kind of related to Jefferson Airplane, Strawberry Alarm Clock—y'know, that kind of thinking. But we hated that one. So Moby Grape sounded good, and it was made up by the band, so we liked that much better."

THE MODERN LOVERS   Jonathan Richman formed the Modern Lovers in Boston in the early seventies. Richman explains, in characteristic fashion, how he came up with the band's name: "The Modern Lovers name came to be the day after Jonathan Richman decided to form a band. Jonathan wanted a name to describe the kind of love songs he was going to make. He figured they would be modern ones."

MOLLY HATCHET   The band began in Jacksonville, Florida, in 1975, and took their name from Hatchet Molly, a legendary, perhaps mythical southern prostitute who lured men to her home, where she castrated and mutilated them.

THE MONKEES   The name was coined by producers Bob Rafelson and Burt Schneider in 1965 in imitation of the Beatles, whose 1964 film, *A Hard Day's Night,* was the inspiration for their TV series.

THE MOODY BLUES   The Moody Blues began as the M&B Five in Birmingham, England, in 1964. Guitarist Justin Hayward joined the band in 1966 and became their lead vocalist and chief lyricist. In an interview, Hayward recounts the group's origins: **How did the Moody Blues come up with their name?** "In Birmingham where we used to work, all of the major gigs were in the back of pubs. The pubs were very, very large in Birmingham, still are, and they'd have a sort of big room at the back where they'd have dances. One of the major breweries in Birmingham was called Mitchell and Butler. The group had a deal working for them, with Mitchell and Butler sponsoring the group some equipment because they were working a lot of the time in their pubs. All pubs in England are owned by breweries, and Miller and Butler owned lots of them in the Midlands. So that's why the original group was called the M&B Five. Associating yourselves with a brewery meant you had gigs made for you really, it gave you one step up on everybody else. Then, when it proved to be a rather sort of nothing name, Mike Pinder, our original keyboard player, thought of the name Moody Blues. We dropped the 'Five' and then became the Moody Blues, but it was really the initials that came first." **How did he pick "Moody" and "Blues?"** "The whole image of the group was kind of dark. The 'Moody' came from the fact that we never smiled in photographs, and they were very dark. If you look at all the early photographs, we're all wearing sort of these dark blue suits, what they call reefer jackets, done up, always done up, with dark shirts underneath. The whole thing was rather sinister. We were a rhythm and blues band, so that's where the 'Blues' came from. And then I wrote 'Nights in White Satin' and it all changed. It was completely different then. The fact that we did a great big left turn was really just to try and find ourselves and discover our own personalities and how to express ourselves before we went completely broke." **That was the turning point?** "It was really, because at that point we'd gone as far as we could go singing about people's problems in the Deep South of America without knowing anything about it, and at the same time worrying about our image and how our hair looked, y'know. It was completely incongruous. And although we loved rhythm and blues, and we were good at it, it just wasn't expressing our own personalities. The songs that I was writing just didn't fit in with the rhythm and blues thing. So that was the big change, when we decided one day in the van coming home from a gig, we thought, 'Oh, sod it, let's forget all that rhythm and blues stuff, let's just do our own songs and see what happens.' Because the alternative was just to split up really and go and get another job." **So you changed direction musically but still called yourselves the Moody Blues. Did you also consider changing the name?** "I don't think so, no. Because you create so many kinds of ties . . . I've often thought about that, whether at that particular point, whether we should've changed the name as well. In the end I don't think it actually would have made any difference. I think that *Days of Future Passed* would have been successful by any group. And the reverse is true, really, that it didn't harm us. It didn't harm us or really help us. But what we had, being known as the Moody Blues, was a lot of contacts and a lot of connections, and we had a record company that was interested in us. I think if we'd have changed our name, maybe they would've thought, 'Well, hang on a minute. . . .' "

MORPHINE Speaking of his band's name, Morphine frontman Mark Sandman told *New York* magazine, "We thought it fit the music because there's sort of like a low, penetrating kind of thing going on with us." Morphine, a drug derived from opium, is a sedative.

THE MOTHERS OF INVENTION   The Mothers of Invention began as the Soul Giants, a band Frank Zappa discovered playing soul and R&B covers at a Pomona, California, bar in 1963. Zappa joined the band, convinced them to play original material—"I talked them into getting weird"—and changed their name to Captain Glasspack and the Magic Mufflers. After getting tossed out of numerous area bars, they changed their name to the Muthers. "It just happened to be Mother's Day [1964]," Zappa recalled in *Frank Zappa: A Visual Documentary* by Miles, "although we weren't aware of it at the time. When you are nearly starving to death, you don't keep track of holidays." The following year they changed their name to the Mothers, and were signed by Verve, MGM's jazz/R&B label in 1966. In *The Real Frank Zappa Book,* Zappa writes: "We were then informed that they [MGM Records] couldn't release the record—MGM executives had convinced themselves that no DJ would ever play a record on the air by a group called 'The Mothers' (as if our name was going to be The Big Problem). They insisted that we change it, and so the stock line is 'Out of necessity, we became the Mothers of Invention.' "

MÖTLEY CRÜE   Mötley Crüe formed in Los Angeles in 1981, but the band's name dates back to 1973 when guitarist Mick Mars was still called Bob Deal and was working as a roadie for a group in San Diego called Mottley Croo. "We were a bar band, rude and nasty," drummer Jack Valentine told *Rolling Stone* in October 1987. "There was one showcase club in town that brought in L.A. bands." In order to play there, Mottley Croo changed its name to Whitehorse and claimed to come from Los Angeles. "Then we got such a big following that we kept the name Whitehorse." After Whitehorse's guitar player left the band, Deal took his place. "Deal was the most destitute being I'd ever met," said Valentine. "The guy was just so poor. He didn't have a car, he didn't have a guitar that was worth beans. He had one set of clothes."

Deal eventually moved to L.A. and hooked up with bassist Nikki Sixx (Frank Carlton Serafino Ferrano), drummer Tommy Lee (Thomas Lee Bass), and singer Vince Neil (Vincent Neil Wharton) after running an ad that read in part, "Loud, rude, aggressive guitarist available."

Nikki Sixx told *Entertainment Weekly* in August 1992 why they added umlauts to the name: "We didn't think about its proper use. We just wanted to do something to be weird, and the umlaut is very visual. It's German and strong, and that Nazi Germany mentality—'the future belongs to us'—intrigued me."

The band's improperly used umlauts did lead to some confusion. During their first tour of Germany, Sixx admitted that "all the kids were going, 'Mutley Cruh!' and we were going, 'Huh?' "

MOTT THE HOOPLE   The band began as the Shakedown Sound in Hereford, England, in 1968, and then changed its name to Silence. Guy Stevens at Island Records took over as manager and producer in 1969 after they sent him a demo tape. He recruited Ian Hunter to replace the lead singer and renamed them Mott the Hoople after an obscure book he had recently read by Willard Manus, published in 1967.

MUDHONEY Grunge pioneers Mudhoney came together in Seattle in 1988 and took their name from the Russ Meyer sexploitation classic.

MUNGO JERRY Formed in London in 1969 as the Good Earth, they named themselves after the mischievous cat Mungojerrie in *Old Possum's Book of Practical Cats* by T. S. Eliot, which was also the inspiration for the Broadway musical *Cats*. Mungo Jerry is best known in the U.S. for their 1970 hit "In the Summertime."

MY BLOODY VALENTINE The band was formed in Dublin in 1984 by guitarist Kevin Shields and drummer Colm O'Ciosoig and was named after a low-budget Canadian horror film.

NAZARETH The band got their start in Dunfermline, Scotland, in 1969, and took their name from the first line of the Band's "The Weight": "I pulled into Nazareth. . . ."

THE NAZZ Todd Rundgren formed the Nazz in Philadelphia in 1967 and Utopia in New York City in 1974. In an interview, Rundgren discusses his bands' names: **Why don't we start with the Nazz?** "Well, it didn't have a lot of significance. We were formed in the late sixties, so most every band was *the* something. It was always 'the This' or 'the That,' so we were looking for some *the* thing to be something kind of simple and iconographic, I guess. We actually got the name from the B-side of a Yardbirds single called 'The Nazz Are Blue.' It was sung by Jeff Beck and it was essentially just some generic sort of boogie, an excuse to play a guitar—the song wasn't anything to speak of. In listening to the song, we couldn't tell what 'the Nazz' was." **Have you since found out what that was a reference to?** "Well, a lot of people said that the Nazz was like a Lord Buckley thing. In [beatnik humorist] Lord Buckley's context, it was spelled with a single *Z* [a reference to Jesus of Nazareth]. I don't know whether it was just some corruption that the Yardbirds added to it, or Jeff Beck added to it when they wrote the song. When we picked it, we didn't even know what it meant. We thought it had just kind of wide-open connotations." **Was that part of the criteria, that it be somewhat ambiguous?** "Not necessarily. It's just that all the things we came up with, most of them seemed too specifically something. A lot of the bands around had these names like the Munchkins, or something that was either too cute or too 'acid,' like the Chocolate Watch Band, or something like that. So we wanted something more or less simple and distinctive, and for some reason that's what we settled on. We just settled on that, not even knowing what the word meant." **Are you glad you did, ultimately?** "Well, it seemed to work out." **I read that Alice Cooper had a band called the Nazz, but he changed it when he found out about you guys.** "Apparently, Alice Cooper did have a band called the Nazz, but we made a record first, so they were sort of forced to change it. I don't know whether theirs was with one or two *Z*s or where they got the name from." **At the time were you aware that there was a band out in the West called the Nazz?** "No, not until much later. Not until, as a matter of fact, we saw Alice Cooper for the first time." **And he said, 'By the way, I had a band called the Nazz?"** "Well, I didn't speak to him, but somehow—I don't know how the information was imparted to me—but somehow I picked up the information that at one time Alice Cooper had been the Nazz." **How about Utopia? Whose idea was that?** "That was mine. That was an idea I had even before there was the band, really. I had an idea that I wanted to do something that went along with the kind of wild and crazy music that I was into. I was taking some psychedelic drugs at the time, and I just had all of these different kinds of visions. The effect on me from taking psychedelic drugs was very sort of 'spiritual.' For some people it was just recreational, but for me it was epiphanal. I had this idea that I wanted to make music a different way and that I also wanted to have a different kind of band structure, and on one particular excursion it occurred to me that the name of the band should be Utopia." **Again, looking back, are you glad you chose that?** "Yeah, we made a lot of use out of the name." **Do you recall any other names that you considered and jettisoned?** "I don't think so. I don't recall any that really stuck out. It was always a kind of meticulous process. In the case of Utopia, there weren't a whole lot of other alternatives, I don't think. Maybe Nirvana was one of them." **I was wondering about that. When I first heard of Nirvana, I thought of Utopia.** "There was a possibility that that was one of the names under review, but I think that it had too much of a strictly Eastern context, at least at the time. At the time nirvana was really a Hindu or Buddhist concept." **I guess now it really has sort of broadened.** "Yeah, it's a more common parlance, so nobody will mistake them for having a particular religious agenda."

NED'S ATOMIC DUSTBIN   The band came together at college in England in November 1988. They found their name in a book of scripts from "The Goon Show," a classic BBC comedy series starring Spike Milligan and Peter Sellers. Recalls bassist Alex, "We got so desperate trying to think of a good name that we decided we'd better just get a daft one. I looked through an old 'Goon's book, and that was the silliest title . . . except one called 'The Spy: Or Who Is Pink Oboe.' It was a tough choice."

NEW ORDER   Following the suicide of vocalist Ian Curtis, Joy Division's remaining members—guitarist Bernard Sumner, bassist Peter Hook, and drummer Stephen Morris—decided to continue performing under a new name. Although the band claimed the name merely referred to their new beginning, some critics believed that it was a reference to Adolf Hitler's plan to conquer Europe, prompted by the fact that Joy Division was also a Nazi term.

THE NEW YORK DOLLS   The New York Dolls (who often performed in drag) formed in New York City in 1971. Guitarist Sylvain Sylvain (born Syl Mizrahi) recalls: "The name, which I kind of came up with, was actually put together before the Dolls ever played together as a whole band with [singer] David Johansen, and even with [guitarist] Johnny Thunders. The original drummer, Billy Murcia—he passed away on our first English tour, and we got Jerry Nolan to replace him—we had a group, me and Billy, called the Pox. When it broke up after one of the guitar players left, we were sort of drawing up ideas for names and stuff.

"Usually, y'know, you come up with a name from either television or maybe a newspaper, or like a current event that's going on maybe, just basically anything that hits you. I saw the movie *Beyond the Valley of the Dolls,* the Russ Meyer film, which was sort of a parody of *The Valley of the Dolls,* and I said, 'Hmmm, "Dolls." ' And of course they used to call pills 'dolls,' especially in the movie: 'Oh, what happened to her?' 'Oh, she took all these dolls.' So I said to Billy, 'Wow, that could be a cool name for a band, just the Dolls, y'know?' When we met David, he said, 'Hmmm, the Dolls, yeah, but how about "the New York Dolls?" ' " **It sort of sounds like a sports team.** "Yeah. Of course, New York really made a lot of sense to us because obviously that's where we came from, and that's where we put the band together. There was a lot of art and all kinds of groovy stuff being stirred up in those days, as New York was basically like your international center." **So you wanted to let people know that you were from the city?** "Yeah, that just came about very naturally, y'know, 'cause the Dolls by itself meant different things to different people. When most people saw us, they said, 'Wow, the Dolls,' and they never really associated the movie, or the fact that it meant drugs, until later on."

THE NICE The band, which included Keith Emerson, later of Emerson, Lake, and Palmer, formed in London in 1967. They reportedly took their name from the Small Faces song "Here Comes the Nice," an ode to amphetamines.

NIGHT RANGER The band formed in San Francisco in the early eighties and by the middle of the decade had a handful of hits, including "Sister Christian." In a 1998 press release issued by the band, drummer and vocalist Kelly Keagy explained the origins of their name: "It's about a guy named Eddie, who was a homeless man in San Francisco that used to hang out around the clubs we played. Eddie was homeless, but he took care of other homeless people. He proved he could have dignity and strength—he fed off the spirit of the streets. Everyone called him the 'Night Ranger,' and when we met him and got to know him and what he was about, he was really an inspiration to us. He's still an inspiration to us."

NINE INCH NAILS   Trent Reznor formed Nine Inch Nails in Cleveland, Ohio, in 1987, as a one-man industrial rock band. The name has been rumored to represent all sorts of things: the stakes that were used to crucify Christ, the standard size of nails used to seal coffins, and what you'll find on the tips of the Statue of Liberty's fingers. Reznor's explanation, as told to *AXCESS* magazine, is a bit more mundane: "I don't know if you've ever tried to think of band names, but usually you think you have a great one and you look at it the next day and it's stupid. I had about a hundred of those. Nine Inch Nails lasted the two-week test, looked great in print, and could be abbreviated easily. It really doesn't have any literal meaning. It seemed kind of frightening. . . . It's a curse trying to come up with band names."

999   The British punk band took their name from the phone number for emergency services in England.

NIRVANA   "Punk is musical freedom," Kurt Cobain said in a press release distributed by DGC Records when *Nevermind* was released in 1991. "It's saying, doing, and playing what you want. In Webster's terms, nirvana means freedom from pain, suffering, and the external world, and that's pretty close to a definition of punk rock."

No Doubt Named after a catch phrase of original member John Spence, who shared lead vocals with Gwen Stefani. He committed suicide in 1987.

Oasis Vocalist Liam Gallagher formed the band, originally called Rain, in Manchester, England, in 1991. Inspired by a nightclub in Swindon that he had come across while working as a roadie for another band, he rechristened them Oasis.

The Offspring The band, which formed in Orange County, California, in the late eighties, were so named because they considered themselves the second generation of California punk rockers.

Oingo Boingo Oingo Boingo began not as a band but as a satirical stage act called the Mystic Knights of the Oingo Boingo that built a cult following in Los Angeles in the midseventies. The show gradually incorporated musical elements until it evolved at the end of the decade into a band with the shortened name of Oingo Boingo.

THE O'JAYS   Formed as the Triumphs at McKinley High School in Canton, Ohio, in 1958, and later called the Mascots, they changed their name in 1961 in honor of Eddie O'Jay, a Cleveland disc jockey who served as their mentor.

THE 101ERS   Joe Strummer's band (before the Clash) took their name from the George Orwell novel *1984*. Room 101 is where Winston Smith is tortured: " 'You asked me once,' said O'Brien, 'what was in Room 101. I told you that you knew the answer already. Everyone knows it. The thing that is in Room 101 is the worst thing in the world. . . . The worst thing in the world varies from individual to individual. It may be burial alive, or death by fire, or by drowning, or by impalement, or fifty other deaths. There are cases where it is some quite trivial thing, not even fatal. . . . In your case, the worst thing in the world happens to be rats.' "

ORCHESTRAL MANOEUVRES IN THE DARK (OMD) The band was formed in Liverpool, England, in 1978 by synthesizer players Andy McCluskey and Paul Humphreys. In an interview, McCluskey recalls their origins: **How did you guys arrive at Orchestral Manoeuvres in the Dark?** "When I was an aspiring musician, before I was even in bands—this is like when I was fifteen or sixteen—I used to write on my bedroom wall, much to my mother's annoyance, just names—song titles, bands, just anything that came into my head. I had a fairly bizarre collection of them up there. Then when I started to join bands, they were usually other people's bands, so that whatever name they had was what was used. I was in a band—the last band I was in before OMD—it was an eight-piece band with a short name, the Id. The guitarist was studying psychology at the time; he got that from his Freudian studies. When Paul Humphreys and I decided to just be a two-piece, using a tape recorder and playing songs that really all our best friends thought were absolute crap, we figured we needed a name that was going to tell people that we were not a punk band, we were not a rock band or a typical pop band, we were something different. So quite simply I just went to my bedroom wall and started looking down the list of all the names and things. Orchestral Manoeuvres in the Dark had in fact been a title of a song which we had intended to do but never did, which just featured recorded war noises and some very, very distorted guitar. We just figured it was such a literally off-the-wall name that people would know that this was a different type of band, this was two guys and a tape recorder playing in a punk club. We actually only got together as the two of us to do one gig. We dared ourselves to go into this punk club and do our synth songs the way we wanted to, instead of having bloody lead guitarists and drummers messing them up for us, as had been happening in the previous bands. So that was how we got the name. It doesn't have any deep meaning as such. It was really just a name to set the band aside as being something different from all the very short names that were around at the time. All the punk bands had very short names, y'know. It was usually 'the Something-or-others,' and so we wanted a great, big, long name to make it obvious that this was something totally different, which at the time it was." **Any regrets?** "Oh, yeah. I mean, it's such a hell of a mouthful, although I do prefer it to being short-ened to OMD. I say OMD myself all the time. It makes it much more convenient for deejays—by the time they've actually told you the name of the band, the track is half over on the radio. It makes it easier. But right from the very start people had trouble with it, not least because *manoeuvres* is spelled differently in America to how it is in England. In all the various European territories, because it's a collection of words, they would actually put it into their own language. I've seen posters in Spain that say OMD and posters that say MOD, because converted to Spanish, the *M* comes before the *O*. I remember they used to do a thing in a rock magazine called *Sounds* which was like a gig guide, and it had a list of all bands playing wherever they were playing, and in '78, just after we'd started, I remember phoning them up, to see if they'd put us in the listings. The guy said, 'Yeah, right, where are you playing, what's the date, what's the name of the band?' And I said, 'Orchestral Manoeuvres in the Dark,' and he said, 'Oh, you've got no fucking chance with that name—you should change that right away!' " **Was the name in any way a reference to ELO?** "It had nothing to do with it. In fact, when we started, we were influenced by German electronic music. I always thought ELO were pretty passé even by then, in the seventies. So the fact that it got shorted to OMD, that was one of the first of three-letter abbreviations. I mean, now there's a million and one three-letter bands around. At the time we were really just about only the second band to have a three-letter abbreviation, and of course the comparison was going to be with ELO, which I hated."

P

PAPER LACE   The band, formed in Nottingham, England, in 1969, and had a number-one hit in 1974 with "The Night Chicago Died," the story of a mythical shootout between the police and Al Capone and his gang. They took their name from their hometown's most famous export.

PARLIAMENT/FUNKADELIC   As a teenager in Plainfield, New Jersey, in the fifties, George Clinton formed a vocal group called the Parliaments, that according to his manager, Archie Bell, he named after Parliament cigarettes. In 1967, the Parliaments had a major hit with "[I Just Wanna] Testify," a straightforward love song. By then, Clinton had begun to rethink the Parliaments' sound after spending time in Detroit listening to psychedelic music and the Stooges and the MC5. That year, after he was prevented from using the Parliaments name due to a legal battle with the owner of the group's defunct record label, Clinton formed Funkadelic. He coined the name by crossing *funk* and *psychedelic,* which reflected the group's new musical direction. Eventually Clinton won the right to use the Parliaments name, which he did, after dropping the *S,* in conjunction with Funkadelic.

PAVEMENT   The band was formed by Scott Kannberg and Stephen Malkmus in Stockton, California. In an interview, Kannberg discusses the band's origins: **Tell me, how did you**

guys come up with the name Pavement? "Well, god, I don't know. It's been so long ago." **When was it, by the way?** "It was actually in—oh god, let me see. Probably like 1986 or so. And I was in college and just trying to . . . I was like an urban planning, geography major, you know. So I was reading a lot of books about suburbia, edge cities and all that junk. And, I don't know, it just came to my mind one day in class. While I was just thinking of band names. I thought of this great name called Pavement. No one used it yet, so . . . lucky." **Now, at that point was it just you and Stephen?** "Yeah. It was kind of before we got together really to actually record. It was a few months before we actually even—I mean we'd been jamming, you know, here and there, but nothing . . . no definite plans or anything." **Nothing formal?** "Yeah." **So, in a way you came up with the band name before there really was a band.** "Yeah, I mean it was a total concept. You know, kind of a project. When we first started, it was kind of just 'Let's just make up these songs and put it on a single and that's *all* we should do,' you know? 'It will be our moment in rock history,' or whatever. And we got greedy and wanted to do more." **Now, when you suggested the name to Stephen, what did he say? Did he have a list of his own?** "No, he didn't. Well, I guess he did, but I mean I had the upper hand, because he went off to Europe for a year. And I ended up putting out the single." **So it was up to you.** "So I said, 'Okay, it's Pavement.' He was actually in a record store in Austria or somewhere when he first saw the single. And he was like 'What's this? What's this?' And he was asking the guy in the record store, he said 'I'm in this band.' And the guy said to him, 'Oh, Pavement. Oh, that name hasn't been used yet?' "
In retrospect are you glad you chose it? "Oh, yeah. I mean

there's so many ways to describe us now. It's an easy name, you know." **Right.** "You know, it coincides with rock. There is this big thing in England—they don't understand the word 'pavement.' They think pavement means 'sidewalk.' That's their meaning for it. So I mean even today, people, in interviews, say, like, 'Why do you call yourselves "sidewalk?" ' " **And what's your answer to that?** "Our answer? Well, now our answer is like, 'Well . . . I don't know.' But before you had to sit there and explain to them. And they still didn't understand." **So there wasn't any point where you called yourselves something else? It was always just Pavement?** "Well, we did this Lollapalooza tour a few years back. We were thinking about changing our name to Pi." **Pi, as in—** "The sign pi. And, we were going to have a big backdrop and everything with Pi." **Where did that come from?** "I don't know. We wanted a change." **It was just a goof for the most part?** "We were pretty serious. But they wouldn't let us do it." **They being . . ?** "Perry Farrell, or whoever's in charge of that thing. He said, 'If you do that, we'll find a way to kick you off the tour.' "

PEARL JAM   Pearl Jam rose from the ashes of two Seattle, Washington, bands, Green River and Mother Love Bone, in 1990. *Rolling Stone* reported in October 1991: "After a brief run under the name Mookie Blaylock (for the New Jersey Nets guard, whose number, 10, also became the title of their debut album) the band members renamed themselves Pearl Jam, after Vedder's great-grandmother. ('Greatgrandpa was an Indian and totally into hallucinogenics and peyote,' says Vedder. 'Greatgrandma Pearl used to make this hallucinogenic preserve that there's total stories about. We don't have the recipe, though.')"

PERE UBU   Singer and lyricist Dave Thomas formed Pere Ubu in Cleveland, Ohio, in 1975, naming the band after the hero of *Ubu Roi,* a play by French absurdist Alfred Jarry.

In an interview, Thomas explains why he chose the name: "Well, the glib remark would be that all the good names were taken already. At the time, Pere Ubu was quite clearly a good name because it met the prime requisites: that it had three syllables, that it didn't mean anything particularly—I mean, obviously it does, but to an audience in the American Midwest, which was where we were, one could be assured that it really wouldn't mean anything—that it seemed to mean something at the same time, that it looked good and sounded good. Those are just about all the things that you need in a band's name. Also, it had another sublevel of groovy art factors attached to it. I liked Jarry's production methods, and the way he required the audience to become involved in the production, and engaged the imagination of the audience with suggestion, and all that stuff. Mainly, it looked good and sounded good and didn't mean anything and had three syllables.

"A band's name is always one of the critical things to me. If you pick a stupid name, it indicates that you haven't thought too much about the whole thing, and it's a clear indication of where you hold yourself and what you're doing in your own mind. If you give your band a stupid, trivial name, then it indicates that you consider what you do stupid and trivial. Obviously, the inverse is true, or the obverse, or whatever it is, that if you give yourself a stupid, pretentious name . . . We can only hope that Pere Ubu is on the good side of all those equations."

PET SHOP BOYS Neil Tennant and Chris Lowe met in an electronics store in London's Kings Road in 1981. Discovering that they shared a love of dance music, they became friends and formed a band called West End. Later, they switched to Pet Shop Boys after two friends of Lowe's who owned a pet shop in the Ealing district. They say they liked the name because they "thought it sounded like an English rap group."

PHISH The band formed in 1983 at the University of Vermont. In the June 1998 issue of *Döniac Schvice,* the band's official newsletter, bassist Mike Gordon explained, "Our drummer's name is Jon Fishman. His peers have favored the nickname 'Fish'—it's the first part. So if I had to guess, I would think that someone, maybe me, maybe who knows, said 'Let's call the band Phish.' The Ph, of course, was a marketing ploy that, by the way, has worked. Of course, if you ask Fish himself, he'll say, 'We liked the Phhhh sound that an airplane makes during takeoff.' But that's a pile of crap."

PINK FLOYD The band formed in London in 1965 to play a mix of R&B and blues. They were named the Pink Floyd Sound by singer and guitarist Syd Barrett after two Georgia bluesmen, Pink Anderson and Floyd Council. As the band's sound changed, so did its name, first shortened to the Pink Floyd, and finally just Pink Floyd.

GLADYS KNIGHT AND THE PIPS   At a birthday party for her ten-year-old brother, Merald, in 1952, Gladys Knight formed a quintet with Merald, their sister Brenda, and their cousins William and Elenor Guest. They made such an impression that cousin James Woods urged them to turn professional and offered to manage them. They agreed and called themselves the Pips after his nickname, Pip.

THE PIXIES   The band formed in Boston in 1986. The name was chosen by lead guitarist Joey Santiago after flipping through a dictionary and was okayed by the band because they liked the fact that it didn't have any real relevance to their sound. About his own name, vocalist and guitarist Black Francis, born Charles Michael Kitteridge Thompson IV, told *Rolling Stone* in March 1989: "I always liked the sort of funny, corny, pompous stage names, like Iggy Pop and Billy Idol, so I wanted one. My father suggested Black Francis; it's an old family name."

THE PLATTERS   The vocal group formed in Los Angeles in 1953. In the liner notes to *The Magic Touch: An Anthology,* bass vocalist Herbert Reed recalls, "I remember coming out of one of the fella's houses thinking to myself, on the radio they always say, 'Here's the latest platter by so-and-so.' And everytime I put a nickel in the jukebox, I'd see another platter come down. It seemed the right name for a group."

PLAYER   Formed in Los Angeles in the mid-seventies, the group topped the charts in 1978 with "Baby Come Back." Lead vocalist and guitarist John Crowley told *Billboard* that year that they chose the name after "we saw the word on television when the players from the show were listed. We knocked off the 'S' and went with it. I think the word holds a certain ambiguity."

Poco   The country-rock band Poco began in Los Angeles in 1968, after guitarists Richie Furay and Jim Messina left Buffalo Springfield. Guitarist Rusty Young talks about the band's name in an interview: "I was just looking at a book on the Beatles that a friend of mine had, and we're in there. It says that John Lennon actually gave us the name Poco—that we had to change our name from Pogo to Poco, and that John Lennon was the one who came up with it—which couldn't be further from the truth. I have no idea where they came up with that. Lennon was around, but I don't think he was around until after we started playing as Poco. Harrison was there in the beginning, we even auditioned for him, but at any rate, it didn't happen like that at all.

"Anyhow, we started off in L.A. We played this hip club called the Troubadour. On Monday nights, a band could come and play for free, and if they really liked you, then they'd book you to be one of the opening acts for a headliner. We didn't have a name, and there were a bunch of names going around. Jimmy wanted to name the band Flintlock Pepperbox—that was Messina's name. Richie's name was Buttermilk. Popcorn was a name that was suggested. Every week there were your joke names. We'd throw all the names in a hat, and the manager would pull one out, and that would be the name. RFD was one we played under once. We played under a bunch of different names.

"Our manager's favorite comic character was Pogo, and he actually looked like the character Pogo. His name was Dickie Davis. Dickie put that name in the hat, and as it turns out, we drew out that name one day. We were always auditioning for labels, and the Troubadour was a club where labels would come looking for new talent, as well. So that particular night, when we were playing as Pogo, Epic/CBS came down to see us, and they liked us, and they started talking about a deal. We kept the name Pogo because they had come down. We couldn't change our name or they wouldn't know who we were. I don't think anyone was really crazy about the name, but we kept it.

"So we were playing some shows, and we got the chance to open for Canned Heat. We were onstage getting ready to play, during sound check, and we were served with papers. Walt Kelly, the comic's creator, sued us, so we had to stop using the name Pogo. We'd only been using the name three months at the most, but he'd got wind of it. We started going, 'Oh, my goodness, everyone knows us now as Pogo, what are we going to do?' And actually I suggested, from my high school Spanish, 'Why don't was just call ourselves Poco?' It doesn't mean anything, really." **Doesn't it mean "small"?** "Yeah, but it didn't mean anything to us. We thought, 'It doesn't have any bad meaning, any meaning other than small, and people will just think it's a typographical error.' So that's what we did. We called ourselves Poco, and everyone seemed to like it."

THE POGUES The Irish band came together in 1981 in London, where they performed punkified versions of traditional Irish folk songs. They began as Pogue Mahone, which is Gaelic for "kiss my arse."

POI DOG PONDERING   The band was formed in 1985 in Hawaii, where "poi dog" is slang for a mutt or mongrel. The name was chosen by the band because their music is a mix of different styles. Singer Frank Orrall says he added the pondering because he "liked the way it rolled or stumbled off the tongue."

POISON   The pop-metal band got its start in Harrisburg, Pennsylvania, in 1983. Bassist Bobby Dall takes credit for the name and explained, in a statement via their management, that "people were always saying that rock & roll poisons the youth of America, so rather than dispute it, we called ourselves that."

BUSTER POINDEXTER   In 1984, former New York Dolls frontman David Johansen took on the persona of an ultra-smooth lounge singer and changed his name to Buster Poindexter, derived from a nickname he earned growing up as an intellectual thug on Staten Island in New York City.

THE POLICE   The Police were named by drummer Stewart Copeland in 1977 as an ironic reference to his father, who served as chief of the CIA's Political Action Staff—the agency's dirty tricks department—in the fifties and later left to form his own "private CIA." Copeland's father boasted to *Rolling Stone* in January 1986 that his organization was the largest private security service operating in Africa and the Middle East, and that "nobody knows more about changing governments, by force or otherwise, than me."

PORTISHEAD   The group was formed in Bristol, England, in 1991 by Geoff Barrow and Beth Gibbons, and is named with irony after Barrow's hometown. "It's a place where the local newspaper headline is Vera's birthday or the flower show," he told *Rolling Stone*. "It looks pretty and twee, but it's actually quite horrible."

PREFAB SPROUT Prefab Sprout formed in Consett, England, in 1982, named by singer and guitarist Paddy McAloon, who claims he had wanted to use the name since he was a child. The name came from his mishearing the phrase *pepper sprout* in a Nancy Sinatra song.

PRETENDERS Singer and guitarist Chrissie Hynde, a native of Akron, Ohio, launched the Pretenders in London in 1978. In a statement taxed via her manager, she explains: "I was hanging out with this guy who was in a motorcycle club. One day while visiting their 'clubhouse,' he took me into his room and bolted the door shut. He wanted to play me his favorite record, but he didn't want any of the 'brothers' to hear it—probably because it wasn't off *Live at Altamont;* it was Sam Cooke singing 'The Great Pretender.' I looked at this white supremacist lowlife, with his hand on his heart and his eyes shut, swaying to that clear black voice, and I thought, 'I'll have some of that!' "

THE PRETTY THINGS After leaving an early version of the Rolling Stones in 1962, guitarist Dick Taylor named his new band after the song "Pretty Thing" by Bo Didley, whose music he sought to emulate.

PROCOL HARUM Procol Harum formed in London in 1967 and are most famous for the hit "A Whiter Shade of Pale." In an interview, lyricist Keith Reid, who was always listed as a full-fledged member of the group on their albums, recalls the genesis of their name: "It's the name of a cat, a Siamese cat. It's the pedigree name, and it belonged to a friend of ours, just somebody that we used to hang out with when we were forming the band. One day, somebody pulled out the cat's birth certificate and said, 'Have a look at this,' and the name of the cat was Procol Harum. And somebody else, in fact a chap called Guy Stevens who was quite instrumental in Gary [Brooker, the singer and pianist] and myself getting together in the first place, said, 'Oh, you must call the group Procol Harum.' And we just accepted that. We never even questioned it, never even thought if it was a good name, we just went ahead with that suggestion. Once we put the record out, people started to say, 'Oh, it's Latin, and it means *beyond these things.*' But in fact, we had spelled it incorrectly. It should have been *P-R-U-C-U-L,* I think, or *P-R-U-C-O-L H-A-R-U-N.* I believe that's right, anyway. If we'd spelled it correctly, it would have meant *beyond these things.* But somehow it seemed quite apt. That was it really. It was the suggestion of a friend and we just stuck with it." **Are you glad you chose it?** "No. I think it was silly—a silly name. And the trouble with it is that people have a great deal of difficulty understanding what it is. One of our favorites is Broken Arm. Broken Arm, Purple Horrors . . . It's very difficult for people to get the hang of." **What became of the cat?** "The cat would now be more than twenty-five years old, so I would guess that it's no longer of this world." **And who owned this cat?** "It belonged to our dealer. We used to score off of him."

THE PRODIGY   Band founder Liam Howlett came up with the name to describe himself in 1987 before meeting the other members of the group. At the time, he was spinning records at local raves in his hometown of Braintree in Essex, England. He says the name did not come from a Moog Prodigy synthesizer, as has been reported. "It was B-boy largeness," he told Chris Heath in *Rolling Stone.* "Like Grandmaster Flash had a grand name, larging himself up with his name. When I first thought up the name, obviously I didn't consider it would be four people. It was just me, faceless in my bedroom, writing music: 'the prodigy.' "

PRONG   Guitarist Tommy Victor, bassist Mike Kirkland, and drummer Ted Parsons formed Prong in New York City

in 1986. Victor says, "We wanted a name that didn't have dark or death or youth or big or black in it. I tried to think of an object that was industrial sounding. Being a three-piece, I thought of a three-prong plug."

THE PSYCHEDELIC FURS   The Furs formed in London in 1979. Singer Richard Butler discussed the band's name in a 1992 interview for this book: **Why "Psychedelic"?** "It was weird—we never thought of ourselves as a particularly psychedelic band. it's just that all the other bands around England at that time were all called the Sex Pistols and the Clash and names like that, and we wanted a name that sort of made it obvious that we were different from that. We weren't like a punk band, we were like the first of the bands that came after punk. I listened to a lot of sixties music, whether it was psychedelic or not, like Bob Dylan and the Velvet Underground, which I would really describe as psychedelic." **So it was just a deliberate gesture to distance yourselves from those other bands?** "Yeah, and I liked the sound of it." **Why "Furs" then?** "It simply sounded good. We thought of Psychedelic Shirts, Shoes, you name it—everything. Psychedelic Furs just rang nicely." **Before you came up with the name, did you consider any others?** "Yeah, we thought of calling ourselves RKO for a while, which was Howard Hughes's old picture company." **You were a big Howard Hughes fan?** "I liked the mystery of him." **Were there any others that you had in mind?** "Not really. It went from RKO straight into the Psychedelic Furs, really." **Did you come up with the name?** "Yeah, it was me. Me drunk. I think I was sitting in a pub, and I was with the rest of the band, and I was musing over all these different names and then came up with Psychedelic Furs."

PUBLIC IMAGE LTD. After the Sex Pistols broke up at the end of 1977, Johnny Rotten reverted to John Lydon and launched Public Image Ltd., named because he wanted it to be perceived as a company rather than a rock band. On early releases, financial adviser Dave Crowe was listed as a band member.

PULP In 1979, the teenaged Jarvis Cocker formed the band Arabicus Pulp in his hometown of Intake, a suburb of Sheffield, England. The name is a coffee bean commodity that he heard about in an economics class. The name was soon shortened to Pulp.

PUSSY GALORE Formed in the mid-eighties and fronted by Jon Spencer, the Washington D.C.–based noise-rock band took their name from Honor Blackman's character in the James Bond movie *Goldfinger*.

PYLON   Pylon formed in the late seventies and was part of the same music scene in Athens, Georgia, that spawned the B-52s and R.E.M. The band took their name from a novel by William Faulkner.

QUARTERFLASH   Led by the husband and wife team of Marv [guitar] and Rindy [vocals and saxophone] Ross, Quarterflash was formed in 1980 by the members of two Portland, Oregon, bands, Seafood Mama and Pilot. The name comes from an Australian expression, "a quarter flash and three parts foolish."

QUEEN   Queen formed in London in 1970, when singer Freddie Mercury joined guitarist Brian May and drummer Roger Taylor, who had played together in the band Smile. Mercury named the band, telling *Rolling Stone* in 1977: "I'd had the idea of calling a group Queen for a long time. It was a very strong name, very universal and very immediate; it had a lot of visual potential and was open to all sorts of interpretations. I was certainly aware of the gay connotations, but that was just one facet of it."

? (QUESTION MARK) AND THE MYSTERIANS   Little is known about the band, which had its one and only hit in

1966 with the million-selling "96 Tears," but that was the gimmick. The name the Mysterians was inspired by a low-budget Japanese sci-fi movie. The lead vocalist, who was never photographed without sunglasses, had his name legally changed to "?". What is known about the band is that the original members were born in Mexico and moved to Michigan, forming the band in Flint in 1966. After a string of flops, the band split in 1968, but recently reformed.

QUICKSILVER MESSENGER SERVICE An early version of the Quicksilver Messenger Service formed in San Francisco, California, in 1964, and by 1965 the lineup included singer Jim Murray, guitarist John Cipollina, guitarist Gary Duncan, drummer Greg Elmore, and bassist David Freiberg. Freiberg discusses the band's name in an interview: **How did you guys decide on the Quicksilver Messenger Service?** "Originally there were four Virgos in the band, and one Gemini. Of the four Virgos, there were only two birthdays: John and I were born on August 24, and Gary and Greg were born on September 4. We were looking for a name, and the ruling planet for Virgo in astrology is Mercury, and it is for Gemini also. So in searching for a name, we said, 'Well, let's see—mercury's the same as quicksilver, right? Mercury's the messenger god? Quicksilver Messenger Service.'" **Whose idea was that?** "Well, of course I think it was mine, and Jim Murray thought it was his, but we were talking together when we came up with it, so I assume it's probably both of ours. Although I'm sure that I was the one who thought of it. [Laughs.] As I'm sure he probably is, y'know? It seemed like too long and complicated a name, so we kept trying to call it something else, and every time we did, our equipment would blow up or something, so we just said okay." **When you first started, were there any other names that you used?** "I think we tried to use Vulcan once, from the missing planet Vulcan." **Looking back, are you pleased with that choice? Like you said, it was a long name.** "It seemed to stick. And everybody was using fairly complicated names anyway—Jefferson Airplane, Big Brother and the Holding Company. It seemed to fit the time. I don't think it'd work anymore, but one never knows." **Did everyone at the time know that it was an astrological reference?** "I think most people knew." **Were you all into astrology?** "Not particularly. I kind of just dabbled. I never did a chart or anything like that. Nobody else was really into it, other than signs and planets and that kind of stuff I took it with a grain of salt. It was interesting, though, and it made for a good name."

QUIET RIOT Heavy metal band Quiet Riot formed in Los Angeles in the early eighties. Singer Kevin DuBrow explains how the band got their name: "Originally it was Little Women, but we didn't even do one show under that name." **Was that from the book?** "It was really Jerry Sherwood, the drummer of Humble Pie, who had a band called Little Women, and we thought it would be funny to have a heavy rock band with such a light name. I was friends with Richard Parfitt, the guitar player of Status Quo, and we were hanging out one day, and I told him I was forming a band. He asked what it was called, and I said Little Women. He said that if he had a band, he'd call it Quite Right. I said, 'Why would you want to call a band Quite Right?' And he said, 'I'll say it with your accent—Quiet Riot.' And I go, 'Really? Wow.' And he said, 'Yeah, we were going to call one of the Status Quo records by that name, but we decided not to,' and he told me that we should use the name for our band. It's so hard to come up with a good name for a band, and the thing that we loved about the name—still do in fact—is that it's one of the few names, like Bad Company or Led Zeppelin, that actually says something about the music the band plays and the people that play it. Few of them are like that." **Were there any other names?** "No, once we got that, that was it. All the band members thought it was great. It was immediate. It sounded like the name of a big band."

RADIOHEAD   The band began in Oxford, England, as On A Friday, named for the day they rehearsed. Signed to Parlophone Records in 1991, they were given two weeks to come up with a new name. At the last minute they chose Radiohead after a track on Talking Heads 1986 album *True Stories,* which they were listening to at the time.

BRUCE HORNSBY AND THE RANGE   Hornsby formed the band in Los Angeles in 1984. In a VH1 interview, he explained how his group got their name: "Originally our band was just called the Range. . . . But the record company, after we finished the record, they wanted it to just be Bruce Hornsby, so we compromised on a rather unwieldy, lengthy name, Bruce Hornsby and the Range, which is no longer. The reason we thought of the Range . . . was that it sounded vaguely sort of folksy and rural, and my music was a bit in that vein then, with the accordions and mandolins and more acoustic instruments. But we used to joke it was 'cause we were into cooking and golf."

PAUL REVERE AND THE RAIDERS Paul Revere and the Raiders began in 1959 in Caldwell, Idaho. Singer and saxophone player Mark Lindsay explains how the band got their name in an interview: "We were a group playing around the Boise Valley area with no name. There was only one other group in that area, called Dick Cates and the Chessmen, and we were just 'the other group.' We played for a bit and then we began to realize, when we started drawing crowds, that we had to have some kind of nomenclature to identify ourselves. Paul Revere's name was Paul Revere Dick. He had a hamburger stand and I'd seen his full name on this health license. I said, 'Paul Revere Dick. Man, you oughtta call yourself Paul Revere!' And he said, 'No, no, I hate that.' His folks were of German stock, they were second-generation immigrants, and they thought, I suppose, it would be great to name their son after a great American hero. Even though Paul Revere never made the ride. Samuel Prescott, a doctor, actually made that ride, but it didn't rhyme: 'Listen my children and you will hear of the midnight ride of Samuel Prescott.' Anyway, he said, 'No, no, I hate that.'

"So I was over at a friend's house, a guy named Lenny who taught sax over at Caldwell High—I'd just bought a new tenor and was getting a couple of lessons on how to hold the horn—and he said, 'Listen to this, Lindsay!' and called me into his music room and had me listen to his headphones—Koss headphones were a big thing then, in the sixties. The headphones were sitting on a stack of Downbeat magazines because he was a big jazz aficionado. And I thought, 'Downbeat, Downbeat, that sounds like a great name for the group, the Downbeats' So we were the Downbeats for about six months or a year.

"So we cut our first tape, vying for a record contract, in Idaho. And Paul took it down to Los Angeles, La-La Land, to try to get us a deal. He went around everywhere and no one would even arrest us. But he went out to Gardena, where a guy named John Guss had a pressing plant and two labels, Apex Records and Gardena Records. And Gardena, I guess, was more or less of a tax write-off label. He said, 'Sure, I'll put you guys on there,' and we signed for a nickel a record. When Paul signed the contract, he signed his legal name, Paul Revere Dick. And the guy looked at it and said, 'Paul Revere, that's great! You gotta use this name. How 'bout calling yourselves Paul Revere and the Nightriders?'

"So Paul came back and said, 'He wants to call us Paul Revere and the Nightriders.' I thought about it for a couple of days and said, 'You know, that sounds like cowboys. What if we called ourselves Raiders? Paul Revere and the Raiders. It sounds more like pirates or something from that era.' He said, 'Yeah, that sounds good.' So we became Paul Revere and the Raiders, and that's where it's been ever since."

RAINBOW Guitarist Ritchie Blackmore formed Rainbow in 1975 after leaving Deep Purple. He named the band after the Rainbow Bar & Grill, a legendary rock-and-roll hangout on Sunset Strip in Los Angeles.

THE RAMONES   The Ramones formed in New York City in 1974. The original lineup, after some minor adjustments, included singer Joey Ramone [Jeffrey Hyman], guitarist Johnny Ramone [John Cummings], bassist Dee Dee Ramone [Douglas Colvin], and drummer Tommy Ramone [Thomas Erdelyi].

The surname Ramone was modeled after Paul Ramon, the alias Paul McCartney used for a two-week tour of Scotland in 1960, when his band was still calling itself The Silver Beatles. "It was exciting changing your name," McCartney says in *The Beatles: The Authorized Biography* by Hunter Davies: "It made it seem all real and professional. It sort of proved you did a real act if you had a stage name." McCartney can't remember why he chose the name Ramon. "I must have heard it somewhere. I thought it sounded really glamorous."

In an interview, Joey Ramone recalls how his band became the Ramones: **I've heard a story or two. Why don't you tell me how you came up with the name?** "Actually, there's a lot of stories—it's multiple stories here, y'know? But I guess I should just state it. When we met Dee Dee, he was callin' himself Dee Dee Ramone and he was a big fan of Paul McCartney. Paul used to check into hotel rooms under the alias of, like, Paul Ramon. So Dee Dee kind of adapted it from there. When we met Dee Dee, the name Ramone was like kind of a cool-sounding name—it had a nice ring to it, y'know? When we were thinking of a name—it's really hard to think of a name—we just liked the name Ramone because it was different. It was distinct and unique and the whole bit. So we kind of adapted it as our surname to create a sense of unity. Then everyone could have their unique personality within their own thing almost like the Beatles kind of did to some degree. Y'know, everybody is a distinct and unique multi-talented individual in this band, but the Ramone surname defines us as a unit, a team." **What were some of the other stories you've heard or told? I know that for a while some people thought your name was associated with Phil Ramone, the producer.** "A funny story I remember is at the Grammys one year, when he won for Producer of the Year and when he accepted his award, he said something like, 'This is for my little Ramones,' or something. And I guess a lot of his mail goes to us and our management and a lot of our mail goes to him. I met him once in the studio with Cyndi Lauper years ago, and it was very cool." **Were you a Beatles fan? Did you happen to know this thing about Paul Ramon? I mean, that's pretty obscure.** "Yeah, it is very obscure. I love the Beatles, they changed my life." **But you didn't happen to know this little bit of—** "I didn't know that about Paul. But Dee Dee was a real Paul McCartney fanatic." So he was already calling himself Ramone when you met him? "Yeah, yeah. I once told this writer a story about how I met the guys in an elevator and found out that we all had the same last name so we decided to form a band." **Did the writer buy it?** "Yeah! You have to tell it so that they buy it. One time I said I had an Uncle Pedro Ramone and we took it from him." **I guess after you're asked the same question a hundred times you just start amusing yourself.** "Yeah, you have to keep yourself amused or else it's boring. Gotta make it fun for yourself. A lot of people didn't know what to make of the Ramones at the beginning. They thought we were a mariachi band or they thought we were some kind of Spanish or Mexican group, y'know what I mean?"

RATT   Ratt formed in Los Angeles, California, in 1981. Guitarist Robbin Crosby told Irwin Stambler in *The Encyclopedia of Pop, Rock and Soul:* "The band initially called itself Mickey Rat after a character in a comic book. But the cartoon writer objected, so we just changed it to Ratt. We thought about changing it, too, but once we got a big following that didn't make sense. We couldn't see using a name with the words *formerly Ratt* in parentheses."

THE RAVENS   The Ravens, consider the first of the R&B vocal groups, formed in New York City in 1946, their name said to have been inspired by the fact that everyone was "ravin' " about their sound.

REDD KROSS   The band formed in Hawthorne, California, in the late seventies. Jeff McDonald explains how the band got its name: "Redd Kross was inspired by the famous masturbation scene in *The Exorcist.*" **Because she's masturbating with the cross and it becomes red with blood?** "Yeah." **Originally it was spelled with a C I believe?** "Yeah, originally it was spelled the very unoriginal way—not the heavy metal way." **In the early days, did you guys play off the symbolism of the red cross?**   "No, it was always just like a silly punk rock name. That was basically it." **Kind of like Black Flag?** "Yeah, we were in a room with those guys, desperately trying to think of a new name. We shared a rehearsal space, the church, with Black Flag and another local group called the Last. We were going to do a show with Black Flag, one of our very first shows in a real club, and we were just like, 'Our name'—we were called the Tourists at the time—'Our name is lame. It's terrible.' We'd found out there was another group called the Tourists, which was Annie Lennox and what's-his-face [Dave Stewart, later of the Eurythmics]. We couldn't think of a name, and that one just kind of popped into my head. I think it was kind of inspired by the Black Flag-ism that we were dealing with at the time." **You guys were from Hawthorne, right?** "Hawthorne, California, the home of Emmet Rhodes and the Beach Boys." **Did the name the Tourists have something to do with that?** "Yeah, if you were from two miles inland you couldn't hang out at the beach. I mean you could, but you'd be hassled by 'the locals.' We were like two miles inland. We could have walked to the beach if we weren't too lazy. We would go and try to ride our boogie boards or knee boards and everyone would just call us 'tourists' and try to run us over. I got run over one time and had to get like six stitches." **Why did you change the spelling? I heard you were sued by the Red cross.** "That was kind of interesting. We were playing an outdoor concert, in the city of Torrance, at a park with another group that was also stealing a name called the Salvation Army, and I guess because it was affiliated with the city it was in the local newspapers. So Steven was in his algebra class, he was a freshman at Hawthorne High, and someone came in from the office and said, 'There's a telephone call for Steven McDonald, and would you please come to the office.' So he went in, and they basically told him that there was nothing personal about it, but if we didn't change our name, they'd have to sue us. He just came home that day like, 'Wow, they want to sue us,' and we were like, 'Oh, my God.' And then they sent us this nice letter, saying that 'From the reviews that we have read, we hear that you're quite a good group. But we have the trademark to the name.' And they made suggestions. They said, 'Now, if the name was Yellow Cross or Green Cross, we'd have no objections.' It was like they were too cool about it, so we were like, 'No problem.' So we were thinking of changing the name, we were thinking in terms of Redd Foxx, all that kind of stuff." **So were they angry when you just decided to change it to a K?** "We never heard from them again, so I guess it's okay. Now don't misspell it, it's two *D*s and a *K*."

THE RED HOT CHILI PEPPERS According to *Rolling Stone*, singer Anthony Kiedis, bassist Michael "Flea" Balzary, and the group's late, original guitarist, Hillel Slovak, were students at Hollywood's Fairfax High when they formed their first group, Los Faces. After playing in a variety of other bands, they reunited several years later to form what would become the Red Hot Chili Peppers. Kiedis told a writer from *SPIN* in 1991: "I guess it was in 1983, the first gig we ever played, and we were called Tony Flow and the Miraculously Majestic Masters of Mayhem. Then after the show we said, 'That name sucks.' Next, it was about a week-long process of trying to find a name, and we went through about a thousand. Finally, Flea came up with Red Hot Chili Peppers, and that seemed appropriate. It was like the sounds and colors that we were emitting were very urban and very much a reflection of the lifestyle we were living—which was basically, you know, completely care-free. We were crazy kids on the street, and we wanted that sort of energy to come through. We didn't pattern ourselves after any other musical entity, we were more concerned with putting out the feelings we'd gotten from watching, like, you know, a beautiful porno film or the Marx Brothers or Woody Allen or Salvador Dali, or, you know, just the Hollywood Hills. We wanted it to be a reflection of our lives."

R.E.M. The band formed in Athens, Georgia, in 1980, choosing the name from a list of ideas written in chalk on the walls of the converted church where they lived and rehearsed. Among the names passed over were Twisted Kites and Cans of Piss. Although the term R.E.M. usually refers to "Rapid Eye Move-ment," the stage of the sleep cycle when dream-ing occurs, the band picked the name because they claimed it could ultimately stand for anything and was therefore appropriately ambiguous. A friend of theirs, a young lawyer named Bertis Downs IV, trademarked their name because, *Rolling Stone* reported, "two other R.E.M.'s, one REM, and one Rapid Eye Movement had already come and gone."

REO SPEEDWAGON REO Speedwagon formed in Cham-paign, Illinois, in 1968, adopting the name of a fire engine designed by Ransom Eli Olds, father of the Oldsmobile. In an interview with Irwin Stambler in *The Encyclopedia of Pop, Rock and Soul,* guitarist and chief lyricist Gary Richrath recalls: "Neil [Doughty, the keyboard player] thought it up while he was going to college there [in Champaign]. REO was the first fire truck built somewhere around 1918–1920 by Ransom E. Olds, who was like a renegade against GM and other big companies. So the symbolism seemed good and it also was a nice catchy name for a rock band. We also stuck with the name because when it was put on a marquee with other band names, those capital letters stood out.

THE REPLACEMENTS The Replacements formed in Minneapolis, Minnesota, in late 1979. Peter Jesperson, who managed and produced the group for the first six years, recalls: "They were originally called the Impediments, which was a dumb name so I'm glad they changed it. They were playing at a chemical-free coffee house in south Minneapolis and showed up intoxicated. They were thrown out by the manager before they had a chance to play—the manager or whoever the camp counselor was at this coffee house said, 'I'll make sure you never play this town again,' so the next day they changed their name to the Replacements. They were replacing themselves. The only other time I heard Paul [Westerberg, the vocalist and rhythm guitarist] specifically refer to it, someone said, 'Well, if you are the Replacements, who are you replacing?' and he said, 'Everyone.' But that was just a glib answer for some reporter. It was a good name because it had a slightly cheeky air to it and they were a slightly cheeky band. They weren't really a punk rock band, but they had a lot of punky attitude."

THE RESIDENTS   The mysterious Residents, who materialized in San Francisco, California, in 1974, have never identified themselves by name or appeared onstage or in photographs without some kind of mask. Hardy Fox, one of the band's managers, explains: "The first audition tape that the Residents ever sent to a record company was to Warner Brothers, and they didn't have a name, they didn't use a name, they didn't even believe in names; they still don't actually. So

```
IN LULULU
CURRENT RESIDENT
F 45TH ST APT 3
```

they sent it in, and when it was returned as a rejection, it was just addressed to 'The Residents' at that address, so they said, 'It must be us, and it has been ever since.'"

RIGHT SAID FRED   Brothers Fred and Richard Fairbrass formed the group in London in the early nineties and had a number-one hit in 1992 with "I'm Too Sexy." Their name was suggested by a friend who had heard the 1962 British hit "Right Said Fred" by Bernard Cribbins. "I think we went for it because we knew it was stupid," Richard told Fred Bronson in *The Billboard Book of Number One Hits*. "It had a good eccentric English sound to it."

THE RIGHTEOUS BROTHERS   Bill Medley and Bobby Hatfield began performing together in 1962. The name came from the reaction to their shows at black clubs in southern California, where they were told, "That's righteous, brother."

THE ROLLING STONES   Formed in London in 1962, the band was originally called Rollin' Stones, named by lead guitarist Brian Jones after a song by Muddy Waters, whose style of music he wanted to play. The following year they added a *G* to their name at the insistence of their new management and became the Rolling Stones. According to Keith Richards, they picked their name by "sheer accident." In a VH1 interview, he recalled: "We finally got a gig, all right? This is, like, 1962. We were rehearsing for like a month, and we'd done a few interval shows, and you know we were pretty good, and people were digging it. But finally we got our own night in a pub in London, you know? So we said, 'Great, call them up, let out the news. . . . How much money have we got? . . . Call up the local magazine, *What's On*, or whatever, and put an ad in. . . . You do it. . . . How much a word?' Brian's doing the business on that. And, like, 'Fine, okay, who's appearing?'— this is the chick on the other end, you know what I mean? I mean, suddenly here it is, we didn't have a name. And just lying on the floor was Muddy Waters, *The Best of Muddy Waters* album, face side down with the track list, you know, the first song is 'Rollin' Stone Blues.' So right off the top of his head, Brian went, well, 'What's the name? This phone call's costing money, man, you know? I mean, man, what's the name of the band?' And he looked and went 'Rollin' Stones.' Okay. Boom. That's the way it happened. I mean, there's no thought behind it. That's the way the Stones operate, man. It's always been—still the same. Things just fall together at the right time."

THE RONETTES Sisters Veronica and Estelle Bennett and cousin Nedra Talley began their career in 1961 in New York City when they recorded their first single as Ronnie and the Relatives while also performing as dancers at the Peppermint Lounge. In her 1990 autobiography, *Be My Baby*, Ronnie recalls: "After we started dancing at the Peppermint Lounge, we decided it was time to change our name again. With all the exposure we were getting, we knew it was just a matter of time before people in New York started talking about us. And when they did, we didn't want them talking about a group called Ronnie and the Relatives. It just didn't have that magic. My aunts and uncles were tossing names around one night when my mother pointed out that the Bobbettes and the Marvelettes had both had hits recently.

" 'There seemed to be a whole lot of 'ettes going around,' Mom said. 'Why don't we call them the Rondettes?'

"Everyone in the room suddenly sat up. 'Yeah,' said Nedra's mother, my aunt Susu, 'that's a good one. It's got a little piece of all three girls' names in it.' We dropped the *D* and shortened it to Ronettes soon after that—no one seems to remember why—and that was the name that stuck."

ROXY MUSIC   Bryan Ferry formed the band in London in 1971, originally calling it Roxy, after a local movie theater. "Music" was added to distinguish them from a U.S. band called Roxy.

RUFUS   The funk group, which featured Chaka Khan on lead vocals, got its start in Chicago in the early seventies. First called Smoke, they changed their name to Ask Rufus, the title of a column in the magazine *Popular Mechanics*, before shortening it to Rufus.

THE RUNAWAYS The Runaways formed in Los Angeles in 1975. Guitarist Joan Jett left the band in 1979 to form her own band, the Blackhearts. In an interview, she explains how both bands got their names: "With the Runaways, that was it. It was the Runaways. It was just one of those names. I said it and that became the name." **Were any of you guys actual runaways?** "Not in the true, really bad sense, no." **Can you remember the circumstances when you came up with the name?** "There really wasn't an anecdote, unfortunately. It wasn't one of those things where we sat down and brainstormed. I just thought 'the Runaways'—all girls—it sounded good. That was it." **When you ran it past the rest of the group, they were receptive?** "Yes." **Were you guys calling yourselves anything before that?** "No, no. Always the Runaways." **When you thought of it, can you remember what it meant to you?** "Rebellion—just kind of like the normal thing that a fifteen-year-old girl would be doing, leaving for Hollywood and playing in a rock and roll band. When we started, we were a three-piece, so I didn't have to run it by that many people." **Why did you choose the name the Blackhearts?** "Because—and this is a really dumb reason—you're on the road and you stop at gas stations and you have to go to the bathroom,

and you go in there and everybody writes on the walls. I just thought that the Blackhearts would make a really cool, easy logo to leave on a bathroom wall. You just get a Sharpie [marker] and draw a black heart and color it in, and it's a Blackheart. For some reason that was important at the time. But also, to be someone who's a black-hearted person means to be a loner. I think it's a nautical term or something, nautical slang. I think it might also be a reggae thing, too." **You're right—the "blackheart mon" is like the boogeyman for rural Jamaicans.** "I had heard about that. Y'know, it was very generic. It wasn't flashy. It was simple and to the point." **Was there a gas station on the road somewhere where you finally decided to go ahead and—** "I do remember writing it in many bathrooms in gas stations in the Northeast, because when we first started, we were based in New York, and we still are, and we did a lot of traveling in Connecticut, Massachusetts, Pennsylvania, and Maryland. So it's probably in countless bathrooms."

MITCH RYDER AND THE DETROIT WHEELS Born William Levise, Jr., in 1945, he formed Billy Lee and the Rivieras in Detroit in 1963. In 1965, after signing to producer Bob Crewe's New Voice label, he picked his new name out of a phone book and rechristened his band the Detroit Wheels to make them sound more up-to-date.

SAVAGE GARDEN   One in a long line of bands whose names are contradictions in terms, the Brisbane, Australia-based duo took theirs from novelist Anne Rice's description of the lush yet brutal world of a vampire. "It's talking about the duality," singer Darren Hayes told Phillip Zonkel in *Cover Story*. "A vampire is someone who is immortal [and] beautiful, yet the harsh reality is they kill to survive, just like a beast in the jungle." Part of the name's appeal, Hayes noted, was his identification with the lord of darkness: "It's not necessarily the obvious, tacky vampire themes. It's a lot about relationships and desires, and in a lot of ways I do feel like a vampire. I think a lot of performers do."

SCRITTI POLITTI   A punk band that turned pop, Scritti Politti formed in Leeds, England, in 1977 and took their name from an Italian phrase meaning "political texts."

THE SEARCHERS   The Searchers formed in Liverpool, England, in 1961, their name taken from the 1956 John Ford western starring John Wayne and Natalie Wood. A catch phrase from the film inspired the title of Buddy Holly's 1957 number one hit, "That'll Be the Day."

THE SEX PISTOLS Guitarist Steve Jones, bassist Glen Matlock, and drummer Paul Cook were calling themselves the Swankers when vocalist Johnny Rotten [born John Lydon] joined the band. It was manager Malcolm McLaren who suggested the name the Sex Pistols, which was partly inspired by his clothing shop, SEX. He wrote in an essay in *SPIN* in December 1988: "The name meant for me all sorts of things. It came about by the idea of a pistol, a pinup, a young thing, a better-looking assassin, a Sex Pistol."

DEL SHANNON Born Charles Weeden Westover in Coopersville, Michigan, in 1934, he changed his name after graduating high school, adopting the surname of a friend, Mark Shannon, and calling himself Del after his boss's car, a Cadillac Coupe de Ville.

THE SHIRELLES In 1961, the Shirelles became the first girl group to have a number-one single with "Will You Still Love Me Tomorrow." The four women met in junior high school in Passaic, New Jersey, in 1958 and formed a group called the Poquellos, Spanish for "little birds." They were signed to Tiara Records, a small label owned by Florence Greenberg, a classmate's mother. She asked them to come up with a new name and suggested the Honeytones, but they wanted something similar to their favorite group, the Chantels, and considered calling themselves the Chanels. Ultimately they chose the Shirelles, although there is some dispute over whether or not they named themselves specifically after member Shirley Owens, who was not the lead singer at that point.

SHOES The power-pop group, which formed in Zion, Illinois, in the mid-seventies, took their name from a wise-crack made by John Lennon, who, when asked about the name the Beatles, looked down at his feet and said, "Well, we could just as well named ourselves the Shoes."

TOMMY JAMES AND THE SHONDELLS Tommy James, born Thomas Gregory Jackson, formed the Shondells in 1960 in Niles, Michigan, when he was twelve years old. In 1962, they recorded "Hanky Panky," a song that would hit number one and sell a million copies four years later. Between 1966 and 1970, the group had over a dozen hits, including "I Think We're Alone Now," "Mony, Mony," and "Crimson and Clover." When asked today how he chose his group's name, James says: "I wish there was a more dramatic story to tell. The name Shondells was simply two syllables that sounded very musical to me as I was search-ing for a name to call my band, on an otherwise boring day in seventh-grade study hall in the spring of 1960."

SHONEN KNIFE Japan's Shonen Knife was formed in the early eighties by guitarist Naoko Yamano, bassist Michie Nakatani, and drummer Atsuko Yamano, and has devel-oped a cult following in the U.S. In an interview in *Seconds* magazine in 1991, Atsuko explained: "'*Shonen*' means 'boy': Boy Knife. The reason is a few years ago I went to English examination and there was a question paper like this [folds a sheet of paper in two]. I had to cut here [gestures to bottom of paper] and open the question paper. I brought a usual paper knife, but girl in front of me brought very old style jackknife. And there was a brand name on the jackknife. The jackknife looked like this [draws a picture of a jackknife with the word *Shonen* on the handle]."

SIMPLE MINDS   The band was formed in Glasgow, Scotland, in 1978 by former members of the punk group Johnny and the Self-Abusers, which included childhood friends Jim Kerr (vocals) and Charlie Burchill (guitar and keyboards). Kerr explained in a VH1 interview: "The origin of our name comes from a David Bowie song. Bowie had a song called 'Jean Genie' . . . and there was a line in it, which I can't remember the full line—but it was 'He's so simple minded he can't find . . . whatever.' And I'm pretty sure that the origin comes from that song."

SIMPLY RED   Vocalist Mick Hucknall formed Simply Red in Manchester, England, in 1984. According to a publicist at Elektra Records, the story goes like this: "Hucknall decided to try singing one night at the nightclub where he was working as a disc jockey. When the manager asked how he wanted to be billed, he replied, just "Red," ' a nickname given to him as a child because of his bright red hair. 'What was that?' the manager asked. 'Simply "Red," ' he replied, and the rest is history."

SIOUXSIE AND THE BANSHEES   Siouxsie and the Banshees formed in 1976 and played their first gigs as part of the One-hundred Club Punk Festival in London. At the time, the band included vocalist Siouxsie Sioux (born Susan Dallion), bassist Steven Severin, future Sex Pistol Sid Vicious on drums, and guitarist Marco Peroni, who would later become Adam Ant's song-writing partner in Adam and the Ants. Severin, who was then calling himself Steve Havoc, recalls: "Of course once we had insinuated our way onto the bill of the One-hundred Club Punk Festival, the most important thing was a brilliant name. With a mere week of preparation, how to sing, how to play, where to plug in, and other such trifles were secondary to the correct 'nom de noise.' Halfway through that week, ITV had shown the film *Cry of the Banshee* starring Vincent Price, and as is the way of these things, some kind of syncronicity occurred (cue light bulbs over Siouxsie and Severin's heads): 'The Banshees—what a great name.' 'No,' I said, 'how about Susy and the Banshees?' Hence began the great misspelling saga. Two days later, Siouxsie said, 'I hate cowboys,' and Souxie . . . Siouxie . . . no, Siouxsie and the Banshees were born.

"As a postscript, I would just like to say that there were no other names or suggestions. No skeletons in our closet like the Nosebleeds or the Bottom Burps or even Johnny and the Self Abusers [see entry for Simple Minds]. How vulgar!"

SIR DOUGLAS QUINTET San Antonio-born Doug Sahm formed the Sir Douglas Quintet in California in 1964, the name an attempt to pass the group off as a British Invasion band. Their hits included "She's About a Mover" in 1965 and "Mendocino" in 1969.

THE SISTERS OF MERCY Formed in Leeds in 1980, English goth rockers Sisters of Mercy took their name from a song by Canadian folksinger Leonard Cohen. Singer Andrew Eldritch observes: "Whenever you get in a taxi, the driver says, 'What's the name of your band then?' It is at that point that I think the name of my band is so embarrassing. The Sisters of Mercy is an actual order of nuns, but I took the name from a Leonard Cohen song which is about prostitutes. I thought that the juxtaposition between nuns and prostitutes was very appropriate for a rock band, still do. But it's very hard to explain that to a taxi driver."

SKINNY PUPPY   Skinny Puppy was formed in Vancouver, British Columbia, in 1983 by Ogre and cEVIN KEY. Their ugly vision of the world, they explain, is one seen through the eyes of a starving mongrel dog. Notes keyboardist Dwayne Goettel, who joined the band in 1986: "It all goes back to the image that cEVIN and Ogre created of Skinny Puppy being this little, scrawny, abused animal that

didn't say very much. Every once in a while the dog would have to scream out or somebody would step on its tail. When it did make a noise, it was something you could understand or feel, too."

THE SMALL FACES   The band was formed in London in 1965 by singer and guitarist Steve Marriott, keyboard player Jimmy Winston, bassist Ronnie Lane, and drummer Kenny Jones. They chose the name because they were indeed

"small"—they were all under five feet six inches; and they considered themselves "faces"—mod lingo for cool guys, as in "I'm the Face," which the Who recorded in 1964, when they were still called the High Numbers.

Marriott left in 1969 to form Humble Pie with Peter Frampton, and singer Rod Stewart and guitarist Ron Wood joined the band. No longer small, they relaunched as the Faces.

SMASHING PUMPKINS Smashing Pumpkins formed in Chicago in 1989. Singer and guitarist Billy Corgan explains in a recent interview: "The name of the band existed before there was a band. I was in somebody's kitchen and we were sitting around talking about something and somebody said something about smashing pumpkins and I thought, 'Oh, that's a pretty good mythical band name, ha, ha.' I thought of *smashing* more in term of glorious or something, not as the physical act. So I began telling people that I was forming a band called the Smashing Pumpkins, as a joke. When I actually formed a band, I said, 'Well, I've got this name but I think it's kind of stupid.' But everyone remembered the name, and that was it, it just stuck. And once you play one show with it, then you go: 'Well, gee, we shouldn't change it 'cause the people who went to the first show . . .' Didn't give it a lot of thought. It was just one of those things. It could have been the Amazing Tomatoes. It just struck some weird chord in me for some ungodly reason. Some dumb joke—that's it. My line on it now is that it's God's cruel joke on me. On the other hand, in some weird way it separates us from your typical band name. And it's ambiguous enough to not hold us down musically, like Metallica, or some metally kind of name. And conversely, in some strange way it kind of describes us."

SMASH MOUTH The band formed in San Jose, California, in the mid-nineties and had a major hit in 1997 with

"Walking on the Sun." The band's name comes from a phrase that football coach and sportscaster Mike Ditka used to describe a particularly rowdy game, "smash-mouth football."

THE SMITHEREENS   The Smithereens was formed in the late seventies in New Jersey by guitarist Pat DiNizio, lead guitarist Jim Babjak, bassist Mike Mesaros, and drummer Dennis Diken. Diken discusses the band's beginnings in an interview: **How did you guys come up with your name?** "In the late seventies, Jimmy, Mike, and I were playing in a band together, and we were calling ourselves What Else at the time. I was walking around with this spiral pocket notebook compiling names for bands. I probably had a couple hundred of them, actually. One that Jimmy came up with was Shag Rug and the Lost Contact Lenses—a lot of stupid shit really. *Smithereens* was just a word that we heard in cartoons when we were kids. Y'know, 'I'll blow you varmints to smithereens.' That was Yosemite Sam, from the Warner Brothers cartoons. I wrote it down in the book, and it really stood out from all the other ones. It sounded like it should be a name for a band. It sounded like it might have been a name for an obscure band in the sixties perhaps, but I never saw anybody else using it. When Pat saw the name, he thought it was worth using. It was pretty simple—it was just a word that we heard from pop culture growing up, in cartoons and in movies and TV." **So are you pleased that you chose it?** "Yeah, absolutely. It's easy to remember, it's unusual. It's actually a real word, y'know, of Gaelic or Irish origin, and it means 'fragments or little pieces.' " **Is the name *the* Smithereens, or just**

Smithereens? "*The* Smithereens." **So you stuck that on there.** "Yeah, 'cause that's what bands usually do—y'know, the Dave Clark Five." **That's interesting, because sometimes you'll see a band like Talking Heads, who I guess are officially "Talking Heads," not "the Talking Heads," and you won't know what's the proper way to say it. And if you look on some bands' albums, you'll see *the* on one and then on the next you won't, like the Pretenders.** People have omitted the *the* a good number of times, on radio or TV and in print, but we do call ourselves the Smithereens. Shortly after we started playing around New York, this movie called *Smithereens* came out, and people to this day ask us, 'Do you have anything to do with that movie?' Actually, we feel that they stole the name from us because we were playing around New York a lot, and that was a New York film." **Yeah, it was set in the New York club scene.** "Right, and the logo that they used was a good cop of the style of the logo we were using." **Did you ever consider any sort of action?** "Not really. We were thinking about doing stuff, making a stink about it back then, going to the movie's marquee where it was playing and writing something up there, but we never did. It would've made some publicity for us, but . . ." **So you've never met Susan Seidelman [the film's director]?** "No, I haven't. I don't know if anybody else in the band has." **I'd forgotten, but now that you mention it, I do remember making the association between the band and the movie and wondering if there was any connection.** "There really wasn't any, except we think they took it from us."

THE SMITHS Singer Morrissey, guitarist Johnny Marr, bassist Andy Rourke, and drummer Mike Joyce formed the

Smiths in Manchester, England, in 1982. They chose the name because of its implied anonymity.

THE SNEAKER PIMPS   The British trio says that they took their name from a comment made in an interview by Mike D. of the Beastie Boys that his band employed a designated "sneaker pimp," someone in charge of finding them footwear. Mike D., however, says he cannot recall making the comment.

THE SOFT BOYS   Singer and guitarist Robyn Hitchcock formed the Soft Boys in Cambridge, England, in 1976 and later formed his own group, the Egyptians. In an interview, he describes the genesis of both names: "The Soft Boys comes from a song called 'Give It to the Soft Boys,' which I wrote in the autumn of 1976. The concept of the Soft Boys were these bloodless, maybe even boneless things that nevertheless had enormous power because they sort of seeped along in the shadows, and you could never see them. They had a lot of influence, but they were invisible—almost invisible—and they had a sexual orientation that was out of this world, but they weren't easily seen. Descendants of something from William Burroughs, really." **Anything to do with The Soft Machine?** "Well, there's *The Soft Machine* and *The Wild Boys,* two of his book titles. So it was essentially a merging of those two titles, although I haven't read *The Wild Boys*. It wasn't exactly along the same sexual lines as Burroughs, but it was the same concept. I imagined the Soft Boys being powerful, spineless, invisible, basically rather sick . . ." **I'm reminded of Balloon Man [from the song on the *Globe* of *Frogs* album].** "No, Balloon Man is very different. Balloon Man is this sort of huge, corpulent, Falstaffian thing that feeds on itself and explodes. Balloon Man is very jolly, he bubbles around the place. The Soft Boys weren't overweight, the Soft Boys—just take out the bones, just try filleting somebody, like. These were filleted corporal human individuals—quasi-human. It kind of summed up the band in the end because we were invisible, but we had a certain amount of influence. It became true. Also, the trouble is that I didn't mean the band to be called that. I had the name of the song lying around. We were

originally called Dennis and the Experts. I was Dennis and the others were the Experts, 'cause they all knew how to play, and I was just, y'know, Dennis. I was the personality. It was a popular name in Monty Python and things. There were always people being called Dennis, a sort of rather weedy, middle-class British kid. Anyway, we became the Soft Boys. We were a bunch of weedy, middle-class British kids, really." **At one point someone said, "Let's change the name"?** "What it was, we were doing a gig as Dennis and the Experts and I sort of announced onstage that we were now called the Soft Boys. I don't know why. It was a more dramatic name. The trouble was, it made us sound—it could be interpreted that we were a bunch of wimps—which we were, too." **The band just accepted it from then on?** "Well, we were a bunch wimps, you know. No one was going to complain about anything. It's better to have a name than be called Robin, Andy, Morris, and Alan, or whatever it was we were called." **Tell me about the Egyptians.** "The Soft Boys faded out. I suppose I turned thirty, and I thought, 'My God, you don't want to be called anything like the Soft Boys.' The Soft Boys were long gone by the time I was thirty, but it wasn't the kind of name that you'd want to be called in later years. I'm really glad that we've never had to reform as the Soft Boys, 'cause, y'know, it's like the Beach Boys— you don't want to be called 'the Boys' when you're thirty-five or something. So that was over and I dropped out of the business altogether for a couple of years, then I made a couple of records and I got back together with Andy and Morris again, and we also had a sax player and a keyboard player. We were going to do a gig, a benefit for a place called the Hope and Anchor in London, a place where the Soft Boys used to play. Loads of people played the Hope and Anchor, you must have heard of it. They were in trouble, and we did a benefit for them at the club. They'd run out of money, and they even ran out of electricity halfway through the set. They'd had their electricity cut, and  their generator ran out of fuel, so Morris played a ten-minute drum solo. We needed a name for the band, and I didn't want to be called the Soft Boys anymore, and it was going to be Robyn Hitchcock and the Somethings, so I called it Robyn Hitchcock and the Egyptians. But we didn't know we were going to carry on doing gigs. It was a one-off sort of reunion." **Where did "the Egyptians" come from?** "Well, I was very keen on Egyptian graphics. I don't know an enormous amount about mythology. I mean I don't know about Thoth, Isis, and Anubis, but I was just keen on the way they looked, really. So we used Anubis for my first, the record called *I Often Dream of Trains*. That had Anubis, who's the god of death. He's the jackal-headed god who admits people to the underworld. Then I had Thoth, who's an all-around good guy, and he's also the god of libraries. When you die, Thoth and Anubis weigh your heart against the feather of truth. Anubis weighs it and Thoth takes the notes. If the feather of truth is heavier that your heart, then you've had it, and if your heart's heavier than the feather of truth, then you're going to move on to the next plane, I think. That's all it was really. It was all a little to do with that. I just wanted a name quickly." **I'd heard a story that you wanted to call yourselves the Psychedelic Jews, but you couldn't do that, so . . .** "That was another possibility. The Soft Boys, two of the guys were half-Jewish, so we could have sort of called ourselves the Psychedelic Jews, but it's the sort of thing that offends Jews and *goyim* alike. You're just going to piss everyone off. That's part of the appeal, really. Like calling an album *Queers for Jesus,* y'know? It's very tempting, if you want to deal with that torrent of misunderstanding that follows. I've always liked the Psychedelic Jews." **I've read somewhere that your name isn't really Robyn Hitchcock. Is that true or not?** "No, I am actually Robyn Hitchcock. For some reason my parents couldn't give us normal names. My sisters are called Lalage, she's an artist, and my younger sister, Fleur, she's a writer."

SOFT MACHINE Formed in Canterbury, England, in 1966, the progressive rock band took their name from the novel *The Soft Machine* by William Burroughs.

SONIC YOUTH   Sonic Youth formed in New York City in the early eighties. In an interview, guitarist Thurston Moore explains: "Sonic came from Fred 'Sonic' Smith, guitar player for the MC5, and Youth came from Big Youth, the reggae toaster, from the mid to late seventies. It's a name that came out of the seventies when I was a teenager, and those were two things that I was really into: Sonic Smith— the high-energy Detroit thing—and then I was really into the reggae thing. I just sort of wanted to use both those worlds. Actually, when we first started, that was one of our concepts, to use big dub rhythms with like sonic guitar. . . . Our first record comes out of that kind of concept. But then it became a total slamfest after that."

SOUL ASYLUM   Originally called Loud Fast Rules, the band formed in Minneapolis, Minnesota, in 1981. In a VH1 interview, singer and guitarist Dave Pirner explained how they came up with the name Soul Asylum: "I had a dream and I woke up and wrote it down. And we talked about it for a long time and couldn't come up with anything better basically."

SOUNDGARDEN   The band, formed in Seattle, Washington in the late-eighties, is named after a sculpture on the beach by Seattle's Lake Washington. "It looks a lot like a *Star Trek* set," singer Chris Cornell told *Rolling Stone* in March 1989. "It's kind of like Stonehenge in outer space. It hums in the wind."

SPANDAU BALLET   The band formed in London in 1979, after an earlier incarnation as the Makers. A spokesperson at the band's management company relates this story:

"Spandau were just about to go onstage, and they still didn't have a name. Then a journalist friend of theirs, who'd just been to Berlin—his name was Robert Elms—apparently, on a toilet wall in Berlin he'd seen the name Spandau Ballet written, so he suggested it and they all said, 'Yeah.' "

THE SPANIELS The group, led by James "Pookie" Hudson, came together in Gary, Indiana, in 1952 and had a string of R&B hits, including "Baby, It's You" and "Good-nite Sweetheart, Goodnite." They first considered calling themselves the Hudsonettes, until somebody pointed out that "ettes" suggested women. They briefly called themselves Pookie Hudson and the Hudsonaires, until Faye Gregory, wife of bass vocalist Gerald Gregory, joked that they sounded like "a bunch of dogs" while rehearsing at their house. That prompted her husband to come up with several dog names, including the Cocker Spaniels. When everyone agreed that "cocker" might leave them open to ridicule, Mrs. Gregory suggested they simply call themselves the Spaniels, because she liked the way it sounded.

SPARKS Formed by brothers Ron and Russ Mael, the band formed in California in the early seventies but moved to England. Russ Mael recalls: "Originally, we were called Half Nelson when we signed with Bearsville Records to record our first album. The album didn't sell very well, and everyone looked around for the problem, and they said, 'Well, obviously the name is too obscure, that's your problem. If you would just change the name, then we could rerelease the album and it will sell tens of millions of copies.' Albert Grossman, who was one of the owners of

Bearsville, thought that Ron and I were just hilarious people, and he said, 'You're not the Marx Brothers—you should be the Sparks Brothers.' We thought that was really horrible, and kind of asinine. So we said, 'Well, we'll compromise and we'll keep the Sparks part of it, but absolutely not the Brothers part.' So that was the birth of Sparks."

THE SPECIALS   Leaders of the British two-tone movement of the late seventies and early eighties, the Specials formed in Coventry, England, in 1977. They took their name from the "special" one-shot records made for the early Jamaican sound systems.

SPIRIT   Spirit formed in Los Angeles in 1966 and were originally called Spirits Rebellious, the name taken from a book by poet Kahlil Gibran.

SQUEEZE   Squeeze was formed in London in 1974, with an initial lineup of singer and guitarist Chris Difford, singer and lead guitarist Glenn Tilbrook, keyboard player Jools Holland, and drummer Paul Gunn. For a while the band was forced to call itself Squeeze UK because there was an American band called Tight Squeeze; when that band split, they reverted to Squeeze. In an interview, the band's manager, John Lay, explains how they chose the name: "Chris Difford originally was in a band called Porky's Falling Spikes. Then they had the idea of calling the band Cum— this, you've got to bear in mind, was when they were sixteen. And then nobody could think of a proper name, so all of them got in a room and wrote their name choice on a piece of paper and put it in a hat, and Squeeze came out. It was a secret ballot, and to this day, not one of them has admitted which one of them it was." **What was the significance of squeeze? Was there any?** "No, there wasn't really, it was just names, they were just looking for names. You know, my theory about names is that the Beatles is a pretty crap name but you associate it with success and it looks like a great name. Same with Duran Duran—what a stupid name, but when they became successful . . ." **I heard that Squeeze took its name from the Velvet Underground album Squeeze.** "There's some truth to that. My suspicion is that Chris Difford was the Squeeze donator—at that time he was massively influenced by the Velvet Underground." **What's strange about that is that by the time that album was released, none of the original Velvets were in the band. So it's kind of a strange album to take their name from.** "Well, it wasn't really taken from it. They were really just looking for a name, they couldn't agree, so the names were just put in a hat."

STEAM Paul Leka, Gary De Carlo, and Dale Frashuer played in a group from Bridgeport, Connecticut, called the Chateaus before recording "Na Na Hey Hey Kiss Him Goodbye" in 1969. That song was meant to be a throwaway B-side for a single to be released under De Carlo's stage name, Garrett Scott, but, to his surprise the record label loved the song and decided to put it out as a single. De Carlo agreed under the condition that it be released under an assumed name, and Leka suggested Steam, recalling the sight that greeted the trio when they emerged from the studio on the night they recorded the song. "When we came out of the studio at five in the morning," he recalled in *The Billboard Book of Number One Hits,* "it looked like there was a big fire. There was a manhole, and someone said, 'Wow, look at that steam!' I put that in the back of my head for a group name." "Na Na Hey Hey Kiss Him Good-bye" by Steam shot to the top of the charts while four singles by "Garrett Scott" bombed. A disgruntled De Carlo refused to record any more songs for a Steam album, so Leka recruited another group from Bridgeport and dubbed them Steam.

STEELY DAN   Singer and keyboard player Donald Fagen and bassist Walter Becker, who met as students at Bard College in 1967, formed Steely Dan in Los Angeles in 1972. They took the name from a milk-spurting dildo in the William Burroughs novel *Naked Lunch*.

STEPPENWOLF   Led by singer and guitarist John Kay, who was born Joachim F. Krauledat in Tilsit, Germany, the band began as Sparrow in Toronto, Canada. After they relocated to Los Angeles in 1967 and were signed to Dunhill Records, at the suggestion of producer Gabriel Mekler they changed their name to Steppenwolf after Herman Hesse's classic novel.

STIFF LITTLE FINGERS   Taken from a song by the Vibrators that referred to the sixties sci-fi TV series *The Invaders*, in which sinister space aliens were identical to humans with one exception: they had unbendable pinky fingers.

STONE THE CROWS   The soul band formed in Glasgow in 1969 and took thir name from a Scottish curse meaning "to hell with it."

THE STONE ROSES   The band began as the Patrol in Manchester, England, in 1980, changing their name to English Rose, after a song by the Jam, in 1983. In 1985, the band combined their name with that of their idols, the Rolling Stones, to become the Stone Roses.

STONE TEMPLE PILOTS   After meeting at a Black Flag concert in San Diego in the late eighties, singer Scott Weiland and bassist Robert DeLeo formed the band Mighty Joe Young, named after the 1949 movie about a giant gorilla, with Robert's brother Dean on guitar and Eric Kretz on drums. One day, inspired by the logo on a can of automotive oil at Weiland's apartment, the band decided to change their name to three words beginning with the initials STP. Shirley Temple's Pussy eventually lost out to Stone Temple Pilots.

THE STOOGES   The Stooges were formed in Ann Arbor, Michigan, in 1967, by Iggy Pop, who was born James Osterberg. He took the name Iggy from his first band, the Iguanas, and Pop from local junkie Jim Popp. Iggy explains

how the Stooges got their name: "We were hanging around, stoned on acid, and had just been watching the Three Stooges on TV. The band didn't have a name, and [guitarist] Ron Asheton, who was a major fan of the Stooges, said, 'How 'bout the Stooges? They can be the Three Stooges and we'll be the Psychedelic Stooges!' "

THE STRANGELOVES   The Strangeloves, whose biggest hit was "I Want Candy" (1965) were originally the studio-based writer-producer team of Bob Feldman, Richard Gottehrer, and Jerry Goldstein. After writing and producing pop songs for a variety of acts, including the Angels' "My Boyfriend's Back," the sudden popularity of the British Invasion almost put them out of business. In response, they decided to release a single under the name of a fictitious British act. Feldman recalls in the liner notes from their greatest hits collection, "Marty Kupersmith, one of Jay's original Americans, stopped by our office while we were deciding what to do with this record. He was wearing these silly dark glasses and giving right-arm salutes, emulating Peter Sellers' character in *Dr. Strangelove, Or: How I Learned to Stop Worrying and Love the Bomb* [1964]. I took his glasses, started talking in my best British accent, and *voila!* The Strangeloves were born." When Feldman's English accent proved shakey, they shifted the band's origins to Australia—mythical Armstrong, Australia, to be exact—and became Miles, Niles, and Giles Strange, wealthy sheepherders who lived to rock.

THE STRANGLERS   The band formed in Guildford, England, in 1974 as the Guildford Stranglers. According to *No Mercy: The Authorized and Uncensored Biography of The Stranglers,* by David Buckley: "The band talked up the idea of the group as a bunch of sexual predators. The band name itself, although coined initially in a half-jokey manner as an attempt to épater les bourgeois, has obvious connotations with violent crime: strangulation is a murder technique used exclusively on women by men. . . ." Pop historian Dave Laing, in his book *One Chord Wonders: Power and Meaning in Punk Rock,* writes: "In an inversion of the other earlier practice of group naming which signifid success or status, the Damned and the Stranglers highlighted the socially undesirable, sinners, and lawbreakers respectively. To say 'Damned' rather than 'Condemned' was to invoke an extra layer of the supernatural. . . . As planned, the name stirred up controversy, especially when the band played in Los Angeles for the first time in 1977. Notes Buckley: "The L.A. gig coincided with the first press reports of the gruesome Hillside strangler. There were curfews in the L.A. region, and massive police presence. Everyone thought the Stranglers were opportunists and had acquired their name expediently as a sick joke. According to Hugh [Cornwell, singer and guitarist], this did the band great harm."

THE STRAWBERRY ALARM CLOCK The band formed in Santa Barbara, California, in 1967, and had a big hit with the flower-power anthem "Incense and Peppermints." Bassist George Bunnel discusses their name in an interview: "Michael Ochs, the rock historian, has this story of how we came up with our name that's really not how it happened. The Michael Ochs story was that we took out a *Billboard* magazine and went through the top one hundred songs at the time, and hit 'Strawberry Fields Forever' and decided to call the band Strawberry Alarm Clock. He said that we wanted to call the band Something Alarm Clock, and that that was how we got the Strawberry." **What's the real**

story? "Well, 'Strawberry Fields' wasn't out yet, so that puts a fork in that one. Actually we were *told* to put Strawberry in our name. The band had a stupid name—it was called Three Sixpence, to be English. We wore English Beatle boots and we wore the preacher jackets with no collar. And then the record company said, 'This'll never work, this is all old, it's already all been done, you're doing stuff that you've seen.' And we thought, 'Yeah, we are.' The music was really unusual. The music wasn't anything like we looked, though we were trying to sing with English accents. That was what we were trying to do when we did 'Incense and Peppermints,' oddly enough, and it came out psychedelic. They wanted us to put strawberries in the name. Russ Regan at MCA specifically said that strawberries were like a sign of the time—they were like the 'peace and love fruit,' the 'fruit of love,' sort of like an aphrodisiac." **Was that the going wisdom?** "No, actually it was to kind of try to create a new one. The predecessor was bananas, with Donovan." **Right, smoking banana peels . . .** 'Yeah, electrical banana. So that whole thing created the fruit thing. They said, 'Put *strawberry* in the name,' and we thought, 'Oh, God, should we even do this?' We decided to do it, and we sat around trying to think of names. Mark Weitz, the keyboard player, his parents built like a guest house for him to live in, and the band rehearsed in it. It was a great little setup. And we were in there, and he had an alarm clock that sat on this table. We were sitting around on the bed trying to think of different names that had strawberry in them, like Strawberry Toilet and stuff like that, and this alarm clock went off and fell on the floor and broke. We laughed and thought, 'Strawberry Alarm Clock.' And it sounded so goofy. So we called Russ Regan and we told him, and he said, 'That's fucking great!' That was that. We thought, 'Oh, my God, we've created a monster!' We couldn't even say the name. When somebody asked us, 'What's the name of your band?' we were like, 'Uhhh . . .' We ended up having a real hard time saying it.

It became a crippling psychological problem for each one of us. We couldn't even say the word *strawberry*—it would kind of slur. We were really kind of insecure about it, even though we came up with half of it. We thought it was a joke." **At some point did you become comfortable with it?** "Never."

THE STRAWBS The band got their start in Leicester, England, in 1967 as the Strawberry Hill Boys, named for the district where they rehearsed.

THE STRAY CATS Rockabilly revivalists the Stray Cats formed in Massapequa, Long Island, in 1979 with Brian Setzer on vocals and guitar, Lee Rocker [Leon Drucher] on bass, and Slim Jim Phantom [Jim McDonnell] on drums. Recalls Phantom in an interview: "When we started in New York about 1979 I think it was, in Manhattan they wouldn't hire you every week. Like, if you played at Max's one week, they wouldn't hire you at CBGBs the next week. So we would change the name of the group all the time to get gigs, and the kids who liked us knew what it was. We were the Tom Cats, and we were the Bob Cats, and the Dead Cats. We changed the name monthly almost. 'Cats' was pretty much the key to it so that the kids who liked us could kind of read between the lines.

"When we moved to England about six or seven months after that, we had nowhere to live, nowhere to go, no food—we were buying a hamburger at McDonald's and

 splitting it three ways and sharing the last french fry. Lee kind of came up with it. He said we felt like stray cats. The name had always fit because cat

was kind of a groovy term in the fifties—you know, Elvis was the 'Hillbilly Cat.' So it was a term of a kind of a hipster. We found ourselves with no money, nowhere to live, nowhere to sleep, nowhere to do anything. So Lee came up with the name Stray Cats and it just kind of stuck. It suited the feeling at the time, as well as what we needed in a name. It's as simple as that."

STRYPER   The Christian heavy metal band formed in Orange County, California, in 1983 as Roxx Regime, then changed their name to Stryper after a passage in Isaiah, "With His stripes we are healed."

STYX   The band formed in Chicago in 1963. Keyboard player Dennis DeYoung discusses the band's name in an interview: **Why did you choose the name Styx? With its reference to the river in hell, it almost seems like a name that a death metal band might choose.** "It was the name no one in the band hated. At the time, we were actually called TW4. There were five of us in the band, so that shows you how stupid we were. It's kind of a quick story. We had been a four-piece for a long time, and we added a fifth member. We had kind of a clientele locally in Chicago, we'd developed a reputation, so we didn't want to change the name. But when we got the deal with Wooden Nickel Records, we had to come up with a new name. Every time we had a list of fifty names that one of the band members would submit, someone, as is always the case, would say, 'I hate that name.' As for the name Styx, I was a schoolteacher at the time. I was teaching music appreciation, how music and art relate to the social upheaval of the times from the Renaissance to the twentieth century, which sounds relatively boring, and it was. Anyway, Dante's *Inferno* was one of the things in the class, and that was one of the names that was mentioned—the river Styx.

"The thing about the death metal, we were never that kind of a band, although in the early days we certainly were a bit more on the art rock, superpretentious side, because there seemed to be a following for that. There was a kind of heavier rock element to the music in the beginning, but really, the river Styx is not necessarily just the river that runs through hell. I guess as the story goes, according to Greek mythology, when you die you get on a boat, and there's this guy and a dog on the boat, Charon, and it circles the underworld seven times, but then it comes out into Elysian fields, which is like heaven. So it's that river that circles the underworld. I guess when you get on the boat, the worse you are the lower it goes into the underworld, something like that. I guess if you're really bad you come out in New Jersey. But anyway, there was this feeling in the band that there was the hard rock element and then there was a softer element in our music, and there was an idea that the river Styx was kind of the bridge between those two places. People over the years have thought Styx was just another way to spell *sticks*. You'd be surprised how few people actually know what the name refers to, so it never really played for one second into our development as a musical act. It was just 'that name.' "

What did TW4 stand for? "Well, this is pretty wacky. We were originally called the Trade Winds. Can you imagine that? We were three kids who lived on the same street, and we picked the name Trade Winds so we could paint a palm tree on the drum. And unbelievable as it may seem, a band in New York a couple years after we chose this name had a hit record called 'New York Is a Lonely Place,' and the name of that band was Trade Winds. After that, we changed our name to TW4 because there were four guys in the band." **Can you remember any of the other names between TW4 and Styx?** "Yes, I can, and you'll see why Styx was such a good choice. Believe it or not, one guy wanted to name it Kelp. It would've been a really seventies kind of thing. It was down to two, and the other name was Torch. It's funny to think about names. When I first heard the names the Beatles, I said—I was a real Beatle hater when they first came out—I thought it was the worst name I'd ever heard in my life. All I could think of was a bug. I didn't get the idea of it being 'the beat.' "

SUPERTRAMP   Singer and keyboard player Richard Davies formed the band in London in 1969 with the backing of Dutch millionaire Stanley August Miesgaes, who spotted him playing in a band called the Joint. After rejecting "Daddy," the band followed the suggestions of original sax player Dave Withrop and took the name Supertramp from W. H. Davies's book *The Autobiography of a Supertramp.*

THE SUPREMES   Diana Ross, Mary Wilson, and Florence Ballard began as the Primettes in Detroit in 1959, formed by manager Milton Jenkins to support his male group the Primes, who would later become the Temptations. In 1960, the women were signed to Motown Records by label president Berry Gordy, Jr., who insisted they change their name despite their desire to remain the Primettes. Ballard picked the Supremes from a list supplied by Janie Bradford, a Motown employee. At first, the women hated it, complaining that it sounded like a male group. In fact, the name was first used in 1957 by a male quartet from Columbus, Ohio, who recorded a single for Ace Records and named themselves after a bottle of Bourbon Supreme.

SWEET   Sweet, whose hits included "Ballroom Blitz," "Fox on the Run," and "Love Is Like Oxygen," formed in London in 1968. Explains guitarist Andy Scott: "The name Sweet was totally *right* for the band because we certainly are not sweet in reality. So we all agreed it was appropriate."

TALKING HEADS   Bassist Tina Weymouth met guitarist David Byrne and drummer (and future husband) Chris Frantz at the Rhode Island School of Design in 1970. After graduating in 1974, they moved to Manhattan together.

Weymouth recalls: "We had a long list of possible band names taped to our wall at the loft on Chrystie Street where the three of us lived. Anybody who wanted to could add a name. Sometimes Chris would try one out by putting it on his kick drum. One of those names was the Vogue Dots. We were looking for a name that wouldn't specifically connote any kind of music. One day a friend from Rhode Island School of Design, Wayne Zieve, was looking through *TV Guide* and came across 'talking heads.' The *Guide* said it was TV-camera jargon for a head-and-shoulders shot, such as would be used to shoot a news commentator. It further said a talking heads shot was to be distinguished from its opposite cousin, action footage, by the fact that it was 'all content, no action.' Wayne added it to the list and everyone liked it . . ."

"Carnivals and circuses used to often have a 'talking head' as well. When I was a little girl, I used to make my siblings and neighborhood kids put on circuses in imitation of *The Little Rascals*. One little kid would crouch inside a cardboard box and stick her stockinged head out of a hole in the top. Members of our audience would be encouraged to ask 'the talking head' questions of prophecy. When they did, she would make hilarious predictions about that person's relationships with everyone else in the neighborhood."

THE TEARDROP EXPLODES   The Teardrop Explodes formed in Liverpool, England, in 1978, evolving from the band A Shallow Madness and taking its name from a caption in a Marvel comic book.

TEARS FOR FEARS   Curt Smith and Roland Orzabal met at school in Bath, England, in 1974 when they were both thirteen and later played together in a band called Graduate. In 1981, the duo named themselves Tears for Fears, inspired by the book *Prisoners of Pain* by Arthur Janov, who pioneered "primal scream" therapy. Janov's theories, which endorsed the confrontation of hidden fears and the release of suppressed emotions, had a profound effect on the pair, who both had unhappy childhoods. In *Rolling Stone* in June 1985, Orzabal recalled his reaction after reading the book: "I rushed out to everybody I knew and started blubbering to them about it. Everybody thought I was a nutter. The only person who could see any sense in it was Curt." Their 1983  debut album, *The Hurting,* further reflected their debt to Janov and included such songs as "Suffer the Children," "Watch Me Bleed," "Mad World," and "Start of the Breakdown."

TELEVISION   Television formed in New York City in 1973, after guitarist Richard Lloyd teamed up with vocalist and lead guitarist Tom Verlaine (born Thomas Miller), bassist Richard Hell (Richard Myers), and drummer Billy Ficca. In an interview, Hell, who left Television in 1975, discusses the band's origins: **You were part of Television in its early stages. Do you know how that name came about?** "Yeah, I contributed it. There'd been a previous incarna-

tion of the band called the Neon Boys that existed for a few months as we searched for a second guitar player. There were only three of us and we wanted a second guitar player and were never able to find anyone. When we finally found the guy who seemed like he would work, we decided to come up with a new name for ourselves, and we had a band meeting and everyone was supposed to bring suggestions. I had a list of a bunch of possibilities, and Television was among them, and I really liked the name. It had only been in the previous few months that my collaborator, my partner in crime, Verlaine, had changed his name to Verlaine, from Miller. When I recited my list of suggestions, Tom immediately jumped on Television. Pretty soon afterwards I realized that it was probably influenced by the fact that his new initials were T.V. So I regretted it slightly, once I realized that."

THE TEMPTATIONS The group was formed in Detroit in 1960 as the Elgins by members of two other groups, the Primes and the Distants. They changed their name in 1961 when they signed to Motown Records. Founding member Otis Williams recalls in his 1988 memoir, *Temptations:* "Not knowing that the name was taken, we christened ourselves the Elgins, after the watch . . . It was only a few days before signing when we discovered that another group was calling itself the Elgins and we'd have to change names again. Switching monikers was the last thing on our minds, but it had to be done. We first figured out what kind of name we didn't want: anything too damned long or hard to remember or meaningless or silly, like the El Domingos or the Siberians. That in mind, the five of us were standing on Hitsville's front lawn [the renovated two-story house where Motown was headquartered] with a guy who worked for Motown, Bill Mitchell. We were throwing around names when off the top of my head I blurted out, 'Temptations.' Bill said he really liked it, but when he asked the other four their opinions, we all took one look at ourselves in our raggedy, long winter coats and cracked up. We knew we weren't likely to tempt anyone or anything, but what the hell, it was as good a name as any. As was typical of Paul [Williams, a fellow group member] he saw something else in it. 'It's just a name,' he said, 'but maybe it will give us something to live up to.' . . . You can see today that it was the perfect name; it was about style and elegance but also suggested romance and frankly, sex, something Paul deliberately made part of our image. Even back then he'd remind us, 'We're selling sex.' "

10cc From an interview with British music industry impressario Jonathan King, who in 1972 gave the band its name, as he did also for Genesis: **Tell me about 10cc and how that came about.** "I started my own label in the early seventies called UK Records, and I picked up this master called 'Donna' by this group that was put together by a guy that I knew from Wayne Fontana and the Mindbenders a long while back [guitarist Eric Stewart]. I had to give them a name there and then because I'd signed the record, and I went to sleep that night and had this dream that a band of mine on my label made number one on the album and singles charts simultaneously in America, and the band was called 10cc. So I gave them that name the next morning. Everybody then decided that this was apparently meant to be the amount of an average male ejaculation [in cubic centimeters]. Which was absolutely far from the truth; it had not been a wet dream, I can promise." **Is 10cc actually the true measurement of . . . ?** "You, I'm sure, would know more than I, since I've never had an orgasm." **I had heard that you, knowing that the average male ejaculation measured 9 cc, had decided to call them 10cc because you**

thought they were above average. Is that apocryphal?
"Totally apocryphal. There's a lot of apocryphal stories about names, and unfortunately, most of them are much more amusing than the ugly reality, which in this case is that the name came to me in a dream, a bit like Joseph. I have to say, though, that one of the reasons that I like names like 10cc is you can immediately see them on the charts, and therefore you don't have to go through all the other boring names. It's short and punchy and looks different. It's all sorts of letters and small figures and things. It makes you sit up and pay attention."

10,000 MANIACS The band formed in Jamestown, New York, in 1981, and took their name from the misre-membered title of the cult horror film *2,000 Maniacs*. They had previously performed as Still Life and the Burn Victims, among others. Keyboard player Dennis Drew told *Rolling Stone* in June 1989 that they selected the name so the locals would know "that we weren't going to do Led Zeppelin covers."

While distinctive, the name initially alienated some radio programmers, who assumed the Maniacs were a punk band or a novelty act. The name even confused one early band member, a sax player who would take the stage wearing pink slippers and a colander on his head, explaining to his bandmates: "We're maniacs, aren't we? I thought we were supposed to be funny."

TEN YEARS AFTER The band formed in Nottingham, England, in 1966, led by singer and guitarist Alvin Lee. Their name is a reference to the birth of rock and roll a decade earlier.

TESLA   The hard rock band got its start in Sacramento, California, in the early eighties as a garage rock group called Earth Shaker, then morphed into the blues rock outfit City Kidd. They changed their name to Tesla after one of their managers lent them *Man Out of Time,* a book about inventor Nikola Tesla, the historically overlooked electricity and radio pioneer. Guitarist Frank Hannon once told a newspaper that "Tesla got shafted by the media." In 1990, the band attempted to convince the Smithsonian Institution to accept and display a bust of their namesake. The Smithsonian declined.

TEXAS   The band formed in Glasgow, Scotland, in 1988, taking their name from Wim Wenders's 1984 film, *Paris, Texas,* which the band felt was evocative of their own sound. It suggested "open spaces, sparseness, that slide guitar," vocalist Sharleen Spiteri told *Rolling Stone* in August 1989.

THAT PETROL EMOTION   The Irish band formed in London in 1985, led by brothers Sean (guitar) and Damian (bass) O'Neill after the demise of the Undertones. Sean told *Rolling Stone* in October 1987: "Our name is deliberately meant to sum up a whole feeling of frustration and anger that you feel living there [in Northern Ireland]."

THE THE   Matt Johnson formed the The in London in 1980. *Rolling Stone* reported in March 1984: "The The, Johnson's nom de pop, has created a few problems for him on the Continent, where no one seems able to pronounce it, but he likes the ambiguous handle: 'It doesn't suggest any particular preconceptions.' "

THEM   Formed in Belfast, Ireland, in 1962 and originally called the Gamblers, Van Morrison's band took their name from the 1954 monster movie *Them!* about giant man-eating ants that terrorize California. The band chose the name because it suggested a sense of menace and mystery, and didn't have a "the."

THEY MIGHT BE GIANTS   Guitarist John Flansburgh and accordion player John Linnell, both natives of Lincoln, Massachusetts, formed They Might Be Giants in Brooklyn in the early eighties. The name comes from an obscure 1972 film starring George C. Scott and Joanne Woodward, which *Halliwell's Film Guide* describes as a "curious fantasy comedy which rather tentatively satirizes modern life and the need to retreat into unreality; mildly pleasing entertainment for intellectuals." In an interview, Flansburgh discusses the band's beginnings: **How did you guys come up with the name?** "Well, we first had a really bad name—a name so bad that John and I have made a vow that we will never tell anyone, even our children. We used it for our first show, a Sandinista rally in Central Park. We had this really terrible, terrible, embarrassing name. So we put together this long list of new names, a page of names, but none of them were that great. This long list of names included Dumptruck, and we liked that one okay. This friend of ours, Raoul Rosenberg, had this act with his dummy, Julius. He's now a political activist, but back then he was a ventriloquist. He was trying to think of a name for his act that would be something more than just 'Raoul and Julius,' and he came up with the idea of calling his act They Might Be Giants, but then decided not to use it. It was a reference to this movie that I hadn't seen at the time, this sort of second-rate seventies cult movie." **What was that about?** "It's about a delusional guy. So anyway, we asked him if we could borrow his name, and he said yes. So we made up two posters for our next gig, and one of them was Dumptruck and one of them was They Might Be Giants, and fortunately we chose They Might Be Giants because there was a band from Boston called Dumptruck, so we would've had to become Dumptruck N.Y.C. or Brooklyn Dumptruck or something. So we named ourselves They Might Be Giants. The key ingredient to its interest to us was the fact that it was a full sentence. It wasn't so much that it had the word *giants* in it, or that it suggested that we had some larger future. In fact, we were kind of surprised that people thought that the *they* was referring to us. We always thought it was an outward-looking name, and that was another point of interest. Y'know, *they* as opposed to *we*. Everyone knows that bands name themselves, so why would you call your band 'they' if you meant yourselves? We just thought it was kind of an outward-looking, paranoid name, and the fact that it was a full sentence seemed kind of interesting. This was at the point where bands had just moved from the Pencils to Pencil Pencil, and there were very few bands who had any names more interesting than that. It was in the era of New Wave. It was like 1983, so still, if New Wave wasn't the most vital thing, it was still influential. The reference to *Don Quixote* didn't seem that important, it seemed pretty obscure." **I only just heard that this afternoon, that "They Might Be Giants" is the title of a chapter in *Don Quixote*.** "Is it a chapter? I think it's just made reference to in the windmill part. I've never read the book, but I have read the passage. It wasn't that big a part of it. We didn't believe that people would catch the reference. It just seemed like a good full sentence." **Any regrets that you chose the name?** "One of the things about our name is that people got the impression that we were ambitious because of it when nothing could have been further from the truth. To us, it seemed obvious that we were destined for the margins of popular culture. It was just a functioning name for a bar band. It actually took us a long time to figure out that people didn't even understand the name. It was so totally uncalculated. I think if we knew then what we know now, we probably would have gone for a more streamlined name. But it does look good on a marquee sometimes, filling up all the space."

THIN LIZZY The band was formed in Dublin, Ireland, in 1969 by schoolmates Phil Lynott (vocals and bass) and Brian Downey (drums) and Eric Bell (guitar). In an interview, Downey recalls the band's early days: "When we started off first in Dublin, we had a three-piece band—Eric Bell, Phil, and myself. We used to sort of rehearse in a place called the Countdown Club. We were sitting around trying to think of a name. We went through various names—the Mod Con [as in Modern Convenience] Cavedwellers, and various other stupid names. We were wracking our brains for days and days, maybe weeks. Eric Bell used to be a big fan of this comic here on sale, an English comic, and there's all these strange characters in it like Dennis the Menace and Mickey the Monkey and people like that. There was also a person called Tin Lizzie. This was *Tin,* T-I-N L-I-Z-Z-I-E. She was like a little female robot. He was a huge fan of this comic and liked Tin Lizzie. That was his favorite character in the comic. So he came up with this idea; he asked me, 'Look, seeing that we went through so many names, and we couldn't seem to figure out what we liked, why don't we call it Tin Lizzie?' We all went, 'Awww, forget it, no way, it's terrible,' y'know? Phil said, 'No, absolutely no way. There's no way you could call the band Tin Lizzie.' So we sort of pondered it over for a couple of days, and Phil came back one day and said, 'Tell you what we do. Why don't we sort of stick an *H* in and call it Thin Lizzie—to confuse the Irish, because people in Ireland don't pronounce the *H* anyway—and call it Lizzy, L-I-Z-Z-Y, put a *Y* at the end instead of an *I-E*.' So he got some guy to draw up this little logo, and it looked pretty good with the *H* and the *Y* at the end. But we still weren't one hundred percent sure. We really weren't completely convinced that it would work, until we played the first few gigs. On the posters, the first pubs spelled it *Tin* anyway. That created a bit of controversy, so we went bank to the promoter and said, 'Look, that's the wrong way to spell Thin Lizzy,' and he said, 'But it's called "Tin Lizzie."' We said, 'No, it's *T-H*—it's Thin Lizzy.' That's basically how we got our name. It was very simple, but it took a while to get it together." **Does that comic still appear?** "That comic is still around, but I don't think Tin Lizzie is in it anymore. The name of the comic was *Beano*. Tin Lizzie was a female robot, looked sort of like a trash can." **Was it set in the future?** "No, it was sort of like the fifties, I think. It appeared in the *Dublin Evening Herald*." There was never any lawsuit from the creator of the comic? "No, I think that was Phil's idea—if he changed the spelling, we couldn't be sued." **Do you recall any of the other names that you guys considered at the time?** 'Yeah, the Mod Con Cavedwellers. I think the other one was the Liffeybeats, after the river Liffey in Dublin, like the Merseybeats, you know? That was thrown out after about two seconds. There's one or two I can't remember actually, it was so long ago—it was 1970, I think, or '69. Before, Phil and I had a band called the Orphanage. We actually did gigs under the name of the Orphanage a couple of months before Thin Lizzy formed. We were going to keep the name the Orphanage going, but Eric Bell and myself said no, with new members there should be something fresh. The Orphanage was very close to becoming our name." **I think Tin Lizzie was also the nickname of a Model T Ford.** "As well, too, right. Obviously, Tin Lizzie from the comic strip was taken from the Model Ford." **So when you came to the States, did people say, "Oh, you're named after the car?"** "They used to tell us that, but we said no, it was after a comic strip character Eric Bell thought of."

THIRD EYE BLIND   Stephan Jenkins formed the band in San Francisco in 1990. Their song "Semi-Charmed Life," an ode to sex and drugs, was one of the big hits of 1998. When asked if the name refers to the metaphysical third eye in Eastern religions, Jenkins told *Rolling Stone*, "Yeah, but it's also kind of taking the piss out of that. I like names with wit and a sense of punk-rock irony. I'm not into that Kula Shaker shit: some guy sitting there in his mantra position—ugh!" He elaborated in an official band press release: "It's not a misiion statement or anything like that. I always have liked names with wit and irony. I was a big fan of Camper Van Beethoven. The name reflects a certain sense of magic and dreams—we thought that was very lacking in music when we started—music for a blind time, if you will. It also takes the piss out of that phony spiritual thing. Third Eye Blind has always been about real things."

13TH FLOOR ELEVATORS   The 13th Floor Elevators came together in Austin, Texas, in 1965, and were one of the pioneers of psychedelic rock. Clementine Hall, wife of jug player Tommy Hall and one of the Elevator's chief lyricists, explained the origins of the band's name in a story in the June 1992 issue of *DISCoveries,* a record collectors' magazine: "There was a lot of confusion about who actually named the group the 13th Floor Elevators, but I clearly remember how it happened. I was sitting in our bedroom with Tommy when he asked what they should call the band. I suggested the Elevators to Tommy, not only because the band was making psychedelic music, but because I thought it would sound like a black band. We would always listen to R&B groups, especially at this one place where we always ate barbecue.

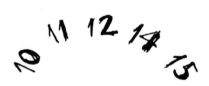

"A day or so later Tommy came back and said that the rest of the band liked the suggestion of the Elevators, but they thought it wasn't long enough. It was then that I suggested the 13th Floor Elevators. Adding the '13th Floor' to the name provided various interpretations, the most obvious being that the thirteenth floor was usually nonexistent in the older high-rise buildings. Also, *M* is the thirteenth letter in the alphabet, and in street vernacular the number thirteen became associated with marijuana. It was also my lucky number."

.38 SPECIAL   Jacksonville, Florida natives .38 Special had a string of best-selling albums in the eighties. In an interview, lead singer Donnie Van Zant, younger brother of Lynyrd Skynyrd's Ronnie Van Zant, explains the origins of their name: "I guess .38 was like most bands; when we first got together, we had a problem finding rehearsal halls. All the places that we found were in residential areas. We'd be there for like a week at a time, and before you knew it, you had the cops on you for disturbing the peace. So we had to go on the outskirts of Jacksonville. We found this place, right on the Florida-Georgia line, a place called Yulee, Florida. We found this abandoned auto warehouse, and we nicknamed it the Alamo. It was on a golf course out there, and the golf course used it to put fertilizer in it. We got this place for about sixty dollars a month. We were out there rehearsing one night—it was like no-man's-land out there—and we heard sirens, and people just ramming at the door. Before we could get our guitars off to answer the door, they'd knocked it open, and it was the cops—they called 'em the constables, that's what they called them out there. They had their .38s out, and they didn't know what was going on. We heard a couple of them reply that they thought there was an orgy or drug party going on. They had their guns drawn, and they told us to walk outside, or these .38 Specials would do their talking for them. So they scared us plumb to death. That's how we really got our name. But it's got a good ending to it. Some of them constables later on joined the Jacksonville Police Department, so when we had a successful record and were able to get another practice house in Jacksonville, they guarded our rehearsal hall there for us. We became real good friends with them." **I heard a story that the name came from this '38 Buick Special your folks gave you for your sixteenth birthday that you used as an equipment van for the band.** "[Laughs.] No, I don't know where that one came from." **Did you guys take the name right on the spot?** "No, we thought about it for about a week after that." **Who said, "Hey, there's a great name?"** "I don't really remember which one of us came up with it, but I'm sure it had to be Don Barnes [the guitarist] or myself." **Were you guys operating under any other names at the time?** "At that time I think we were calling ourselves Skin Tight." **Are you glad you went with .38 Special?** "Yeah, y'know, I don't advocate guns or anything like that, but I think the whole thing about it is that the .38 Special is pretty powerful, and we felt that we were a pretty powerful band. We had dual guitars and dual drummers and thought that was perfect for .38 Special."

THE THOMPSON TWINS The Thompson Twins began as a trio in Chesterfield, England, in 1977. Led by keyboard player Tom Bailey, they were named after a pair of hapless detectives in the *Tintin* comic books, which are wildly popular in Europe, but haven't made much of an impact in the United States. By 1981 the lineup had expanded to include seven members, but returned to a trio the following year comprised of Bailey, Alannah Currie (vocals, sax, and percussion), and Joe Leeway (percussion). In late 1986, Leeway left the group, leaving the Twins, at last, a duo.

THREE DOG NIGHT Vocalist Danny Hutton, who was born in Ireland but raised in the U.S., formed the band in

Los Angeles in 1968. The name comes from an Australian colloquialism: in the Outback, the colder the night, the more dogs you need to sleep beside you to keep you warm, a three-dog night being the coldest.

311   Police code for indecent exposure, allegedly inspired by the band's involvement in a skinny dipping incident in a public pool.

THROBBING GRISTLE   Formed in Yorkshire, England, in the late seventies, the prolific and musically confrontational band took its name from local slang for an erection. They reportedly chose it because it was the most embarrassing one they could imagine customers going into a record store to ask about.

'TIL TUESDAY   Best known for the 1985 hit "Voices Carry," the band formed in Boston, Massachusetts, in 1983. According to drummer Michael Hausman, the name did not come from a line in a David Bowie song as had been rumored: " 'Til Tuesday, the name, did not come from anywhere in particular. There's no great story. We were sitting around the rehearsal space, we were talking about names and we got onto this thing about days of the week. And 'Til Tuesday—maybe it was the alliteration, I'm not sure what it was—but that's what just kind of popped out and that was the name. No secret meaning. Sorry."

TIN MACHINE   David Bowie formed Tin Machine in 1989, with guitarist Reeves Gabrels, and brothers Tony and Hunt Sales, sons of comedian Soupy Sales. In an interview, Gabrels explains why the band chose the name Tin Machine: "Well, the popular response is, 'Because Helen Hayes is already taken.' The fact of the matter was we needed a name, and we had a song called 'Tin Machine,' and it appealed to us on a few different levels. It appealed to us from the point of view of, like, the Monkees and 'Hey Hey We're the Monkees'—this gave us 'Hey Hey We're Tin Machine,' and we already had Davy Jones [see separate entry for David Bowie]. The other thing was that it harkened back to the heavy bands like Led Zeppelin and Iron Butterfly, but was a send-up at the same time. For Hunt and me, Led Zeppelin contained his favorite drummer and one of my favorite guitar players. That whole era of music had that improvisational thing that we're trying to resuscitate." **What was the song "Tin Machine" about?** "It's just a series of fairly abstract images. We don't really know what that one's about." **Do you remember any other names that were considered?** "Oh, yeah—the Feldmans." **Where did that come from?** "Well, there's a couple of things that it kind of grows out of. Anybody in any law or business or a record company is a 'Morty.' Now 'Morty' comes from this character Mort Feld, who is just a generic business guy. Your worst nightmare, kind of. And 'Feldmans' came from being in different countries where the Sales brothers could never remember what the name of the currency was. So it was always like, 'Hey, you got any Feldmans you can lend me?' To this day, it's one of those things that you use when you can't remember a name. It's like, 'Louie Feldman called.' 'Louie who?' 'Your friend Louie.' It's the substitute last name." **Are you glad you went with Tin Machine?** "Yeah, it's hard to find a name that somebody else is not going to have already, or something very close to it. I have a band up here in Boston that's called the Atom Said. It's a fragment of a line from a song of ours. And we thought, 'Well, that's good, it's a little off kilter, nobody else is going to have a name like that.' And then a couple of months later, there's a band in England called the Atom Seed.

"The name thing is very strange. I had friends up here who had a band called Wild Kingdom. Then Mutual of Omaha said—this was about eight years ago—'You can't use Wild Kingdom.' So they changed their name to the Gospel Birds. Then a couple of months later someone gets a hold of them and says, 'You can't use Gospel Birds because there's a gospel group called the Gospel Birds.' So then they became the Zulus, and nothing's happened, they've been all right—except their record label dropped them.

"What really shocks me is the shortsightedness, the lack of imagination, in choosing band names. I was in the rest room at a place called the Rat up here, and I was looking at the wall. There's all these band names on the wall, and someone had written 'My Tires Are Bulletproof,' and I didn't know whether that was a sentence or a band name, and I thought, 'Why not?' "

TOAD THE WET SPROCKET The band was formed in 1987 in Santa Barbara, California, by four schoolmates and became the house band at a local bar called the Shack. In a Columbia Records press release, the band discusses the origins of their name: " 'It's a Monty Python skit,' explains [bassist Dean] Dinning, 'from an album called the *Contractual Obligation Album*. It's on the one called "Rock Notes." It starts out'—and here Dinning slips into one of the comedy troupe's snippy British accents—'Rex Stardust, lead electric triangle for Toad the Wet Sprocket, has had to have an elbow removed following their recent worldwide tour of Finland.'

"All of a sudden, all the Toads are talking at once. 'It's not that we're all huge Monty Python fans,' begins [guitarist Todd] Nichols.

" 'It was kind of an excuse for not being able to think of anything better,' finishes Dinning.

"Then [drummer Randy] Guss chimes in. 'We thought it was funny. And then, when we had our first gig comin' up, we had no name. We thought it was so funny that in the newspaper it said, "At the Shack: Toad the Wet Sprocket." '

"Phillips, meantime, is vaguely apologetic about all of this. 'We were gonna think of something better,' he says. 'We were going to think of a good name, and a real name, but it just never happened." '

TOM TOM CLUB Talking Heads bassist Tina Weymouth and drummer Chris Frantz, who married in 1977, formed the Tom Tom Club in 1980. Weymouth remembers: "In 1980, Chris Blackwell, who owned Island Records, wanted to build an apartment building to house artists and musicians working at Compass Point Studios in the Bahamas. He wanted to create a small artistic community, which Chris Frantz and I wanted to be a part of when we weren't away working with the Talking Heads. In the Bahamas, people name their houses instead of giving them numbers. Blackwell's house is Terra Nova, and the beach house  across from the studio where many bands have stayed is called Press On Regardless (but it has been called Pass Out Regardless by insiders). Since we were the first occupants of the new building, Blackwell gave us the honor of naming it. We chose Tip Top for the building, in reference to its location and view; and Tom Tom Club for our own space because it was where we played and wrote our music. We put drumsticks in the walls in the style of Shaker wall pegs. Even the toilet paper holders are drumsticks. We had many great jams and parties there with a lot of different musicians, including Ian Dury and Chas Jankel, Lee 'Scratch' Perry, Wali Badarou, 'Sticky' Thompson, Tyrone Downie, Robert Palmer, Adrian Belew, and many others who eventually played on our records. The band was just such a natural outgrowth of that creative, fun scene that we just kept the name Tom Tom Club for the record and the bands we had afterwards.

"I believe we were the first of the *Club* bands—even ahead of Culture Club—that were to follow in the eighties. Someone told us that there exists an old black-and-white film that contains scenes that take place at the Tom Tom Club. Perhaps we had seen that film and loved the name, but we can't remember. We thought we were inspired by Peanuts Taylor's Drumbeat Club in Nassau. Peanuts is a really good conga player, and tourists regularly go to see him and his fire-eating limbo dancers."

TOO MUCH JOY The band formed in high school in Scarsdale, New York, in the early eighties. Guitarist Jay Blumenfield explains: **How did you guys come up with the name Too Much Joy?** "We were in high school, and we had never tried [hallucinogenic] mushrooms, and we had always heard that they were really cool. So we got all these mushrooms and then we got all these pads of paper and pens and records and stuff, and we took the mushrooms. The plan was to just write our neat thoughts and lyrics and poems and whatever. Something happened that night—we don't remember exactly what—but it was like the best night of our lives. And when we woke up in the morning, the only thing written on any of the pads of paper was 'Too Much Joy,' We all looked at each other and said, 'That's the name of our band.'" **This is the *real* story.** "That's the *real* story, and it's probably better than any of the ones that we've made up." **Did you consider anything else?** "Well, before that, like in ninth and tenth grade, we had gone through a bunch of names. We had gone through the Raves, and we called the band Ton Ton Macout, which is the Haitian secret police, which in French means something like 'My aunt is watching me.' The strange thing is, we read this article about Sinead O'Connor recently, and it turns out when she was younger, she was in a band called Ton Ton Macout, too, which is really weird. So we sometimes tell people we used to be in a band with Sinead O'Connor. But the name since eleventh grade on has been Too Much Joy." **Any regrets?** "No, it's been pretty perfect. It kind of sums it all up."

T'PAU This band is named for a character in "Amok Time," an episode of the original *Star Trek* TV series.

TOTO Toto was formed in Los Angeles in 1978 by six veteran session men. Lead guitarist Steve Lukather debunks an enduring myth about the band's name in an interview: **Tell me how you guys ended up with the name Toto.** "Tell me what you've heard and I'll tell you the truth." **I heard that [lead singer] Bobby Kimball's last name was really Toteaux, as in T-O-T-E-A-U-X.** "[Laughs.] That's total bullshit. The bottom line, how the whole thing really started, we were doing demos for our first record in early '77, and we needed something to write on the demo tapes, because we didn't have a name for our group. So we said, 'We need to get a name like Toto, something really simple, easy to remember, and easily identified in every language, that if you hear once, you're going to remember it.' Always with the intention of finding a better name, 'cause I think the name doesn't fit the music at all. I think it's actually been detrimental to our career more than anything." **Who suggested Toto and how did they come up with that name?** "David Paich and Jeff Porcaro. They came in with the idea, and then we found out that in Latin it means 'everything,' and we play lots of different kinds of music so . . . A lot of us were like, 'We gotta find a name, we gotta find a name.' It was one of those kind of things, shit happened so fast for us, the next thing you know people said, 'Y'know, that's not a bad name.' I was going like, 'Man, the word doesn't fit what we're doing.' " **So Bobby Kimball's name really isn't Robert Toteaux.** "No that's a joke, that's a wank. Someone's pulling on your willie on that one. I remember years ago, making jokes about it, but it was never a legitimate explanation. We found out it meant a lot of different things in a lot of different languages, and it was sort of interesting, it was one of those kind of things that just stuck, and the band became the name." **Who do you think made up the bit about Kimball's last name?** "Oh, that was our old bass player David Hungate. Bobby Kimball . . . those guys haven't been around for ten years. I could give a fuck where they are, actually." **Did you call yourselves anything else when you were just jamming?** "There were a couple of names early on. I think Jeff had one called Ripe Jack, which I always liked, which refers to a man's hard penis. I thought that was a much better name. It was just

271

one of those things where we were making a record and the record was out before we even really had a chance to get deep into thought about it. We just thought, 'Oh, yeah, okay.' Believe me, compared to a lot of other names, it's not so bad. I mean, look at some of these now—the Butthole Surfers, which is a personal favorite of mine. Back then, in the mid to late seventies, people took their names a lot—you can get away with a lot more now. You can come up with phrases now ten years ago you'd never consider as a name. Our name is not quite as bad as some of these are."

In an interview, Billy Kimball confirms Lukather's story: "Jeff Porcaro and David Paich were sitting around watching *The Wizard of Oz* one day, and they came up with the name from the movie." **So they brought it to the band, and everyone said . . .** "We said, 'We love it.' " **I read that your name was originally—someone has since told me that it's not true—but that your name is actually Robert Toteaux.** "That may have been a thing we did with *Rolling Stone* just as a joke—told them my name was Robert Toteau, T-0-T-E-A-U—and we all had a big chuckle about it. Next thing you know, I was seeing it printed everywhere that my name was Toteau." **So you were born Robert Kimball?** "Yeah." **Were you pleased that you picked the name Toto in retrospect?** "Oh, yeah, I thought it was great because as we went around the world, we found—I think we ended up with about seventeen different connotations. It's a betting term in Europe—Toto Lotto. There's a cartoon character in France named Toto, and I think it means 'child' in Swahili. And *toto* means 'all-encompassing' in some language. It's pretty wild. Also, it's the name of the largest toilet manufacturer in Japan. So the first time we went to

Toyko, we saw our name early every morning." **At the time I guess you guys didn't realize that.** "Oh, no, not at all. We had no clue."

TRAFFIC Steve Winwood formed Traffic in 1967 after leaving the Spencer Davis Group. The name was coined by drummer Jim Capaldi while standing on a street corner one day watching the cars go by.

T. REX Marc Bolan, who died in an auto accident in 1977, formed the band as Tyrannosaurus Rex in London in 1967. Producer Tony Visconti, who worked very closely with Bolan, explains in an interview: "Marc Bolan was always impressed as a youngster by the *Tyrannosaurus rex* skeleton in the British Museum of Natural History. I'm sure all of us have had a similar experience. When you finally see those bones firsthand, it just knocks you away that something was actually that big, and that's what he said. He said he couldn't believe that. He said *Tyrannosaurus rex* was like 'the warlord of the royal crocodiles.' He said it was the most powerful beast. Of course he set it up as his idol because he was into power, and also he had a very rich imagination. He was very much into Tolkien, Middle Earth, and all that. So in some way, *Tyrannosaurus rex* fitted in with his whole mythology of great, wondrous beasts that lived millions of years ago. He always said when he got a band together, a band of his own, he was going to call it *Tyrannosaurus Rex*—which is exactly what he did." **So it wasn't the result of all the band members**

putting fifty ideas into the hat. "No, there was only one band member—that was Marc Bolan. It's what he always wanted to call it. There's some references to that in some of his early lyrics, to 'the warlord of the royal crocodiles.' He really did worship this beast; he gave him that nickname. His poetry was marvelous—what a poetic way of describing *Tyrannosaurus rex.*" **How did the name evolve from Tyrannosaurus Rex to T. Rex?** "We did four albums as Tyrannosaurus Rex. Then one day he came into my office and noticed that I had been writing 'T. Rex' in my diary. For every day of the week that I was in the studio with them, I didn't want to write out 'Tyrannosaurus Rex.' In my diary and also my wall chart. Y'know, every producer or A&R guy has a chart on the wall, so it actually was in public view. And he was actually insulted by that. He said, 'It's Tyrannosaurus Rex and you shouldn't shorten it.' So I said, 'I'm sorry, but this is the way I'm going to keep doing it. I can't write that out, it's too long.' But I think the writing was on the wall, so to speak, and other people began to shorten it to T. Rex. Deejays especially could not pronounce it, being the illiterate idiots that they are. They could not say the words Tyrannosaurus Rex, which limited our airplay. The British deejays would stumble on it and make jokes of it. So after this little incident when he told me off about shortening the name, the very next album was called *T. Rex.*" **Was there a day when he said, 'Okay guys, I'm sorry, it's T. Rex now, or did it just appear and you were like,** 'Oh . . . ?' "He said, 'I'm shortening the name of the group to T. Rex.' I said, 'Why?' 'It's easier to say,' he said. That was his excuse." **Did he ever say, "Look, I'm sorry about goofing on you that day?"** "No, he never apologized for anything. He was quite a character."

THE TROGGS The Troggs began as the Troglodytes in 1964 in Andover, England, and were discovered by the Kinks' manager the following year. In 1966, the band changed their name to the Troggs, lead singer Reginald Ball changed his name to Reg Presley, and their single "Wild Thing" shot to the top of the charts. In an interview, Presley recalls how they came up with their name: "Well, we were looking for a sort of earthy type of name because you had your Stones, and that was a sort of hard, aggressive name in those days, and we were looking for something like that. Everybody had their own opinions on what the band should be called. We picked up a couple of student schoolteachers that were hitchhiking their way to London when we were going up there to get some new equipment, and I asked them for name suggestions. They said, 'Why don't you call yourselves the Grotty Troggs?' 'cause we were sat in the back of an old Ford transit van, y'know. I kind of liked the name the Troggs, and then we voted for it, quite a while after that, and I picked the longest straw, so I was able to choose the band name. Grotty Trogg, you know, *grotesque*. I liked the name, and I got the vote, so that was it. *Trogg* is short for *troglodyte*— a mythical cave dweller, it says in the Oxford dictionary. So we thought caves, rocks, rock, roll—it sort of went in there somewhere." **Is _trogg_ common slang in Britain?** "No. Anybody who lives in caves though, they do call them troggs. Around the same time we started, there were some caves up in Derbyshire that were taken over by some hippie-type people, and they locally got called troggs." **Are you pleased you chose that name in retrospect?** "I am now, yeah. It's a good name."

THE TUBES   Lead singer Fee Waybill (born John Waldo) explains the band's origins in an interview: **How did you guys settle on the name the Tubes, and what does it signify?** "When we first got together back in San Francisco in like '72, we were two different bands from Arizona that had kind of combined. We'd moved to San Francisco one after the other, and I was the roadie for the band originally called the Red White and Blues Band that had changed its name to Arizona after the move to San Francisco. The other band was called the Beans, and after the band that I was the roadie for lost its bass player, our trio decided to join their quartet and became Beanizona. I became a background singer because there were too many roadies. They said, 'Here, take this tambourine and, like, sing in the back,' and I eventually worked my way into being the lead singer.

"After we were Beanizona for a while and that didn't work, we changed it back to the Beans. We were playing gigs and didn't have a deal or anything when a band from the East Coast called the Beans came out with a record on United Artists. It was a New York sitar rock band or something like that. We were freaked out and wrote a letter saying, 'We're the Beans—you can't call yourselves the Beans!' And they said, 'Well, by virtue of being published first, we own the name—not you.' So we had to change our name, although we didn't want to. We thought of changing it to something that included beans, like the Laserbeans or the Holybeans, but then decided to come up with something new.

"Everyone's assignment was to come up with a full page of names. We had thousands of names, we went through tons of them. We were almost called the Gasmen and some other horrible names that I can't remember. Somebody, I think it was either Mike [Cotten, synthesizer] or Prairie [Prince, drums] was looking through a medical dictionary for names of body parts and came across tubes, rods and bulbs—the bones inside the inner ear. We thought, 'Oh, inner ear, it's perfect for a rock group, how perfect—Tubes, Rods and Bulbs.' And then we thought, 'No, that's too long, and it's too hard to say.' So we shortened it to T.R.B.—another initial band, we hated that. So someone suggested, 'Why not just Tubes?' We all like it because it had so many different connotations. You couldn't pin it down. It could be inner tubes, TV tubes, laser tubes, Fallopian tubes . . ."

THE TURTLES The Turtles evolved from a high school surf band formed in Los Angeles in 1963 that was first called the Nightriders and then the Crossfires.
The following year, with both the British Invasion under way and folk rock gaining in popularity, the band stopped

playing surf instrumentals and began passing themselves off as an English group and played several folk gigs as the Crosswind Singers. In 1965, when local White Whale records offered them a deal but asked them to change their name, manager Reb Foster suggested the Tyrtles, in imitation of the Byrds. The band initially balked, but agreed to the conventionally spelled Turtles.

24-7 SPYZ   The band formed in New York City in 1986. Guitarist Jimi Hazel explains: "When we started the band, we thought about what each person was all about. We seemed to like different kinds of music, so we figured if you take something from each kind of music that you like and you kind of put it together, it's kind of like being a spy. It's kind of like infiltrating a specific kind of music and picking the elements that you like and bringing them back. At the time, '24-7' around the block was slang for something you did all the time, like 'We used to drink 40s [40-ounce bottles of beer] 24-7,' or 'I used to chase girls a lot, 24-7.' It was also a brand name for blow. So it became 'twenty-four hours a day, seven days a week musical spies.' "

U

UB40   UB40 formed in Birmingham, England, in 1979, taking their name from the British unemployment-benefit card. Brothers Robin and Ali Campbell explained to *Rolling Stone* in April 1984 how they chose the name: " 'A friend said, "You're on the dole, so why not call yourselves UB40?' " recalls Robin. 'We didn't realize it at the time, but it was a stroke of genius.'

" 'It meant we had three million fans automatically,' adds Ali. 'It's probably up to five million now. But it wasn't a calculated political move. Individually, we're politically motivated, but as a band . . . we never set out to be the spokesmen for the unemployed youth of Great Britain. We set out to play reggae and make money.' "

UGLY KID JOE   The band formed in 1990 in Isla Vista, California, and played under a variety of names, including SWAT (Suburban White Alcoholic Trash), before settling on Ugly Kid Joe. The name was inspired by Pretty Boy Floyd, an L.A.-based glam band, for whom they had been scheduled to open. Guitarist Klaus Eichstadt told *SPIN* in August 1992: "We'd used, like, three names in the past month, so we were like, 'What

are we gonna call ourselves for this one?' I said, 'Let's go for something dumb like Ugly Kid Joe, you know, opening for Pretty Boy Floyd.' Everybody kinda chuckled and we were like, 'Yeah, it'd look funny on the marquee, and we could give, like, a dollar off for ugly chicks or something.' "

As luck would have it, the show was canceled. The other band members thought it was pointless to keep the name, but Eichstadt had sketched a cartoon character he called Ugly Kid Joe. The cartoon was polished by a friend, Moish Brenman, who did artwork for local skateboarders. Eichstadt explains: "The design was done by Moish for, like, fourteen bucks. That was all we had. We gave him, like, a bag of Doritos, a candy bar, a Mountain Dew, and fourteen bucks. That was the coolest—to have our own logo. Then we had him do the drumhead and suddenly we knew we were a real band."

U.K.   See **Asia**

THE ULTIMATE SPINACH   Reportedly the name is a reference to pot; one concert poster for the band featured Popeye the Sailor smoking spinach.

GARY PUCKET AND THE UNION GAP   Gary Pucket formed the band in San Diego, California, in 1967, naming them after the town of Union Gap, Washington, near where he grew up.

URGE OVERKILL   The band formed in Chicago in 1986. In a VH1 interview, singer and guitarist Nash Kato explained that their name "was off a Parliament record. I believe it was the title track off *Funkentelechy* [1977's *Funkentelechy Vs. The Placebo System*]; 'Mood control is designed to render the funkable ideas brought to you by the makers of Mr. Prolong—better known as Urge Overkill, the pepping of the pleasure principle'—something like that." Said bassist "Eddie" King Roser in the same interview: "When people see the words Urge Overkill, they sort of think it's—we used to get this all the time—like, 'Are you hardcore?' I mean, it couldn't be farther from what it is, what the sound of the name was. [Parliament's George] Clinton predates hardcore, that's for sure."

URIAH HEEP   Uriah Heep formed in London in 1970, having evolved from a band called Spice. They named themselves after the unctuous Dickens character in *Great Expectations.*

UTOPIA   See **The Nazz**

U2   U2 evolved from a band called Feedback formed in Dublin, Ireland in 1976 by vocalist Bono (born Paul Hewson), guitarist the Edge (David Evans), guitarist Dick Evans (the Edge's brother), bassist Adam Clayton, and drummer Larry Mullen, Jr., all friends from the Mount Temple School. Later that year Dick left to form his own band, the Virgin Prunes, and Feedback became the Hype.

Clayton, acting as the band's manager, sought advice from Steve Rapid, singer for the local band the Radiators, who suggested they change their name. When Clayton agreed, expressing a desire for a name that was somewhat ambiguous, Rapid suggested U2. There was a U2 spy plane, a U2 submarine, and a U2 battery made by Eveready, in addition to the suggestion of "you, too" and "you two." When Clayton suggested the name to his bandmates, they were somewhat skeptical, but eventually accepted it.

Bono was initially called Bonovox, after a local shop that sold hearing aids. Bono gave the Edge his name, allegedly inspired by the shape of Evans' head.

VAN DER GRAAF GENERATOR Formed in Manchester, England, in 1967, the art rock band was named by drummer Chris Judge Smith after a machine that creates static electricity.

VANILLA FUDGE The band formed in New York City in 1966. Drummer Carmen Appice recalls: "We were white guys doing rhythm and blues stuff, and one day this girl in this club said, 'You guys are like white soul—like vanilla fudge.' And we said, 'Yeah, that's an interesting name.' Before that we were called the Pigeons, and as we were signing to Atlantic Records, they said, 'Well, the name the Pigeons isn't really that good.' Actually, maybe it was the producer, Shadow Morton, who said change the name. It was somebody from that end of it, from the record end, who said, 'This name's no good. We need something that describes you guys better.'" **Why were you called the Pigeons in the first place?** "The band already had the name when I joined. It had something to do with the Byrds. We actually played a show one time with the Byrds and the Seeds—the Byrds, the Seeds, and the Pigeons. It was pretty funny." **So you dumped the name.** "It wasn't a very strong name, and it didn't describe what we were doing. So when this chick came up with this Vanilla Fudge name, we went, 'Hey, that's a great idea!' " **Who was she?** "She was a fan. It was at a place called the Page Two, in Oceanside, New York, in the beginning of '67." **You guys were one of the pioneers of the whole contrasting-name phenomenon with Iron Butterfly and Led Zeppelin. Were you at all conscious of that?** "No, not really. We were just white guys doing a lot of black music in our own way—y'know, like 'Hangin' On,' 'Take Me for a Little While,' 'Hold On I'm Comin'.' We did a lot of stuff like 'The Tracks of My Tears' and we rockified it, a blue-eyed soul sort of vibe. That's basically what we did, but we didn't want to call it 'white soul.' So when Vanilla Fudge came along, we thought, 'Yeah, that's pretty cool. Yeah, this might sell.' "

THE VELVET UNDERGROUND An early incarnation of the Velvet Underground formed in New York City in 1964 featuring Lou Reed [vocals, guitar], John Cale [viola, bass, keyboards, vocals], Sterling Morrison [bass, guitar], and Angus MacLise [drums], who was later replaced by Maureen Tucker. After performing under a variety of short-lived names, including the Primitives and the Warlocks, they settled on the Velvet Underground, from an obscure paperback that Cale's friend Tony Conrad found on the sidewalk of the Bowery in Manhattan. The book claimed to chronicle the seamy sexual underside of everyday America.

In *Up-tight: The Velvet Underground Story* by Victor Bockris and Gerard Malanga, Sterling Morrison notes: "We had a name at last! And it was adopted by us and deemed appropriate not because of the S&M theme of the book, but because the word *underground* was suggestive of our involvement with the underground film and art scenes."

In an interview in *Rolling Stone* in 1988, Lou Reed recalls: "There was a place in Philadelphia we used to play, the Second Fret. One of the weirdest stories about that is that I had taken the name Velvet Underground from this paperback book I had seen, just this junky book with a great title. I went into the Second Fret, and this girl was there taking tickets. She said to me, 'My father just died.' 'Oh, I'm sorry to hear that.' 'He wrote that book.' Small world."

THE VENTURES   The instrumental rock band began in Seattle, Washington, in 1960 as the Versatones, soon changing their name to the Ventures because they were "beginning a new adventure."

VERUCA SALT   The Chicago-based band named themselves after a character in the children's novel *Charlie and the Chocolate Factory.*

THE VIOLENT FEMMES   Guitarist Gordon Gano, bassist Brian Ritchie, and drummer Victor De Lorenzo formed the Violent Femmes in Milwaukee, Wisconsin, in the early  eighties. In an interview, Ritchie discusses their origins: **How did the Femmes get their name?** "Well, it's a very mundane story. Everybody wants to look for some sort of social or political motivations for our name, and we've usually tried to mislead people and tell them the wrong story. I suppose since this is a real, official name encyclopedia, I'll give you the truth. There was this guy named Jerry Fortier—he's a musician and he's a photographer, he did the photography for our first album—and he started talking to me about my family. He asked me, 'What's your brother like?' and I just started to lie. I don't know why, but I just decided to lie. I said, 'Well, he's just like me. He's got the same haircut, he dresses like me, he's got a punk rock band, and everything.' And it's not true at all. My brother's straight—he works for an insurance agent, doesn't look anything like me. So then Jerry caught me by surprise and he said, 'Well, what's the name of your brother's band?' And I said, 'Um, uh, the Violent Femmes!' It was just, y'know, one of these spur-of-the-moment, flow-of-consciousness, Freudian-slip-type pronouncements that I made—and he accepted that at face value. Then I went over to Victor's house, and I said, 'Hey, listen to this weird name that I just came up with today.' And I told him, 'Violent Femmes,' and Victor was quite taken with that. So originally, when we started, we were free-lancing as a rhythm section. We played with Gordon Gano and we played with a lot of other people, too. So we just called our rhythm section Violent Femmes and that's how it started. Of course, after a while we just adopted it as the name of the whole band." **What were you guys called before you were the Violent Femmes? Did you have a name?** "Oh, we had a lot of different names: the Romboids, Hitler's Missing Teste, Nude Family Portrait . . ." **What were some of the more unusual stories that you guys fabricated to explain the name?** "Usually we just refused to talk about it, but then sometimes we would say that it was a schoolyard thing, like Milwaukee slang. The work *femme* is slang for sissy. I don't know if it's slang all over America, but it was in Milwaukee in the fifties, *violent* obviously being the opposite of that connotation. So the name ends up having a nulled effect. I mean, it really doesn't make too much sense. Violent Femmes—it's a non sequitur. The interesting thing about the name is that we would have never chosen that name except for the fact that we didn't give a shit and we didn't expect the band to survive. We intended to just do a couple gigs and then we were going to split up and move on to other things. We figured that this Violent Femmes moniker was okay for a few gigs, it would get a lot of attention, it was ridiculous, and everything like that. But I think if we had considered the fact that we'd be together for, now, eleven years . . . We're getting to the age where it's not exactly as dignified as we'd like. I never appreciated Crosby, Stills and Nash until I realized how smart they were to name themselves that. We just lost a gig because of it. We were supposed to play in England with this band James, who I guess are pretty big over there. They asked us to open up one of their big shows in London, and it was at some kind of a family-type place, like an amusement park or something like that. When the venue heard about our name, they refused to allow us to play there. It's strange that a band that's been around for eleven years— y'know, that would be as if the Rolling Stones couldn't get a gig because of their name in 1972. It's like, it's been around for a while, let's move on to more important issues. And of course we wonder about how much airplay and how much attention we've lost because of the name, but certainly we've gotten a lot of attention because of the name as well."

Richard Hell and the Voidoids   After he founded the Neon Boys with Tom Verlaine, which later became Television, and cofounded the Heartbreakers with Johnny Thunders, Richard Hell launched the Voidoids in New York City in 1976. In an interview, he recalls: "I was sitting in a restaurant on Second Avenue with Tom Verlaine after a rehearsal one night, just watching the parade go by, and to amuse ourselves we began calling each other names, attaching *oid* to different words, like, 'You're a bulboid,' 'You're a transmissionoid.' I was wracking my brain for the best *oid* I could conceive of, and that's when I had the brilliant illumination and conceived the original *voidoid*. It turned up in a novel I was working on at the time that I called *The Voidoid*. That word was used to describe a certain kind of personality. I meant it was a sort of late-twentieth-century human mutation that had taken place from the influence of all the pollution and broadcast waves filling the air." **It's not a very positive term then.** "It's hard to tack a value to it. It's just sort of the way things are." **Did you consider any other names that you can remember?** "Oh, tons of them. In a book of mine that came out a year or so ago [*Artifact,* Hanuman Books, 1990], there's a long list of names, maybe thirty, forty names [including the Scream, the Droolers, the Facial Expressions, and the Teeth]. The Beauticians, that was one of my favorites."

THE WALKER BROTHERS Launched in London in 1964 by three Americans, nobody in the group was born a Walker or related in any way to a Walker. It's been reported that British music industry impressario Jack Good dubbed them the Walker Brothers, but *Scott Walker: A Deep Shade of Blue* by Mike Watkinson and Pete Anderson tells a different story. According to the book, in the early sixties bassist Scott Engel and guitarist John Maus, who were then living in Los Angeles, had to use fake ID's to get in and play local clubs because they were underage. Maus' card was in the name of Walker, which he preferred to his given surname, which is German for "mouse." Because he and Engel looked alike, they adopted the name the Walker Brothers, as did drummer Gary Leeds when he joined the band. The group had several hits in the mid sixties, including "Make It Easy on Yourself" and "The Sun Ain't Gonna Shine (Anymore)."

THE WALLFLOWERS Jakob Dylan, son of Bob Dylan, formed the band in Los Angeles in the early nineties. Through a spokesman he denies the rumor that he took the name from one of his father's songs. He refuses, however, to pinpoint its origins.

WALL OF VOODOO   Wall of Voodoo formed in Los Angeles in the late seventies. Leader Stan Ridgeway recalled in a recent interview: "In 1975, I was out of work. I had been playing in a lot of Top 40 and country and western kind of bands around bars in Whittier with names like the Three Little Pigs and the Come On Inn and stuff. But I really wanted to get out of that and I had this idea to start this soundtrack company that would just service sci-fi and horror films, where we would undercut the competition because we were so cheap. We might even work for free—it didn't make much difference. But I needed a façade, so I rented an office on Hollywood Boulevard that ended up being right across the street from the Masque [the seminal L.A. punk Club] when it started in '77. So a lot of characters were flying around then, and I would kind of collect them and bring them up to the office, and we'd try a lot of things out up there. The name Wall of Voodoo was actually a twist on Phil Spector's wall of sound. I had a big collection of rhythm machines, and I thought that what we were doing was not a wall of sound but really a wall of voodoo. It was a company long before it was a band, but after a while people wanted us to come out and play, and so we did."

WAR   In 1969, after leaving the Animals, singer Eric Burden met Danish harmonica player Lee Oskar, and together they recruited Night Shift, an all-black band they spotted playing in an L.A. nightclub. In an interview, the band's longtime manager and producer, Jerry Goldstein, explains: "We were in the middle of the peace movement, and Eric

Burden used to do a lot of weird things. We figured if we called the group War, people would notice it. At first the idea was War Is Music. You wouldn't believe the outcry. People were like, 'How can you call a bunch of brothers blah, blah, blah!' We had so much static that when we did the first album, UA [United Artists Records] wanted us to make the letters mean something, like We Are Righteous. We all fuckin' laughed and said, 'We'll just make hit records.' "

When asked about the name, Eric Burden comments: "Well, I didn't like the name at first. I thought it was capitalizing on a conflict, but I let myself get talked into it because the guys in the band thought it was aggressive and thought it was hip to 'take a negative word and turn it into something positive,' as they put it. But *war* spelled backwards is *raw,* and that's what I got—a raw deal. So, what's in a name?"

WAS (NOT WAS) Multi-instrumentalists Don Was (Don Fagenson) and David Was (David Weiss), who grew up together in Detroit, formed Was (Not Was) in the early eighties. Don discusses their name in an interview: **How did Was (Not Was) come about?** "Well, it's actually the living embodiment of Piaget's reversibility theory. Basically, my son was a year-and-a-half old at the time and was starting to grasp onto the concept of opposites and found it amusing to point to something that was blue and say, 'Red,' and wait for a disapproving face and go, 'Not red.' So this motif provided the template for the name. The only thing missing was that we had to hallucinate a decent verb." **So how did the "Was" part come about?** "That's the verb hallucination. Then we just took our names based on the band—figuring that it was a one-off twelve-inch. 'Hey, it's—funny—you'll be David Was, I'll be Don Was, it'll be great.' Ten years later, we're registering in hotels under that name and I can't understand why we can't pick up prepaid tickets under the name of Was." **Any other names that you considered at the time and jettisoned?** "Oh, man. No . . . I think there were different forms of punctuation though. It's kind of an homage to Allen Ginsberg, the parentheses—y'know, to take on that 'beat' look. But I think that was it. What else could it be?" **Are you pleased about your choice, ten years later?** "Everyone said it was the stupidest possible name because people wouldn't be able to remember it, and as a result the band would be forgotten. My argument was always, 'No, it doesn't matter if you call it something very simple if you don't have records that stick with people—then they'll forget the name no matter what. But if you actually have a hit, and you're called something impossible, people are going to be forced to remember the name, and once they remember it, they'll never forget it.' We get a lot of people who say, 'Which one of you guys is Was and which one is Not Was?' Like a vaudeville team. When we got to Europe, we found that the accepted theory was that we were correcting people's pronunciation of our last name—that it's 'Vas, not Was.' The name's probably the coolest thing about the band. Someday I hope to live up to the originality of the name. It's been downhill since then." **Did your label try to—I know they've tried to tamper with who sings and who doesn't and all that—has a label ever said, "You've got to got rid of the name"?** "No one ever forced the issue. I think the attitude with most of our record labels has been to like—I picture a record company president sort of throwing up his hands and shaking his head as he tosses the album into the 'C' priority bin. That characterizes our careers."

W.A.S.P.   The abbreviation allegedly stands for "We Are Sexual Pervets."

THE WATERBOYS   The band was formed in London by Scottish-born Mike Scott in 1981. He named the group after a line in the Lou Reed song "The Kids" from the album *Berlin*.

WEEN   Mickey Melchiondo (Dean Ween) and Aaron Freeman (Gene Ween) began recording together in 1985, when the two were in junior high school in New Hope, Pennsylvania. Their name is a cross between "wuss" and "peen," as in penis.

WET WET WET   Wet Wet Wet formed in Glasgow, Scotland, in 1982, and took their name from a line in the Scritti Politti song "Getting Having and Holding."

WHAM!   George Michael (born Georgios Panayiotou) and Andrew Ridgely met in school and played together in a band called the Executive in 1979. When that band broke up, the duo recorded a demo tape that included a song that would become their first single, a rap parody called "Wham! Rap," from which they took their name in 1981. The song, which jokingly endorsed unemployment, was their first hit.

WHITESNAKE   Singer David Coverdale left Deep Purple in the midst of a problem-plagued British tour in 1976, after which the band broke up. Due to contractual constraints that prevented him from performing live or recording solo in the U.K., Coverdale moved to Germany and cut an album called *Whitesnake,* which flopped. After working on a second album in Germany, for which, like the first, he recorded vocals in Munich over backing tracks cut by other musicians in London, he returned to England in 1978. There he assembled a band called David Coverdale's Whitesnake made up of the session musicians who had worked on the albums.

THE WHO   Singer Roger Daltrey, guitarist Pete Townshend, and bassist John Entwhistle began performing together with Doug Sandom on drums as the Detours in London in 1962. Late in 1963 they met managers Helmut Gorden and Pete Meaden, who gave them a better-dressed mod image and renamed them the High Numbers, mod slang for stylish. In 1964, after Sandom was replaced by Keith Moon, filmmakers Kit Lambert and Chip Stamp took over the band's management and rechristened them the Who, a name they had used previously for a short time.

WILD CHERRY   Best known for the 1976 hit "Play That Funky Music," the band was formed in the early seventies in Steubenville, Ohio. Lead vocalist and guitarist Bob Parissi was laid up in the hospital when inspiration struck. As his bandmates prepared to leave his room, someone mentioned that they needed a name, and Parissi, spotting a box of flavored cough drops, jokingly suggested Wild Cherry.

WINGS   Following the breakup of the Beatles, Paul McCartney formed Wings in 1971. McCartney initially planned to call the band Turpentine, then the Dazzlers, before settling on Wings. The name was reportedly inspired by the difficult birth of his second child, Stella, whom he prayed would be delivered "on the wings of an angel." In the 1991 book *Blackbird: The Life and Times of Paul McCartney* by Geoffrey Guiliano, McCartney recalls: "It was dodgy at the time, so rather than just sitting around twiddling my thumbs, I was thinking of hopeful names for a new group, and somehow this uplifting idea of 'Wings' came to me."

THE WOODENTOPS The band formed in Northhampton, England, in the early eighties and took their name from a children's BBC-TV show that starred crudely-fashioned wooden figures.

THE WONDER STUFF The band formed in Birmingham, England, in the mideighties. Singer Miles Hunt reveals: "We've never told anyone this. We've never gone into it. My father and his brother were actually involved in music. When I was a youngster, John Lennon often used to come around to our house, and it was basically a Lennon quote. When I was about nine or ten, just running 'round the house, he said, 'The kid sure has the wonder stuff,' and often as I grew up my dad used to remind me of this story. Y'know, to me, he was just like a friend of my dad's." **What does your dad do?** "Well, I can't say what he does really. But his brother, my uncle, he was in a British glam band that had a lot of hits, and they were very friendly with the Beatles. So when the Beatles split up, Lennon used to hang out a lot when he used to come back to England from

New York. This one time when I was a kid, I was just running around the house like a maniac with my friends, and he said, 'Your boy sure has the wonder stuff.' You're getting an exclusive here. We've never told anyone this. The British press doesn't consider this sort of thing." **So what was your dad's name? Is it Hunt as well?** "Yeah." **Just for the record, what was his first name?** "Oh, you can't print that. Just say Lennon was a friend of my uncle. My uncle was in a band called Wizard, my uncle Bill."

X The band formed in Los Angeles in 1977 after singer and bassist John Doe met guitarist Billy Zoom via a classified ad and singer Exene Cervenka at a poetry workshop. Adding Don J. Bonebrake on drums, the band became X in honor of Exene.

X-Ray Specs The seminal English punk band was launched in 1976 by lead singer Poly Styrene (Marion Elliot) and saxophonist Lora Logic (Susan Whitby). Best known for the song "Oh Bondage, Up Yours," they took their name from the novelty eyeglasses advertised in the back of publications like *True Detective* that supposedly gave the wearer the ability to see through clothing and other barriers.

XTC The band formed in Swindon, England, in the mid-1970s. They changed their name from the Helium Kidz after singer and guitarist Andy Partridge reportedly saw an old film in which Jimmy Durante discovered "the lost chord" and exclaimed "Dat's it, I'm in XTC!"

THE YARDBIRDS The band came together in London in 1963 and was originally called the Metropolis Blues Quartet. According to *Yardbirds: The Ultimate Rave-Up* by Greg Russo, it was vocalist Keith Relf who, despite his initial reluctance to change the name, found the term "yardbird" in the liner notes for a Jack Kerouac record. A yardbird was a person, a hobo, who made his home around railyards. It's worth noting that the group had its origins in two bands that played at the Railway Tavern in London. For a time, the band was billed as the Most Blueswailing Yardbirds. They did not name themselves after jazz great Charlie "Bird" Parker, as has been reported.

YES Yes formed in London in 1968. In the liner notes to the *Yes Years* box set, singer Jon Anderson explains, "Yes got pulled out of the bag, I think. We wanted to display a strong conviction in what we were doing. We had to have a strong and straight title for the band."

YO LA TENGO   The band was started in 1984 by guitarist Ira Kaplan and his wife, drummer Georgia Hubley, and was part of the Hoboken, New Jersey, rock scene in the eighties that made the club Maxwell's its focal point. The name means "I have it" or "I have her" in Spanish. Kaplan told the *New York Times* in May 1992: "We called it Yo La Tengo because we didn't want a name in English. We didn't want to be called, oh, the No. 2 Train, we didn't want something that would have an image. And we didn't get far enough in our thinking to realize that everyone would ask us why."

THE YOUNGBLOODS   Formed in Boston in 1965, the Youngbloods, who had a Top 10 hit in 1969 with "Get Together," were named after founder Jesse Colin Young. Born Perry Miller, he took his name from Wild West figures Jesse James and Cole Younger, and Grand Prix race car driver Colin Chapman.

THE YOUNG RASCALS   The group formed in New York City in 1965. They planned to call themselves the Rascals until it was discovered that there was already a group called the Harmonica Rascals. Without their knowledge, Atlantic Records changed their name to the Young Rascals with the release of their first single in early 1966. In the spring of 1968 they convinced Atlantic that they could legally shorten their name to the Rascals. Their name had no connection to the TV show *The Little Rascals*.

Z

MAURICE WILLIAMS AND THE ZODIACS   Best known for the 1960 hit "Stay," Maurice Williams and the Zodiacs got their start as the Gladiolas. When they switched record labels, they were forced to give up the name, and one of the members of the band suggested the Zodiacs, after a make of car had caught his eye at a repair shop.

ZZ TOP   After his psychedelic band the Moving Sidewalks broke up, guitarist Billy Gibbons formed ZZ Top with bassist Lanier Greig and drummer Dan Mitchell in 1969. Managed by local promotion man Bill Ham, the band recorded their first single, "Salt Lick" b/w "Miller's Farm," on Ham's one-shot Scat label. Later that year, the lineup was finalized when Greig was replaced by Frank Beard and Mitchell by Dusty Hill, both former members of the American Blues.

According to the 1985 book *ZZ Top: Bad and Worldwide* by Deborah Frost, Greig says the name was inspired by a poster of Texas bluesman Z.Z. Hill, one of several photos of blues players that hung in the apartment shared by Gibbons and Mitchell, and *Top* came from Top rolling paper. It has also been reported that *ZZ* came from Zig Zag, another leading brand of rolling paper.

In a story on the band in the February 1991 issue of

SPIN, novelist Terry Southern, after attempting to confirm the Zig Zag reference, was told by the band's press agent: "No way, Jose. These are clean-living boys. End of story."

But in an October 1991 issue of *Goldmine,* Billy Gibbons told Cub Koda: "We wanted somethin' real bluesy soundin', I like B.B. King, you know? There was this R&B singer named Z.Z. Hill and that seemed like a good place to start. We also wanted the name to suggest the best, the ultimate. For a while, we were just gonna call ourselves Z.Z. Brown. I thought that sounded pretty right. We knew Z.Z. King or Z.Z. Queen wasn't going to work! Then one day I was driving with a friend of mine and we passed by an old barn with the hayloft doors open, facing out. He pointed up at the two doors that had those old-fashioned Z-shaped beams on 'em and said, 'Look, Z.Z. Top!' I knew right then we had our name."

Illustration Credits

The Cavedogs: Marc Burckhardt
The Dead Milkmen: Marc Burckhardt
Skinny Puppy: Marc Burkhardt
All others: James Victore